ALSO BY MICHAEL LEWIS

Liar's Poker

The Money Culture

TRAIL FEVER

TRAIL FEVER

Spin doctors, rented strangers, thumb wrestlers, toe suckers, grizzly bears, and other creatures on the road to the White House

by Michael Lewis

Alfred A. Knopf   New York   1997

THIS IS A BORZOI BOOK
PUBLISHED BY ALFRED A. KNOPF, INC.

Copyright © 1997 by Michael Lewis

http://www.randomhouse.com/

Portions of this work were originally published in slightly
different form in *The New Republic*.

Library of Congress Cataloging-in-Publication Data
Lewis, Michael (Michael M.)
Trail fever : spin doctors, rented strangers, thumb wrestlers, toe
suckers, grizzly bears, and other creatures on the road to the
White House / Michael Lewis. — 1st ed.
p.   cm.
ISBN 0-679-44660-5 (alk. paper)
1. Presidents—United States—Election—1996.
2. Presidential candidates—United States.   3. United States—
Politics and government—1993–   I. Title.
E888.L49   1997
324.973'0929—dc21   97-5444
CIP

Manufactured in the United States of America
First Edition

To my father,
J. Thomas Lewis

As a boy I thought you could be elected president.
Now I'm not so sure.

Democracy in this age has become more demanding than ever before in U.S. history. One has to choose it as a way of life rather than a party affiliation. And in choosing one may well have to make some sacrifice in other things, such as opportunities to make a lot of money, exercise a lot of power and enjoy an enviably high status. . . . The experience of democracy is not ultimately about winning but about deliberating and acting together.

—SHELDON WOLIN,
Professor of Political Theory Emeritus,
Princeton University

People are always asking me like "Krist are you gonna run for state legislature or city council or something?" and I'll say no I'm gonna run for my life.

—KRIST NOVOSELIC,
former bass player for Nirvana, May 1996

CONTENTS

INTRODUCTION

If you look long and hard enough at ugliness, you often find real beauty in it. On a clear dawn the toxic swamps that lie between Manhattan and Newark Airport are breathtaking, the more so because you expect them to repel. The presidential campaign of 1996 had, for me, the same surprising appeal. Most of what I had seen of the process I'd witnessed from the usual mediated distance. And so I expected to find empty speeches, hollow candidates, dirty tactics, and political operatives who made their living by telling people things that were not true. But I did not expect to find passion, or heroism, or heart-stopping eloquence, or a candidate, included in debates with Bob Dole, who called himself the Grizz. I did not expect to find on the campaign trail so much of American life.

From the moment I walked into the campaign I had to keep in mind that in all likelihood I was about to witness the Making of Chester A. Arthur. It was not, to put it mildly, a moment of obvious historical importance. Despite the usual rhetoric about Crises, Crossroads, Turning Points, New Beginnings, and Radical Departures, the nation was chugging along, on autopilot as it were. The indifference to politics is the signature trait of our times: no issue or cause, it seems, is too great to be ignored. In America there is a great tradition of big political questions being ignored—or at any rate being addressed only by people regarded as crackpots. The guts of the New Deal came to Franklin Roosevelt not from his advisers but from the early Socialist Party platforms. The direct election of United States senators first was proposed by the Prohibition Party. In this regard, the campaign of 1996 was no exception. The two major candidates for president in the world's most influential democracy exhibited virtually no interest in big problems: wealth disparities, inner-city despair, Medicare and Social Security budget crises, the expanding demand for money in politics. Both Clinton and Dole displayed an astonishing ability to feign engagement with the world around them when, in fact, they were hiding. The level of artifice and pretense hit new highs.

That does not mean the campaign lacked drama or importance. Far from it. Its importance arose out of its unimportance. It was a rare case study of what happens in a democracy when the majority prefers not to participate. A whole society took its eye off the ball, mainly because it could afford to, or thought it could afford to. But here's the point: *nothing inside the presidential election insisted upon being paid attention to.* Whatever native interest many people felt toward political questions was bored out of them by the process. The spin, the shifty convictions, the fear of risk, the lack of imagination, the inability of small minds to see that it is better to lose pretty than to win ugly, all added up to the worst show on earth. The widespread boredom with our politics is not a neutral event. It serves the interests of *someone.* It deters outsiders from becoming too interested. It keeps things quiet on the inside.

Maybe the best way to introduce this book—a journal I kept during ten months of 1996—is to explain why I set out to write it in the first place. I had no grand scheme. I had no theory, of the Twilight in America variety, that needed facts to support. I had no specific qualifications, just three days of experience as a campaign journalist, but they made all the difference. I had spent those traveling with Vice President Dan Quayle back in the summer of 1992. It wasn't so much what Quayle had said that hooked me. It was what he had done—what the conventions of the campaign trail required him to do. Every few hours of every day, to take a tiny example, the vice president's campaign plane, *Air Force Two,* came to rest on the tarmac of a military base on the outskirts of some medium-sized city, and Quayle appeared in the open door. He waved. It was not a natural gesture of greeting but a painfully enthusiastic window-washing motion. Like everyone else in America I had watched politicians do this on the evening news a thousand times. But I had always assumed there must be someone down below to wave at. Not so! Every few hours our vice president stood there at the top of the steps of Air Force Two waving to . . . nobody; waving, in fact, to a field in the middle distance over the heads of the cameramen, so that the people back home in their living rooms remained comfortably assured that a crowd had turned up to celebrate his arrival.

After three days with him I had a tall stack of similar mental snapshots of our vice president behaving in ways that no person in his right mind would behave were he not running for office. The artifice astonished me, and made me wonder: When a process becomes this phony, how do people on the inside of it ever know what is real?

In late 1995 the editor of *The New Republic* asked if I'd like to drive up to New Hampshire and document the Republican primary. My ambition was to describe political people as they appear right up close, as opposed to how they appear on television or in the newspaper. The problem, of course, is that political people often don't wish to be seen up close. As a rule, the more important they are the less they care to be watched. The only solution I ever found to this problem was to treat the campaign less like a day job and more like a guerrilla war. When I learned from old hands that the point of a press badge is to enable political operatives to identify those to be kept far away from the action, I chucked away my credentials. I abandoned also the usual literary methods. I found that a simple journal enabled me to cram in all sorts of detail and incident that somehow was squeezed out of more highly structured compositions.

But in ten months on the campaign trail I never was able to escape my first, crude question: What happens to politics in unpolitical times? What becomes of the great issues, the great causes, and the great men?

The short answer, I think, is that they survive. Finding them is not easy, however. And a funny thing happened once I knew what I was looking for: the more I searched, the farther afield I was led. The winners— political insiders like Dole and Clinton—came to seem mere reactionaries, almost irrelevant to the great questions of the day. They did not lead the country; the country led them. Each morning they raised more money, paid for more polls, and then sat down and composed more ads. The daring we commonly associate with great politics they left to lesser candidates and braver men. If a new idea happened to take hold (a flat tax, a curfew, a trade barrier, a better fence along the Mexican border), they pretended it had been theirs all along. The 1996 presidential campaign was governed by the logic of a food chain: steal from those beneath you; attack those above you. Clinton stole from Bob Dole who stole from Pat Buchanan who stole from Alan Keyes. Morry Taylor attacked Steve Forbes who attacked Lamar Alexander who attacked Bob Dole who attacked Bill Clinton, who remained as detached and aloof as a hot-air balloon on a placid summer day. Indeed, for both Clinton *and* Dole the most honest campaign slogan would have been: Vote for Me! I Won't Change Anything Except My Own Convictions!

The viewpoint in books about presidential campaigns is usually the view from the top of the food chain: the Making of William Jefferson Clinton; the Tragedy of Bob Dole. What is astonishing is how stilted and, ultimately, uninteresting that view has become. Bravery, adventurousness, engagement, a passionate devotion to ideas and principles, seem to be handicaps in politics, if your goal is to win. The view from the bottom of the political food chain was far more edifying. The man at the bottom of the food chain launched his rockets directly at the political process; he struggled with the great issues of the day—or, at any rate, what will very likely be the great issues of tomorrow. If you cared to glimpse the plight of the American workingman, you were better off trailing around behind Pat Buchanan. If you cared to see the heroic possibilities of American politics, you were far better off seeking out the senator that Dole did *not* chose as his running mate (John McCain). If you wanted to hear a speech, you were well advised to seek out the obscure black former ambassador to the United Nations running for the Republican nomination (Alan Keyes). And if you wanted to see a truly representative citizen, who felt genuinely the same desires and ideals that motivate the mythical average American, you followed the Grizz.

Every author has his ideal reader. The ideal reader of this book, the troubled figure I kept perpetually in mind as I wrote it, is someone struck numb by modern presidential campaigns. If he votes, it is not because he feels any genuine enthusiasm but because he feels guilty not voting. Dear reader, you have my sympathy. Half the time you feel like you don't belong; the other half you feel glad you don't belong. But you do; and you shouldn't. There's a lot more going on out there than any of us know.

TRAIL FEVER

PRELUDE

The People

Until the moment Moses put the idea into his head it had never crossed Morry Taylor's mind to run for anything. Certainly he wasn't the type who ran for president: the joiner, the networker, the back-scratch artist. Often Morry would say, accurately, "I'm not a member of nuthin'. I don't owe nuthin', I don't have nuthin' to hide. I'm what you call an empty refrigerator——you open it up and there's nuthin' inside." To be president you had to spend your whole life stocking the refrigerator, preparing other people for the idea that one day you could be president. You couldn't just . . . run.

And yet: Why *not?* Moses had a point.

Moses worked on the factory floor at Titan Wheel International, the billion-dollar company Morry Taylor had built from a scrap heap. One day late in June Morry was walking through one of his wheel factories complaining about the idiocy of Washington politicians, as he often did. But this time Moses overheard him. He popped up from behind a steaming machine and said, "Hey Morry, you fixed this place. Why don't you go fix the country?" Morry laughed, of course. "You see, Morry," Moses had said, "that's why we always get the shaft. No one ever stands up."

That's what first got Morry thinking.

For the next few weeks the statistic that kept popping into Morry Taylor's brain was that 70 percent of all Americans hate Washington and anything else having to do with politics. Or so they claim. He'd lie awake at night considering that number, in the same way he'd think of some huge, untapped market for farm wheels. Ross Perot had done it, of course, but Ross had made the fatal mistake of running as an independent rather than a Republican, the only sane thing on earth to be, in Morry's view.

3

Morry didn't have as much money as Ross, but he had tens of millions of dollars, more than enough to scare the hell out of the professional politicians in the Iowa and New Hampshire primaries. He also had ideas about how to fix the government and an inspiring real-life American dream story to tell. He wasn't soft like a lot of so-called businessmen: he could still operate each piece of machinery in every factory he owned. The sons of millionaires had now taken to describing themselves as "self-made men," but he actually was. He had started out as a lowly tool-and-die maker, the son of a blue-collar worker. He took a few engineering courses at Michigan Tech, then made a career selling wheels for farm equipment. In the early 1980s, in his late thirties, he began to buy up distressed tire and wheel factories. Every factory he bought was, when he bought it, either bankrupt or approaching bankruptcy, but by the end of 1994 Titan Wheel International had $620 million in revenues, no debt, and one of the highest profit margins of any company listed on the New York Stock Exchange. In manufacturing circles Morry Taylor was viewed as a miracle worker. Every one of his 5,500 workers credited him with saving his job.

In the end Morry decided that the country finally was ready to elect a president who was a serious businessman. The only question was: Which businessman?

A few weeks later, on August 7, 1995, Morry started down the road to the White House: he flew to Dallas in one of Titan's jets to speak to the United We Stand delegates assembled by Ross Perot. The People, as Ross called them. Perot's idea was to invite everyone down to Dallas and make them compete for the People. Morry was hardly alone. Just about everyone who felt the little suck of presidential ambition in his chest in August 1995 flew to Dallas: Pat Buchanan, Senator Bob Dole, Lamar Alexander, Alan Keyes, Senator Dick Lugar, Senator Phil Gramm, Governor Pete Wilson. Even Bill Clinton sent an emissary, his old friend Mack McClarty. Morry was by far the most obscure of the bunch. The politicians he met before the event took him either for a potential contributor or for one of the People. He was the only one who didn't have the patter and the body language of a professional politician. He was the only man backstage, for instance, who found it strange and unnatural to configure his hand into one of those funny thumb-wrestling gestures to stress his points. The other guys were, to a man, thumb wrestlers.

Just before he took the stage it dawned on Morry that in his entire life he'd never before done anything like this. He'd always thought of people who ran for office as some kind of joke. One way or another they were all like the cute little twerp with the overly groomed hair who stopped you on the way to football practice and told you he was running for junior-class president. But from the moment Morry settled in behind the podium his stomach flip-flopped and his mouth felt like someone had filled it with Elmer's glue: politics wasn't as easy as he'd imagined. He nearly made it through his allotted twenty-five minutes, however. The TelePrompTer broke two sentences into his speech, so instead of reading from his prepared text he just said what he had to say. This required exactly sixteen minutes. He couldn't have told you precisely what he said, or where the other nine minutes of his speech went, but he made it through. He was fairly certain he'd told the sea of strangers about his plan to eliminate the budget deficit in eighteen months, and maybe also his belief that congressmen should live in their districts year-round and telecommute like everyone else in America. One of his lines had brought down the house: "The question I get asked more than any is, How can you win? The answer is simple. If Bill Clinton can win, so can I." Otherwise his speech was a streaky blur of disconnected phrases punctuated by the thunderous applause of the People.

Then he left, fled for Lombardi's in downtown Dallas. His campaign staffers stayed behind to hand out free food and drinks to any delegates who stopped by the Taylor for President suite.

Not unreasonably Morry had assumed that no one but a few kooks would care to see him. After all, even the big-time politicians who did this for a living had failed to win over the People. Just a few hours earlier, after his own speech, California governor Pete Wilson with his far larger and better greased campaign drew to his suite exactly twenty-three potential supporters. Twenty-three! Phil Gramm pulled in even fewer. In Texas! His own home state! Gramm and Wilson just stood around like fools waiting for a crowd that never showed. Morry found it too embarrassing to watch it happen to a thumb wrestler to experience it himself.

A few minutes after tucking into his dinner Morry got his first call from the hotel: the Taylor for President suite was crowding up. Maybe Morry should think about coming back. Morry ignored the request and went back to his meal. Ten minutes later his newly acquired campaign manager Bill Kenyon called him. "Get the hell back here right now," Kenyon said.

Morry returned to find one thousand of the four thousand United We

Stand delegates trying to cram themselves into his hotel suite. At that very moment, inside the banquet hall, Ross Perot was speaking. The People were missing Perot's closing speech to meet . . . him. They had run through all his food and booze, and still they were waiting for . . . *him!* Once they spotted him hovering in the doorway they started a chant: "Morry! Morry! Morry!" Almost to a man they wore Morry's favorite campaign button: MORRY TAYLOR AND I VOTED FOR ROSS PEROT IN 1992. Die-hard Perot volunteers——the few people in America who actually cared who became president, the sort of people whose enthusiasm put Perot on the ballot in every state—were walking up to Kenyon with that look in their eye and saying things like "I will do everything I can to help Morry Taylor become president." In their eyes at least, Morry was the rightful heir to the strange and passionate political movement once led by Ross Perot. Four hundred of them signed up to work for Morry on the spot.

A month or so later Pete Wilson withdrew from the race. Phil Gramm had gone nowhere, spending millions of other people's dollars doing so. Morry had spent only a few hundred thousand of his own dollars and was on just about every ballot in the country. He hadn't done a thing. The People had done it for him. Almost before he knew how it had happened, Morry was running for president.

ONE

Trailers

It is hard to believe that the race for the Republican nomination, or any other race for that matter, could begin in Manchester, New Hampshire. When I arrive at eight in the evening the streets are buried beneath a foot of snow, and the only signs of life are several dark stooped figures on foot, all making soundless tracks in the same direction. Without even knowing it, they are building a trail. I follow on the assumption that if there is only one place in Manchester to go I want to be there. The footprints end at the front door of a porn-video store called Forbidden Fruit. Here lies the first hint of the presidential politics to come. Immediately in front of the store a vending machine displays the front page of the Manchester *Union Leader,* the state's largest paper. Alongside the front-page endorsement of Pat Buchanan a reader writes, "May God in heaven help our country if Clinton gets another four years in office."

Then in the distance I spot a light: Phil Gramm's campaign headquarters. A young man toils behind a desk at the back of the office. I knock and do my best to explain my business, even though I am not exactly sure what that is. I suppose I want to see up close what it looks like to spend $20 million trying to become president. Happily, the young man seems almost to be expecting me. Instead of just handing me Gramm's schedule, he sits down and laboriously copies out by hand what he feels I need to know. Tomorrow Gramm is coming to New Hampshire.

The thumb wrestlers convene. Phil Gramm in the center.

JANUARY 2

The phone rings at seven o'clock the next morning. It's another eager Gramm aide wanting to know if I would like to attend a breakfast at eight o'clock at which Gramm is speaking. "I can come pick you up," he says, with a hopefulness that gives him away. I may be new to the campaign trail, but I'm not new at life. The first rule of life is that you never accept the first offer in a new and uncertain market. I roll over and go back to sleep. Outside, the snow falls.

Already the Texas senator has spent $20 million of other people's money to persuade voters that he is more fiscally responsible than anyone else in the race. The main result has been to frighten off serious contenders like former vice president Dan Quayle and former education secretary William Bennett, who failed to keep pace with Gramm's fundraising. "When Phil Gramm said to me, 'I'm going off to do three hundred receptions in the next forty days,' I couldn't think of *anything* I'd rather do less," said William Bennett, explaining his decision not to run. (Bennett went on to say, "I thought of that movie *The Mosquito Coast*. I mean, this guy's sort of a charming nut, and he takes his family to this horrible place. That's what it's like in a presidential run—it's like taking your family to the Mosquito Coast.")

Two hours later I discover that all you need to do to become a campaign journalist is call the campaign headquarters, find out where the candidate is going, and say you want to come along. By eleven I am booked to travel with Gramm, Pat Buchanan, Bob Dole, Lamar Alexander, and Steve Forbes; with a bit more planning I would have bagged the rest of the nine-man field—Dick Lugar, Robert "B-1 Bob" Dornan, Alan Keyes, and Morry Taylor. No one in this business seems to care very much who you are or where you are from just as long as you agree to play your role and whip up some public attention. If you insist, they will fetch you at your hotel and drive you halfway across the state. For free.

This evening's event is an hour passed with a family of undecided voters in a nearby town called Salem, and if you want to know why Americans change the channel when a politician appears on the screen, you need look no farther than this encounter. The victims are a couple in their late thirties named Matt and Kate Conway. He sells hockey equipment; she is a "housewife or homemaker or whatever the correct term is," as he puts it. Fifteen reporters, along with Gramm's campaign staffers, cram into the pleasant powder-blue living room to document the event. Before Gramm turns up in the flesh, Matt tells the assembled journalists, "We are a typical Middle American Ozzie and Harriet family; we really are." This is a fortunate coincidence, since the Gramm campaign is advertising the meeting as a chance for Phil Gramm to demonstrate his commitment to a balanced budget to "a typical Middle American family."

Gramm arrives beneath a handsome camel-hair coat and stomps the snow from his shiny black wing tips onto the carpet. Within five minutes the Conways are guests in their own home. The senator from Texas treats the Conways as archetypes—a Typical Middle American Family. He says things to them that no human being ever would say to another outside of a democratic election. "I don't want to take up too much of your time," he says, for instance, "since I know you are busy with your family." Busy with your family? The phrase jars until I twig its subtext: Phil Gramm is pro-family. You could spend years traveling the earth without running into anyone who is antifamily, but Gramm still insists on his sentiment. This is just the sort of artifice that causes normal people to despair of ever taking a sincere interest in politics. The Conways, being polite, do their best to play their part. In the context of what is meant to be a perfectly ordinary conversation Matt offers up perfect little sound bites. He says, "This house was about two hundred thousand dollars to get our piece of the American dream."

Soon enough Gramm sits down between them at their dining-room table and begins to make magic with charts and numbers. Gramm does not explain *how* he would balance the budget or even *why* the budget should be balanced—except for a felonious diagram he uses to show how much money the typical American family would save from the resulting decline in interest rates. He peddles his balanced budget idea like an Amway salesman; from the moment he pulls out his foot-high laminated chart I find myself waiting for him to offer them a new line of steak knives or household disinfectants, but no, he just keeps rambling on and on about the budget, digressing only to say what a terrible president Bob Dole would make. Even when the typical eight-year-old twins who belong to this typical American family rush into the dining room and demand to play with Mommy and Daddy, Gramm says, wittily, "Let's see how good they'll feel when they find out they'll have to pay one hundred ninety-seven thousand dollars in income taxes just to cover the interest on the public debt." I believe one of the children flinches, but perhaps I am mistaken.

Gramm is charming enough, but even here in this modest setting you can see he's no match for Clinton, who hovers over the Republican primary like a hot-air balloon with a smiley face painted on its side. Gramm lacks the gift for seeming interested in what other people have to say, much less the ability actually to be interested in each and every one of us 250 million Americans. His mouth gives him away. Hard, tiny dimples frame his pucker like parentheses, which suggests he is about to laugh at whatever anyone is about to tell him. Talking to Phil Gramm is like being in on one endless humorous aside. But every now and then the senator gets wrongfooted and greets the news of some terrible human tragedy with his little mouth-dimples. He's nearly caught chuckling, for instance, about an illness in the Conway family. Then he quickly has to change his expression, to exhibit the proper emotions. The trouble is, he doesn't really have another expression. He wants to put everything that is said inside his parentheses. Whenever the Conways say something, he holds his breath until they are finished—offering an encouraging nod and his endlessly taut ironic mouth—and then launches into some speech entirely unrelated to their point. ("Well, let me tell you the point I want to

make . . .") The best he can do with their conversational sallies is to relate them to his own life:

MATT: I was born in Pearl Harbor.
PHIL: Oh, really? My wife is from Hawaii.

But maybe I have him all wrong; it can happen, especially with people so determined, as presidential candidates apparently are, to hide
their true selves from view. I recall reading somewhere about Gramm's
upbringing in Columbus, Georgia. After his father became ill his mother
used to take little Phil from their lower-middle-class house to the rich
folks' neighborhood, where she would point to the houses and say, "If
you work hard you can live in one of *those!*" Gramm's teeth are very bad;
he has the worst orthodontia by far in this campaign. They are discolored
and look as if each and every one has been sharpened to a point—more
like animal teeth or pumpkin teeth than human teeth. They alone give
you some idea of the poverty he experienced as a child. Perhaps Senator
Gramm clenches his mouth the way he does because he wants to convey
bonhomie yet is uncomfortable with his smile. If so, it shows how physical traits can lead to emotional ones. Gramm has worn his wry look for so
long that he has become permanently wry.

Whatever its cause, the effect of Gramm's lip tic is to make people
feel that they are in on some joke they probably don't quite get, except
he's chosen the wrong people to do this with. Kate Conway is fairly nervous, as anyone would be who is suddenly facing a dozen people she does
not know asking her questions about the future of the Republic. But
Matt is Mr. *Capital Gang.* Twenty minutes into the visit he is offering
Gramm plausible advice about how to beat the big boys. "The advantage
you have is that you are up here campaigning while Dole and Clinton are
down in Washington hiding," Matt says, accurately, before revealing that
already he has become friendly with the campaign heads for Alexander,
Lugar, and Dole. In passing he mentions that he lives near "George
Bush's FEMA head," whatever that is, and then says—I swear—that "we
came very close to buying the house next to John Sununu's," referring to
the former New Hampshire governor.

New Hampshire hosts the first primary in part because it did the last
time but also because it is uniquely prepared. The state must contain the
world's most professional electorate. Every candidate knows that ten
thousand New Hampshire votes might be the difference between win-

ning the White House and ending one's days in obscurity. Every voter knows this, too. The state has organized itself so that it is not organized: no one can deliver many votes. Every single citizen must be thoroughly sucked up to, one at a time. The primary is therefore a painful extortion: the people may say they are for less taxes and smaller government, but they are engaged in the shakedown and are only just worth what they are paid for their votes. And it works. Half of New Hampshire seems to have pictures of itself shaking hands with a president on its living-room walls; the other half actually gets political appointments after the election. New Hampshire currently is one of the biggest per capita recipients of discretionary Medicaid dollars, for instance. The Portsmouth Naval Yard is one of the few naval facilities to remain open during the current government shutdown.

The state is famous for surprising election results, and no wonder. Everyone in New Hampshire has an interest in making this campaign interesting—thus attracting reporters, attention, campaign promises, and money to themselves. Every New Hampshire reporter—indeed, every New Hampshire resident—is like a sports announcer trying to keep his audience glued to the box during a rout. The other day the local offices of the Clinton campaign, for example, received a call from a fellow named Carl Cameron, the *only* local New Hampshire television reporter (ABC affiliate) and thus a person of influence. He told the campaign the piece he wanted to do that night. He'd lead with the fact that Dole *seems* to be running in the lead, but New Hampshire has a habit of upsetting front-runners. Then he'd assert that Dole's support is not terribly enthusiastic—cut to man on street who says he isn't very enthusiastic about Dole—and feed the Clinton campaign a question about Dole, which it can put away. So there! You see! Dole's in trouble.

At the end of the home visit I overhear Matt ask Gramm about fuel subsidies and Gramm say he is doing what he can for the state. While Matt and Phil chat privately about other ways the federal government might help out New Hampshire, it becomes clear that though Gramm may not listen he is acutely observant. Unlike everything else in the house—and the house itself—the dining-room furniture appears old and cherished. At the end of his disquisition on fuel oil Gramm asks, "Did you get this furniture from your parents?" They did! After Gramm leaves, the Conways tell the journalists that though they are genuinely undecided they liked Gramm immensely and may well vote for him.

One other odd trait of Gramm's: the moment he climbs aboard a plane or into a car he removes his shoes and massages his feet. His feet don't smell, but it is still a revolting habit, like chewing tobacco. Gramm is a foot masturbator.

JANUARY 7

It is a special day—the day of the New Hampshire Republican State Committee Dinner, which will gather all the candidates in one room at the Manchester Holiday Inn. By 8:00 a.m. the Morry Taylor people have planted signs for their candidate in all the best places, consigning four teenagers with BUCHANAN FOR PRESIDENT signs to a frozen street corner, and everyone else to the question: Who is Morry Taylor? It is thirteen below zero with the windchill factor, and yet the Buchanan people seem perfectly happy to stand there and jab their little signs up in the air in an attempt to catch the eye of passing motorists. Driving past them with the chauffeur from the Holiday Inn, I ask whom he is for. "I don't pay much attention to voting," he says. Then, later, "Clinton seems to be doing about as good a job as you can do. I guess I'd like him to stay there." I can see he feels bad about not having an opinion. This is an example of another strange New Hampshire phenomenon: people who have no natural interest in politics feel guilty about it. Half of America does not bother to vote, but here people acquire political opinions to avoid social embarrassment.

By four-thirty a big crowd awaits the candidates. Along the corridor leading to the grand ballroom, campaign aides open booths and distribute literature. There is one nonpartisan booth, called the GOP Shoppe. It sells candidate paraphernalia: buttons, ties, sweatshirts. The owner, a young Republican, tells me that while business has been booming in Forbes and Buchanan material he has not sold a single Dole item in the last three weeks. Nary a button. Even though Dole is the clear frontrunner, Republicans remain less interested in plastering Dole's name onto their bodies and automobiles and lawns than just about any other candidate's. The other wrinkle in the button market is Morry Taylor. Taylor is giving away his stuff for free. Across the room a table groans with Taylor buttons and Taylor hats and, oddly, Taylor beer. The elderly woman in charge of the Taylor booth hands me in rapid succession a T-shirt, a baseball cap, a bandanna, and a little lesson in political commitment. She celebrated her sixtieth birthday planting signs in the snow on Taylor's behalf. "It was so cold I couldn't feel my hands and feet," she says, hugging herself. I offer my condolences.

"Oh no," she says. "Do you know Mr. Taylor?"

I say that I don't.

"Well then," she says, brightly, "you couldn't understand how much fun it was."

All around me Republicans mingle. Ostensibly they are enjoying a cocktail hour, but in fact they are mourning the absence of the front-runners. Dole, Gramm, and Forbes all are snowed in down in Washington. Jim Courtovich, Gramm's campaign manager, comes over and spins me till I'm dizzy. "You've heard of the A Team," he says. "Well, what we've got here is the B Team." But here even the benchwarmers are celebrities. A crowd gathers in a bar to one side of the hotel, and you would think from its size and enthusiasm that Michael Jackson is about to turn up. "We're waiting for Dick Lugar to arrive," one of the enthusiasts explains. People are actually asking Morry Taylor for his autograph. Morry Taylor!

At length I spot Matt and Kate Conway, Phil Gramm's typical Middle American couple, standing alone in the middle of the vast ballroom. Matt, who just three days ago was leaning toward Gramm, now explains a bit sheepishly that he and his wife are sitting tonight at a table for Steve Forbes. It turns out that his other next-door neighbor (the one who doesn't work for Gramm) works for Forbes. He realizes how fickle he appears, what with his having sung the praises of Gramm in his foyer to the national press just three days earlier. "The Gramm people called and asked if I wanted to sit next to the senator," he says, "and I would have liked to . . . I really would have."

Matt has a confession to make, a confession often heard in New Hampshire this month. The Typical American Family was no accident. Gramm's visit to their home wasn't as spontaneous as it was made to appear. The Gramm people called Matt to prep him before the senator arrived. Alarmed by how well and broadly informed Matt was, they pleaded with him to stick to talking about the federal budget. "They especially didn't want me to ask anything about Bosnia," Matt now admits. I ask Kate if she noticed that Gramm looked her in the chest as he spoke to her. She did; it was one of the things she noticed most about him. Matt seems slightly shocked. "I didn't want to tell you," she explains to her husband.

At the dinner I am seated not with the press but with the Buchanan supporters, who occupy a large corner at the back of the ballroom. Unlike the Forbes supporters, who clearly are wearing what they do every night, the Buchanan supporters appear to have dressed up for the first time in years. The more you look at it, the more the Buchanan section reminds you of the cast of some morality play waiting to take the stage. In addition to the jowly, red-faced old men and the paunchy, bench-pressing young men, the section contains a real live minister in collar and a young woman who is a dead ringer for Brooke Shields. The young woman has no interest whatsoever in the priest, the politician, or the speeches; indeed, she works at cross-purposes with them. She is busy winning the competition with them for the attention of the New Hampshire Republican mind.

Nothing much happens the first half of the dinner, but then Alan Keyes carves a path through the Buchanan section, probably aware that the only thing more sensational than a black man at a New Hampshire Republican dinner is a black man among Buchanan supporters. Just as Gramm has been hammering away at his single notion that he is the only true fiscal conservative in the race, Keyes has been arguing over and again that he and he alone is the true social conservative. Keyes has no interest in economic issues, only social ones. He is the moralist in chief of the campaign trail. He wants the government to make people behave themselves, more or less. This seems to mean principally not having sex with anyone who is not your spouse.

Casually, more like a prince than a politician, Keyes works every table in our corner of the room. He shakes the hand of every Buchanan supporter. He tries to get off cheaply, as they all do, by shaking my hand and telling me how good it is to meet me. I explain to him that I write for *The New Republic* and that, if he buys a subscription, I will write an article about him. I want to test his range, to see if the moralist can also be the ironist. But Keyes turns and says, quite seriously, "You are easily bribed." True enough, I think, but I don't stay bribed for long. Before the thought is aired, however, all hell breaks loose. Buchanan's press director, Mike Biundo, jokingly asks Keyes what it would take for him to quit the race and endorse Pat. Keyes flips out, yelling and screaming and accusing Buchanan of racism. A week or so ago Buchanan included in one of his speeches a story from the Nixon years about John Dean, John Mitchell, and the Hopi Indians. (The gist of it was that Dean plea-bargained with the court to stay out of jail with charitable work for the Hopi Indians. After Dean cut his deal Mitchell's lawyer followed. But before he spoke to the judge, Mitchell leaned over to him and whispered in a voice loud enough that the whole courtroom heard, "If they offer you the Indians, turn them down.")

"Why is this funny?" screams Keyes at Biundo, so loudly that all of a sudden our table is the focus of attention for half the ballroom. "Will someone please explain to me why this is funny?"

Certainly, the way Keyes tells the story, it isn't funny at all, but who knows? With a little less indignation and a little more wallop in the punch line, it could work. You can't help but pity poor Biundo. He is sitting there with a kind of nervous nausea on his face, staring up at a black man raving on like a lunatic about the importance of Indians to the Republican Party. If you saw this scene unfold on the street you would cross over to avoid the man who is shouting and wonder why they ever let those people out of the mental institutions in the first place. But here it is a major media event, the temporary centerpiece of the Republican primary. Reporters with notepads and bearded guys with TV cameras come racing to capture the moment. The New Hampshire primary is passing before Mike Biundo's eyes. You could see him thinking: I'm going to be remembered as the guy who hates Indians.

If Keyes is faking it, he's doing a great job. He's ranting on about how he just met with Native Americans who *wept* at the thought that abortion was legal——natural Republicans!—and yet he couldn't persuade them to join the Republican Party because Pat Buchanan was running around America having fun at their expense. *"Do you find that funny?"* he shouts again. Now virtually every camera in the place is lined up so that Keyes can repeat his rage to CNN, WMUR, the Boston stations. And he does. He gets angry all over again. It's delicious: it's probably not the first time that a black man has charged Buchanan with racism, but it may be the first time that a black Republican has charged Pat with racism against Native Americans. The world of fiercely held political opinions is a more complicated place than that depicted on the six o'clock news.

I spy Buchanan making small talk across the ballroom and beat a path to him.

"What have you got against Native Americans?" I ask.

He has not the faintest idea what I am talking about. I relate as best I can what Keyes on the other side of the room is telling the world's media. He dimly remembers, then he fully remembers, telling the story about the Hopi Indians. "Oh, Christ," he says. "That wasn't a joke. It happened. Mitchell actually said that!"

16

"What exactly did you say?" I ask him suspiciously.

He starts to explain but then pulls himself up like a man who has just been read his Miranda rights. Anything he says, he realizes, will sound absurd. What he does say is "There's no point in going over this," then turns away.

Later during the ceremony the only surprises are Lamar Alexander's speech (surprisingly dull) and Keyes's speech (surprisingly electric). Every candidate explains why Dole would make a terrible president, and, even more ominously for the front-runner, the Dole supporters cheer nearly as lustily for the other candidates as they do for their own man. Buchanan is typically popular, bringing down the house with a joke about how Steve Forbes couldn't make it tonight because his polo ponies had caught the flu. Richard Lugar is auto-enthusiastic; he shouts and waves and does all those things a genuinely passionate speaker might do, except be genuinely passionate. He resembles a mechanical toy into which someone has inserted batteries one size too large.

But by far the most distinctive speaker is the candidate who until now I've barely heard of, Morry Taylor. From a great distance he might just pass for a politician: his suit is sufficiently gray, his jaw sufficiently prognathous, his salt-and-pepper hair sufficiently kempt and swept back off his forehead, in the fashion of powerful men. Otherwise he is a kind of antipolitician. When you look closely, for instance, you can see that his necktie is not the standard made-for-television red but a wild explosion of colors around an illustration of a giant, golden, grinning grizzly bear waving an American flag. When he speaks he does not turn back and forth pretending to address the entire crowd; instead he picks out a few people down in front and speaks directly to them. To stress his views he does not make strange thumb-wrestling gestures; rather, he points menacingly at the audience like a cop making an arrest.

He doesn't sound like a politician either, or anyone else for that matter. Between his brain and his mouth something happens to his words. "GATT" becomes "gaffe"; "humanity" becomes "humaninity"; "the sultan of Brunei" becomes "the sultan of Borneo"; "America, the shining city on the hill" is transformed into "America, the shining city in the sky." Deriding Forbes as the child of privilege he extrudes the phrase "rich money and old families." Once he is finished speaking he does not smile modestly and wave in the manner of the polished diplomat but struts from the stage for all the world like a man who is certain he will be the next president. As he does this I half expect him to raise his index finger in the air and hurl himself into the crowd, like a wide receiver who has just caught a bomb deep in the end zone.

It's nearly midnight before everyone clears out and I am left sitting with Phil Gramm's New Hampshire campaign manager, Jim Courtovich. Like most of the professional political people who landed jobs with the heavily financed candidates (Dole, Gramm, Alexander), Courtovich is consumed by strategy. Whatever beliefs or principles or character traits distinguish his boss from his rivals mean far less to him than the trick of winning. Strategy is the soul of modern politics. At the top of the game few principled differences survive. A Democratic president has just delivered a State of the Union Address in which he advertised the end of big government and stole the few remaining Republican issues (welfare, crime, values). He did this so well that the Republican front-runner (Dole), when it came to be his turn to talk to the cameras, could think of nothing to say. It wasn't his fault. There was nothing to say. Truly serious politicians no longer occupy the old-fashioned political spectrum with a right wing and a left wing. They slide up and down a greasy pole with a top and a bottom.

But even as the differences shrink, the battles rage on. The United States government has been shut down while the two sides haggle about a few billion dollars in the federal budget. An outsider might think that the fate of the earth was at stake, but it is more important than that. Careers are at stake. And political careers depend on strategy.

Once he is sure we are alone Courtovich produces a pad and draws a series of concentric circles upon it. The innermost circle, he explains, represents the fifteen thousand New Hampshire political junkies who have followed the race all along and already are committed to vote for a candidate. The next circle contains the twenty-five thousand friends of the political junkies who now are tuning into the race but pretty much know whom they will vote for. The final circle holds the seventy-five thousand ordinary people who will make up their minds in the next six weeks. These are the ordinary Americans most susceptible to the charms of Phil Gramm, says Courtovitch. "These," he says, "are the Matt and Kate Conways."

He is prepared to go on, he says, if I remain unconvinced. But sadly I now remember that I promised to meet Pat Buchanan at eight o'clock tomorrow morning in a small town called Wolfeboro, well north of Manchester. Another blizzard is on its way and so am I. The roads are, once again, in crisis. On the way up in whirling snow, cars zip past me on the highway as if immune to danger, as they have since I first arrived in New Hampshire. Every twenty minutes or so one of them spins out of control and goes plunging soundlessly off the road and into a snowdrift, where, in a silent tribute to the American taste for risk, it is buried right up to the motto on its New Hampshire plates: LIVE FREE OR DIE. I arrive at two and check into a motel; at three a burst pipe triggers the motel's fire alarm. Well after five in the morning the lights of the Wolfeboro fire department strobe the ceiling of my room, as if there were a crisis near at hand. Pat Buchanan is on his way.

JANUARY 8

There are two things I've never heard anyone say about Pat Buchanan but that become apparent the moment you start hanging around with him. The first is that he has difficulty with children. He has no ability at all to enter into their world. At a breakfast with local New Hampshire activists this morning an adorable six-year-old girl is put forward by her mother to ask a question. "What will you do to take all that bad stuff off TV?" she asks. This is not the sort of question that children think up themselves but that activists teach children to ask. In response Buchanan puts his hands apart as if he's just been thrown a basketball and is looking to pass it on, the way he does when he's delivering an impassioned speech, and says, "Maybe we can use the bully pulpit of the presidency to clear that TV up." Then he launches into a powerful diatribe of the sort that leveled grown men for years on *Crossfire.* The little girl shrinks behind her mother's skirt, as well she might.

Balancing oddly against this is Buchanan's other surprising trait: his gift for telling people what they want to hear, or, rather, for not telling them what they don't want to hear. Buchanan is famous, of course, for saying exactly what he thinks no matter whom it offends. This is only because he is being judged by the standards of politics, which are different from those of real life. On a Wall Street trading floor, for instance, Buchanan would be regarded as a mild fellow, a man of compromise. There are all sorts of subjects that he doesn't care to take a stand on. One small example: A man slides into a booth beside him at a diner, announces he is a supporter, and asks Buchanan what he thinks of New

Jersey governor and Dole supporter Christie Todd Whitman. Buchanan flinches slightly, as if his mouth caught whatever he was going to say instinctively on the way out and stored it somewhere in his cheek, and asks, "Tell me, what do you think of her?"

"I *love* her!" the man enthuses.

Buchanan just nods as the man sings her praises and then changes the subject. He never does say what he thinks. He does this sort of thing a dozen times in a single campaign day.

Buchanan alone has ventured up into northern New Hampshire; with the exception of Lamar Alexander, who is doing some light lifting in the southern part of the state, the other candidates are either trapped by the blizzard down south or drinking hot chocolate in their hotel rooms. The other candidates fear they might be trapped by the snow for days if they come north, and their fear only further emboldens Buchanan. "If we're snowbound and can't get out of here, we'll just do talk radio from here," he says, "Ollie, Rush, Liddy . . ." Northern New Hampshire is transformed into Lunaticville, U.S.A. Hundreds of miles of blue highways are lined with Buchanan signs planted by his advance team until, after a while, you have the impression that there is no one else in the race. I travel with a Buchanan aide behind a van carrying Buchanan, listening to Buchanan on talk radio. We stop in small town halls and libraries and are met by groups of twenty and thirty people carrying Buchanan signs and known by the Buchanan campaign as "activists" (by definition, anyone who bothers to walk through a foot of snow to get to Pat). Men who haven't shaved or bathed squeeze in beside Buchanan in roadside diners to tell him how pissed off they are.

Our politicians tend to imagine the country geographically (North, South, East, and West), but political life is more subtle and elusive than that. In political life we do just as well to consider the country's emotional partitions (anger, despair, hope, apathy). For just as surely as Dole enjoys a lock on Kansas, Buchanan rides herd on rage. His campaign is a tour not of New Hampshire on a snowy afternoon but of American anger. One of Buchanan's supporters, a middle-aged man with a dry fly sticking out of a Boston Red Sox baseball cap on his head, even says, "I'm so angry that I got to go to anger classes." He just sits there at a counter drinking coffee and talking about how angry he is *all the time.* Pat thinks this is a joke of some sort, but it's not: some local judge has sentenced the guy to anger therapy. As the man makes room for another angry follower he tells me that in the past five years he has had emphysema, cancer, triple-bypass surgery, and "the knocks," whatever those are. His best friend put a bullet through his head last year. "Mr. Buchanan is a good man," he says, in conclusion. "Fuck all other countries."

Buchanan sits in the center of his campaign like an eye at the center of a hurricane. His stump speech is always the same: He starts out by teasing a small child in the front row until she looks like she's ready to cry, at which point he turns his attention to the giggling adults. He attacks NAFTA, Japan, federal judges, Pat Schroeder's $4.2 million government pension, and companies that shut down factories and move jobs overseas. He supports the Founding Fathers, term limits for everyone, including judges, and campaign finance reform. He is extremely articulate and, I imagine, persuasive. If you had to distill his message into a single sentence it would be this: Vote for me and the world will return to the way it was before honest American workers lost control of their country.

A nostalgia salesman—that's what Buchanan is. Like all nostalgia salesmen he appeals to everyone who knows nothing about the past and is unhappy for whatever reason with the present. His most devoted followers brim with the feeling that something good in the world has been lost. They are not so very wrong: something has been lost; something is always being lost. The question is what. And why? People who attack Buchanan as an ugly man with ugly views miss the whole point of him. He is enormously likable, and I'm sure that most of the people who loathe him in the abstract would like him in the concrete. This is what makes him so strange and interesting. He weds an open, friendly, inclusive manner to a closed, hostile, and exclusive set of policies. He is able to engage with everyone he meets but is nonetheless capable of demonizing just about every human being on the planet except for his mythical American working people. That is why he can sell his message; coming from him in the flesh it sounds almost friendly.

It's dark by the time we arrive in the Tamworth Union Hall. Another blizzard has crashed down upon New Hampshire, and there's a couple of inches of snow on the ground. For the past half an hour we have been the only cars on the road, wending our way silently on white highways through green pine forests dusted with fresh powder. Buchanan has delivered essentially the same speech five times in person and another half a dozen times on the radio. But instead of winding down he becomes more animated with each delivery. When you listen to Buchanan you have to remind yourself that most people become tired of hearing themselves say the same thing over and over again. Even some politicians—Dole is a case in point—grow weary of their own beliefs. They stop speaking and start reciting. (In Dole's case he has almost stopped speaking altogether.) At some level, they cease to believe in what they are saying. Buchanan is just the opposite: he is more fully engaged with his views the tenth time he has offered them up than he is the first. It's one of the essential traits of the dogmatist that he acquires faith in himself through repetition.

Thirty people have somehow made their way to the town hall to hear him out. The sum total of political commitment in that one room already is greater than anything in the entire Dole campaign. Buchanan starts by poking fun at a four-year-old boy in the front row who is yawning. The kid for once enjoys the attention; he hams it up, pretending to yawn for the next five minutes, but Buchanan has moved on. He's on fire, and no one is safe. Not Bill Clinton: "The army is not his plaything. They aren't the Arkansas state troopers." Not the Supreme Court: "The Supreme Court has usurped power and authority all across the country from the American middle class. Can you imagine what the Founding Fathers would have done if the Supreme Court had thrown out prayer from all the public schools? *Lock and load!*" Not Oliver Stone: "He's poisoning the well against his country with these terrible movies." Not Japanese prime minister Ryutaro Hashimoto: "Who is this guy? I'll tell you who he is. This guy is a samurai warrior. He's cleaning Mickey Kantor's clock!" Not the Fortune 500: "Some of the biggest companies in America don't care about America. They care about profits. The company's got their loyalty, not their country."

Once he lands on corporate America, Buchanan has found his strongest theme: national socialism. Big companies are betraying our country. As he lays into the rich corporate elite, his southern accent comes and goes. Now it comes, with the rhythm of a prose poem:

> AT&T lays off forty-thousand workers
> Did you see that?
> Well, lemme tell ya
> No one is lookin' out
> No one gives a hoot
> Clinton dudn't
> And the Republicans dudn't.

He grows hotter and hotter until he has arrived at his favorite moment. Suddenly, I know exactly what he's about to say. I've seen him say it once before, and I have no doubt I will see him say it many times again. He's going to explain that the American workingman needs Pat Buchanan because the only other guy in the whole country who even *talks* about his problems is . . . a midget. Actually, he puts it a bit more delicately: "Oh, yeah. There's Robert Reich down in the Labor Department. He's this . . . little guy." As he speaks he holds out his hand about three feet off the floor, a full foot and a half below the place the labor secretary's head would reach. "Reich talks about the problem, but he's not going to do anything about it."

Everyone nods. No midget is qualified to deal with such a big problem. The people give Buchanan their grim approval. They nod and clap and purse their lips like they are determined to take charge of their country. I've seen that look before, through a thousand snowy windshields in New Hampshire. These are the people who go hurtling through blizzards at seventy miles an hour but who also refuse to fly on airplanes after a bomb goes off somewhere in the world. Pat makes them feel like they're back in control.

When I sit down to a meal with Buchanan and the small band of young men who travel with him, the conversation drifts onto the subject of Bob Dole's health, and I mention that I was watching Dole speak in Washington not long ago and he didn't look as young as he once did. This kind of talk plays into every Republican candidate's fantasy: every one of them has a scenario wherein Dole drops out for reasons of health and he wins. Buchanan says he doesn't yet need this for consolation: he thinks he can beat Dole in New Hampshire straight up. But his campaign aides squirm with silent pleasure until finally one of them, nicknamed Hollywood because he has been filmed over the past week by both MTV and ABC, says, "Well he is, what, seventy-three?"

That's the signal to start tossing the dirt on the coffin.

"Yeah, seventy-three," says another of the aides. No seventy-two-year-old in American history has been accused so often of being seventy-three as Dole has been over the past few months.

"An injury like that will take a lot out of you," says a third aide.

"He is not looking very well," concludes Hollywood.

"He had that operation on his prostate, too," says Buchanan, thoughtfully, before changing the subject. He's less interested in Dole's health than in the upcoming battle in Iowa. In Des Moines, exactly six days from today, the candidates will debate for the first time. The first debate, says Buchanan, is the place where a candidate—and his ideas—can find an audience. In Iowa anyone might break out.

"Anyone?" I ask, looking down the list of the candidates I am supposed to get to know.

"Anyone," he says.

TWO

The Grizz

Within minutes of landing in Des Moines you know that you have arrived in the American Midwest. The Midwest is the straight man of the Western world, millions and millions of square miles peopled with Abbotts without their Costellos. It's not that midwesterners lack a sense of humor; it's just that they regard humor as second-rate behavior, the opposite of, rather than a complement to, seriousness. It's no wonder that professional midwestern humorists—Garrison Keillor, David Letterman—have the feel of men who have spun out of some orbit. The great conceit of this place is that it is normal, while everyplace else is just a little bit odd. Hence the phrase "solid midwestern values." (When was the last time you ever heard anyone refer to "solid southern values" or "solid eastern values"?) Anyone who believes this about the Midwest, however, must explain how it came to produce Morry Taylor.

It is not long before eight in the morning when the unlikeliest presidential candidate sets out down a desolate stretch of Iowa freeway inside a thirty-five-foot Airstream Land Yacht plastered all over with his favorite screaming-eagle logo—the one his campaign staffers plead with him to abandon. A ferocious-looking bird flies out of the *T* in Morry's last name, painted in huge letters across the side of the colossal machine. Morry's campaign manager tried to talk him out of it, but Morry insisted that the best way to start running was to buy six of these motor homes and race them in a convoy across each of Iowa's ninety-nine counties and into every New Hampshire hamlet: six monstrosities all jammed together and churning down the highway at eighty miles per hour, with Bruce Springsteen's "Born in the U.S.A." blaring out of a speaker on top of the lead vehicle. The way Morry saw it, he'd roll his Land Yachts into town, surround the local courthouse, flip on the rooftop speakers, tap a few kegs of beer, and have everyone talking for weeks about the new Republican candidate for president, Morry Taylor. He was right.

This morning as we speed past cars and the trucks abandoned in drifts during the most recent snowstorm, the noise of the Land Yachts drowns out everything, right down to the squeals of the baby pigs in their tin bunkers beside the highway. Everything but Morry, that is, perched high up in a captain's chair at the front of the lead Land Yacht. He's on his cell phone conducting his usual round of early morning radio interviews. Specifically, he's telling a New Hampshire disc jockey about a recent poll in which several thousand ordinary Americans were asked blindly about the candidates' platforms, without being told which platform belonged to which candidate. The Morry Taylor platform—roughly describable as one part economic conservatism, one part social liberalism, and one part titan of commerce—won in a landslide. Taylor's platform beat Dole's. It beat Clinton's. It beat everyone's. In theory at least, Morry Taylor is the most popular politician in America. He celebrates this achievement with a slow drag on an enormous cigar, then shouts back at Lenny, a resourceful young man whose job is to race around sorting out the chaos that Morry creates wherever he goes in Iowa and New Hampshire, "Hey piss-boy. Are we in the Connecticut primary?"

There's some shuffling in the back of the Land Yacht. "I'm not sure," says Lenny.

"I'm on about the same as Dole," says Morry into the phone. "Dole and I are on the most ballots." Which is true. Although Morry's strategy is to focus on Iowa first and then New Hampshire ("If I win Iowa, New Hampshire's mine, too"), the Perot people have created a truly national organization for him. And while the other marginal candidates in the nine-man field—Senator Richard Lugar, Congressman Bob Dornan—are running to win their 2 or 3 percent of the vote, which they can then cash in like chips in a casino for prestige and appointments, Morry has no interest in anything short of total victory. He is also the only candidate who is the least bit persuasive when he says he has no interest in being president for more than four years. "Why the hell would I want to do that?" he says. "I like my life." And he does. "Anyone who wants to come and help, call 1-800-USA-BEAR," he hollers into the cell phone. The talk-show host on the other end of the line asks him the obvious question. "Well," replies Morry, "I use the bear number because my nickname is the Grizz."

"Why do they call you the Grizz?" I ask, after he hangs up. It seems the natural first question.

"I got that when I took Titan public," he explains. "At the closing they gave me this plaque. It says—and they did it in Latin, which language I can't speak—but this is what it says: IN NORTH AMERICA THERE IS NO KNOWN PREDATOR TO THE GRIZZLY. So I became the Grizz. Then I thought about it. Up until that time I kind of liked my other nickname, Attila. 'Cause of Attila the Hun, you know. People think Attila the Hun was a barbarian, but he's not. He's the guy who ran the Roman Legion out of town."

"History says what happened," he continues, drawing inspiration from an unexpected place. "The Romans, they figured 'This barbarian, we'll just give him some gold and tell him to go away.' So they got together this whole delegation and all the gold and they went out to him and Attila listened to them. They had all the gold and they said, 'If you don't back off we're going to annihilate you. So what'll it be?' Attila just kind of smiled, walked up to the Roman, took his knife, and slit his throat. Took the gold, put the guy's head in a sack, and sent it back with a messenger." (Those looking to confirm this version of Roman history should consult not Gibbon but the management text *The Leadership Secrets of Attila the Hun.*)

Morry Taylor leans back in his captain's chair with his cigar in his mouth and a look of perfect completion on his face. End of story. Whatever it means, I think, it doesn't bode well for the opposition.

At 9:00 a.m. the Land Yacht rolls up beside the front door of Ames High School and disgorges Morry. Morry then does his usual trick of startling the locals. He bursts through both double doors leading into the school, which, like all the doors he will open for the rest of the day, slam violently against the wall behind them. He marches off down a long corridor with the rest of us trying to keep up, leaving a trail of startled adolescents in his wake. He swaggers like a quarterback on the way to a huddle. To watch him you'd never know that he was on the wrong end of a rout.

"Did you play sports in high school?" I ask Morry or, rather, the silver streak running through the dark mane on the back of Morry's head. He doesn't even look around. He's shaking his head; I have no trouble imagining the scorn on his face. My question is plainly ridiculous. *"Did I play sports?"* he asks. "I am the biggest jock who ever ran for president. I can beat you in anything." And with that he blows through the double doors leading into the auditorium. High school probably was not prepared for Morry Taylor the first time he passed through, and it most certainly is no match for him now that he's sitting on $40 million–plus of Titan stock and a fully fueled presidential campaign. About thirty kids file in, slump down into their seats, and settle in for a snooze they'll never have. In Ames, Iowa, democracy is about to spring back to life.

"Your school is too big," booms Morry, and as the kids jolt and stir he enters his stream of consciousness. "This is what is wrong with America," he says, pointing at the kids. "Big, big, big. You don't see no little kids in here. No little kids with the big kids so that the little kids don't have anyone to look up to. When I was in school the third graders looked up to the eighth graders, and the eighth-grade boys were in love with the senior girls. The senior girls just thought they were cute little twerps, but it was good for them. Some kid comes to school with orange hair, you don't have to call the parents. Hell, we'll take care of the orange hair. A place like this breeds weirdos."

The students are now fully alert.

"I never could enjoy going to a school like this," concludes Morry. The kids seem to concur.

"How many of you ever take accounting?" he asks. The kids are now squirming and ducking: he's breaking down their resistance, making them nervous. Two hands go up. Morry shakes his head, a little sadly. "I know you got a lot of these teachers"—he waves nonchalantly at a couple of uneasy-looking older men in the rafters—"and they tell you a lot of . . ." (he doesn't use the word "crap," but he might as well) "*things* . . . but in your whole entire life you are only going to *use* one or maybe two of those things. Hell, I took two hundred fifty-seven engineering courses, and I never *used* one of them."

He pauses and seems to reconsider. I wonder if he's about to make a little plea for the joy of learning for its own sake, the importance of a liberal education, that sort of thing. He isn't. "Now we all agree that the most important thing in your life is your family," he says. "Your momma and your daddy, your brothers and your sisters. But right after that there's something else. We all know what it is, and it's . . . *green.*"

With that he reaches into his pocket and produces a fat roll of hundred-dollar bills. He holds it high so that everyone can see. Five grand. Cash. The kids are now perched on the edge of their seats, giggling nervously, probably wondering what they feed presidential candidates.

"It all comes down to accounting," says Morry. "Accounting and money. You can't live without it. And the minute you make it someone is trying to take it away from you. So *for God's sake,* find out about money!"

"Can I have some?" asks a kid in the front row.

"It's *mine!*" booms Morry, and puts the money back in his pocket, a nice illustration of some general business principle.

It's time to talk politics.

In the context of the Republican primary Morry's positions are somewhat quixotic: He's pro-choice (rousingly so, if asked), against sending troops to Bosnia, and keen on turning the Pentagon into a hotel for visiting congressmen, who, in a Taylor administration, will remain in their districts. He believes that CEOs of publicly held corporations should never be paid more than about twenty times the wages of their most menial workers, and behaves accordingly. No economics professor is a match for his dissection of fellow candidate Steve Forbes's plan to cut the capital gains tax rate to zero. "I sold fifteen million dollars' worth of stock to get into this thing," he says. "I paid five million dollars to Uncle Sam. Under Steve Forbes's plan I woulda paid nuthin'. The guys who work for me would pay seventeen percent on what they earn, and I would have paid no tax at all. And that's wrong." But the biggest difference between Morry and the others is the nature of the struggle. In Morry's view the campaign isn't so much a battle between Democrats and Republicans; to his way of thinking the Democrats aren't much different from the Republicans he's running against. "Clinton's okay," says Morry, when asked by one of the students about the man he plans to face off against in the fall election. "It's just that he's like the rest of them." The campaign, as Morry sees it, is a war against politics as currently practiced.

Here he arrives at the source of his political outrage: politicians. "The problem with government is that it is run by lawyers," he tells the kids. "The even bigger problem is that it is being run by the *stupid* lawyers. The smart ones become partners in big law firms. In other words, your government is staffed mainly by the rejects of the legal profession." Morry is running mainly on his promise to balance the federal budget in eighteen months not by eliminating programs but by firing a third of the lawyers, or at any rate the best-paid government employees. Having balanced the budget, he will then cut both programs and taxes.

"How many of you want to give the government forty percent of what you earn after you get outta here?" he asks the crowd.

29

One of the kids—a weirdo with a wispy beard—raises his hand.

"Mark his name down," says Morry. "An institution needs him. We're going to study his brain. He's not human. He's an alien."

All the kids laugh—even the weirdo—and Morry grins broadly, then distributes his poll. The Morry poll is an oversized glossy white sheet that he passes out wherever he goes in Iowa and New Hampshire. He explains that there is no way that he is going to pay some clown twenty-five thousand a year to do a poll for him. He's going to do it himself. "How many of you want to make five thousand dollars?" he asks. He's got the roll of hundreds out in the open again. Every hand under the age of eighteen goes up.

"On February fifth in each of the five congressional districts I'm going to hold a lottery," says Morry. "Five grand a pop. I'll put up the twenty-five grand. All you got to do to is show up and fill in my poll. The odds of winning the five grand are *much* better than the odds of winning the lottery."

All the students in the room are now busy reading Morry's poll. Some have started filling it in. Someone—one of the teachers—asks Morry if it is legal to raffle off twenty-five thousand dollars to the voters of Iowa. Morry smiles a Cheshire Cat smile and says, "All of the other campaigns have called the state attorney general's office to ask the same question. How *stupid* can they be? I've paid more in legal fees than all of them combined. Of course it's legal. I had my lawyers check it out."

The teachers of Iowa have now been stripped of the last shred of their dignity, but the kids are more riveted than ever as Morry heads toward his familiar conclusion. Ten times each day Morry Taylor, like every other presidential candidate, faces a television camera, or a microphone, or a crowd who has no idea who he is, and explains that he's different from and better than the other eight guys running in this year's Republican presidential primary. "I'm not a politician," he says. "And I'm not a lawyer. I'm a businessman." Usually he leaves it at that. But today for whatever reason he decides to elaborate.

"Whatta I got?" he shouts to his slightly bewildered Lenny (the piss-boy) who sits off to the side, unsure whether he's supposed to answer "forty million plus," "a dozen lawsuits," "two percent of the vote," or "zero self-doubt." It doesn't matter. The question is rhetorical. "I got three talk-show hosts, four lifelong politicians, and an heir," says Morry, in a neat summary of the Republican field. "I got Alan Keyes and Pat Buchanan. Alan talks real loud; he'll blow out your eardrums. Pat just wants to dress people up in uniforms, and he might have you goose-stepping a bit too. Steve Forbes. He ain't going anywhere, he's too nerdy." (Morry puckers his lips and makes owl eyes; the kids break up.)

"What else I got? Richard Lugey." The kids don't seem to notice the mispronunciation of Indiana senator Richard Lugar's name. "Lugey's running these ads about nuclear terrorism. Well, if he was president maybe you *would* have that problem. Phil Gramm. Not a pretty sight. Bob Dole. He's been running for president for twenty years and spent thirty million of your dollars doing it. Which one has ever created any jobs? Thousands of jobs? Only myself. Which one has any foreign experience? Only myself. They're all talkers. Better than me. I'm a doer. That's why they call me the Grizz."

And so it goes for fully forty minutes more until Morry ends with a rousing call to arms: "This is it, folks! This is the only time you have a choice: by November the only choice for president is between light gray and medium gray."

Tonight I was meant to hear former Tennessee governor Lamar Alexander speak but decide at the last minute to go with Morry Taylor, on the assumption that Lamar will be giving speeches for the rest of his life while Morry will probably be done by the end of February. We fly in one of Morry's private planes to a Republican county dinner at Storm Lake, in northwestern Iowa. It is held in a large warehouse disguised as a convention hall. We're a bit late, and everyone is hungry, but before we can eat we must do the usual Iowa Republican ceremony: first we pledge allegiance to the flag, then we sing the national anthem, and finally we join in a prayer, which concludes with a modest request that God "bless the people but not the bureaucrats." The moderator then instructs "the folks on the west side of the room" to line up for the buffet. "I apologize to the folks over here on the east," he adds. "But you'll have to wait." The obsession with points on the compass is another one of those strange midwestern traits. Iowans are distinguished less by race, creed, or gender than by the direction they are heading.

Morry, who is sitting at the head table (south), pops up and beats the crowd from the east to the buffet table (north), where he snags a fried chicken breast, green beans, mashed potatoes, and an anemic-looking salad. Surveying the crowd, he allows, "This is going to be wild tonight. There's going to be some smiles and some people pissed off. A lot of

Buchanan people. That guy at the end of the table—crazier than hell. He writes for the conservative paper." I point out that, out of 150 people, two have availed themselves of the cash bar. The rest drink cold tea without ice. "If you were a Democrat," I say, "you'd have a lot more fun."

"You know something about these people?" he says. "Your wife gets sick, and every one of these people would visit her. They'd take turns bringing meals by your house. Maybe not that many of them dance"—a Cheshire Cat smile—"but they would *love* watchin' me dance." Then just as I am starting to feel remorse for having struck such a condescending note, he drives my condescension into the sea. "Anyhow," he says, "do *you* know how to milk a cow?"

I shrug: How hard can it be to milk a cow?

"Okay, smart guy, let's say you are standing behind the cow," says Morry. "Whaddya do?" I gaze down the row of Republican dignitaries solemnly devouring their chicken breasts. The conservative newspaper editor sits glaring at Morry, goggle-eyed. "Here?" I say.

"Here," says Morry.

I get up from the table, establish the position of the cow, and walk around the right side. But before I can grab for the udder I am pulled up short by Morry's cackle.

"First of all," he says, "cows are never milked on the *right* side. Second of all, you never approach a cow from the *ass*."

"Mr. Taylor?" says the moderator, now at the podium. But Morry doesn't hear him; he's illustrating his point, milking the air, making yanking motions with both hands. "You grab those udders and you start yanking," he says.

"Are you ready, Mr. Taylor?" says the moderator.

"I'm ready," says Morry, ending the lesson and starting his speech. "I've been laughed at all my life in business—all I've had is losers," he begins, on his way to drawing an elegant analogy with his political predicament. Within minutes he has the crowd laughing and clapping at his descriptions of Washington idiocy. They appear to agree with him about everything, especially the lunacy of Steve Forbes's plan to eliminate the capital gains tax. Then in the midst of the fun a brave woman rises and challenges his position on abortion. She believes that abortion should be outlawed.

"It's a religious issue," Morry says, "not a matter for the federal government."

The Grizz: Morry Taylor in his natural habitat.

She presses him: you can see she's used to making public speakers either come around to her way of thinking or regret ever opening their mouths. But then she is used to dealing with people who run for office for a living—for whom losing is a disaster rather than a chance to go back to normal life. Instead of backing down or wiggling, Morry goes on the attack: "Look, ma'am, I think ninety-nine percent of women never want an abortion. They go through a lot of mental anguish. They suffer a lot. I say leave it to them." The woman tries to speak again but Morry interrupts her: "I said, *leave . . . it . . . to . . . the . . . women.*"

And there, at a banquet filled with Republican Party hacks, the sort of people who are meant to be rabidly pro-life, whom Morry *expected* to be rabidly pro-life, a volcano of spontaneous applause erupts. All over the room women are clapping so hard I think they'll break their hands. Here, I think, is the benefit of having someone around who feels free to speak his mind. He liberates, however momentarily, those who don't.

We leave before the other speeches are over. As Morry slams shut the door of the private plane he says, "One guy came up and said, 'I really appreciate you running. I *really* appreciate you running.' That makes you feel good. At least somebody. Better than someone coming up and telling you what a dumb shit you are." We sit quietly until the plane levels out over a carpet of clouds. Then Morry asks me how I think he did. I tell him the truth: He had the audience where he wanted it after his remarks on abortion. He lost it by insisting that if the people failed to vote for him they'd spend the rest of their lives with the word "stupid" tattooed on their foreheads.

"I'm too used to making a sale," he says. "I get 'em right up close and I say: 'Now I got you. And when I got you I want to nail you down.'" He waves his hand in the air as if he were batting away a bee. "All these people are telling me I gotta leave them wanting more."

"It's true," shouts Lenny, from the front of the plane.

"I ain't gonna change," says Morry.

JANUARY 14

It's the day of the first Iowa debate, during which any dark horse might emerge into the sunlight. I am waiting at the front desk of the Des Moines YMCA when Morry arrives just before 9:00 a.m.: "What, you thought I wouldn't show?" The racquetball game takes just under twenty-two minutes. Morry wins: 15–0, 15–5. I figured that between the twenty-five extra pounds he's carrying around and the sixteen years he has on me I could outhustle him. I was wrong. He knows every angle and trick on the court and played each one with relish. "Too good!" he'd shout after he'd dropped the ball into the corner for the tenth time. As the rout progressed he shouted to his aides—who had at length turned up—to come and watch. "Fourteen to zip, not bad for an old guy," he shouted. And then, under his breath, "Some of my guys are betting on you. Dipshits." As we crawl through the hole out the back of the court he says, "Don't you go write that you lost because you were nervous the presidential candidate was going to have a heart attack." Camus identified the love of winning at games as one of the prerequisites of happiness in the modern world. And he did that without ever meeting Morry.

I go over to Titan about an hour before the big debate—the Des Moines *Register* Forum, it is called—and find Morry still in his sweatclothes with his feet up on his desk, scratching out his two-minute closing statement. On the other side of his desk his campaign manager looks on with a mixture of affection, anxiety, and disbelief. "Hey," Morry says when he sees me, "tell me what you think of this," and over his manager's protests he reads his closing remarks aloud. Half of it isn't bad, but the other half is a series of wisecracks about Bob Dole that doesn't seem to belong in a presidential debate.

I offer my first strategic political advice: Cut the Dole stuff; stress the unfairness of Forbes's tax plan compared to his own by drawing on his own life experience; and let people know loudly that he's pro-choice. His manager winces. The Taylor campaign feels the surest way to turn off Republican primary voters is to be loudly pro-choice, and it's true that it didn't exactly work for Senator Arlen Specter, who withdrew from the race not long after the United We Stand convention in Dallas. I make two points: (a) half the people at the Storm Lake event—party hacks every one—had to restrain themselves from leaping to their feet and cheering when Morry came out with his beliefs; and (b) it's not as if Morry has any votes to lose.

Outside the Des Moines television station there are two chanting mobs of about two hundred people each divided by a street. One holds bright orange signs that say EXPOSE THE RIGHT; the other waves signs for Dole, Gramm, and Morry Taylor. From the crowd noise a casual observer might surmise that Taylor and Gramm were vying for first place with Dole running a distant third. I slide past and into the studio, where I present myself as an arm of the Taylor campaign. Someone signs me in reluctantly, but to check me out the attractive woman in charge insists on walking me down to Morry's studio. But as we enter the back corridor we bump into Morry on his way to the stage. He's strutting. Both arms are swinging, and a cluster of six people are failing to keep up with him. "He can stay," he says with a magisterial wave, and moves on.

The debate puts a fine point on the current state of play. Very little separates the other candidates—it's merely a matter of emphasis. Light gray and medium gray, as Morry puts it. Keyes and Buchanan stress their pro-life message. All the other candidates except Morry agree or at least refuse to disagree. The exchanges feel tentative, provisional. It's like one of those pickup basketball games in which everyone who loses pretends he wasn't trying. Since everyone, including Clinton, claims pretty much to believe the same thing, the campaign boils down to a popularity contest. But it is an unusual popularity contest. The winner will not be the man who genuinely appeals to the most people but the man who seems the most presidential.

But then something happens: Forbes, in a word. Alexander, Gramm, and Dole each attack Forbes's tax plan. And with each fresh blow Forbes physically rises in his seat. The man started out nervously pulling down his coattail as if he were waiting for his mother to inspect his dress. Now all of a sudden he's a *player*—taken seriously by the guys who have raised the most money from other people. With each inch Forbes rises, Morry and the other long shots shrink. How organic and fluid this process is! Anyone who lands upon an issue and proves its electoral merit is likely to have influence. Anyone who is capable of attracting attention to himself can stick a wrench in the public debate for weeks. Every one of the candidates stands a chance of shaping future policy. Either he will win, or his issue will be poached by the winner, adopting the same style with which Clinton has poached so much of the Republican social agenda. If Forbes succeeds in getting his flat tax accepted, for example, it hardly matters that he loses the race. Just as if Morry succeeds in making Forbes's tax plan look ridiculous he will have struck one of the great blows for fairness, even though no one will remember his name.

As we near the ninety-minute mark Morry is invited to offer his closing remarks. He is seated exactly where he wanted to be, between Dole and Gramm. His situation facilitates one of his best lines, "I got a couple of million bucks of government pensions sitting on either side of me." The studio loves it, but it is entirely lost on the TV audience, since the camera keeps to tight shots of the candidates; no one watching at home has any idea whom Morry is sitting next to. Otherwise he has cut the jokes about Dole and stressed his views about the Forbes tax plan with a personal anecdote.

As I realize what is happening a little shiver of concern runs down my spine. No, I think, he couldn't be so foolish as to take my advice. But then he says, "Since it has come up so often I think I should say a few words about a woman's choice."

"Time's up, Mr. Taylor," says the moderator.

Every other candidate, when told that his time is up, simply ignores the instruction and plows right along. "Okay," says Morry, then leans back, crosses his legs, wholly devoid of interest or even feigned interest in what the others are saying.

Afterward I rush to the airport in an attempt to beat Steve Forbes back to New Hampshire, hauling along for the ride all the stuff Morry gave me: T-shirts, baseball caps, candy, literature. The American Airlines ticket counter is empty. As I stand there, up comes a man who looks a little like Bob Dornan and asks if there are any seats left on the Chicago flight. He *is* Bob Dornan. B-1 Bob. His bright red furnace face ignites a brushfire of red hair. Even in repose the former marine pilot and current congressman from Orange County, California, looks as if he's about to blow a gasket. Once again I wonder if politicians, like actors, mold their personas to their faces. Dornan is typecast by his appearance: when he is smiling, he can't look anything but drunk; when he is not, he can't look anything but angry. Either way he seems just about to insult someone.

The ladies behind the counter fail to recognize him. Dornan drops a hint: "I was just participating in the presidential debate," he says. This means nothing to the women behind the counter, who have found a seat for him but are now demanding a ticket and identification, which Dornan can't find. "I'm a congressman," he says, as if this explains anything. The women are not impressed by this fact. "I think I won the presidential debate," he says. They ignore him completely. It is a nice illustration of a general principle: If a politician falls in the woods and the witnesses do not know who he is, no one hears him. Finally I say, "You did really well," which is only a slight exaggeration, and then explain to the ladies behind the counter who Bob Dornan is. His credibility skyrockets. They treat him as a big shot. You never can tell who might be president one day.

Together Dornan and I walk to the end of the concourse. There we stand alone with a clear view of a row of private jets across the tarmac. Dornan flew jets for the marines in Korea; more recently he asked to fly missions during the Gulf War. Now he points lovingly to a Learjet. I tell him it belongs to Dole. He reddens right up to his roots. "You'd think the guy could give me a ride back," he says. "When I quit doing this he'll expect me to endorse him and act as a surrogate, and he can't even give me a ride back to Washington."

Bob Dornan: the Mad Bomber's final run starts
as a publicity stunt and ends in disaster.

The prospect lingers in the air between us. Then perhaps by way of explanation he says, "If I get two percent in New Hampshire I'll have done well." I feel bad for him: he's just sat in the middle of national politics and an hour later he is reduced to obscurity. He finds a pay phone, calls home collect, and asks whoever answers if they saw him on the debate. He returns with rising spirits and tells me that "the first caller in to C-Span said Dole for president, Dornan for vice president."

But even as he speaks, the words are silenced by actions. Out from a hangar on the far end of the tarmac rolls the long green-and-gold jet that flies Steve Forbes to his campaign events. The man to watch! Stenciled along the side is its gloriously shameless name, *Capitalist Tool.* The other planes are mere toys beside the *Capitalist Tool,* and Dornan's lips part slightly as he watches it pass. "Rakish," he says, then goes silent.

THREE

The Crystal Owl

Time and *Newsweek* are here in Iowa, gearing up to put Steve Forbes on their covers. David Broder is here from the Washington *Post*. Gene Randall is here from CNN, not so much to ask as to *perform* a few questions on the TV screen beside Forbes. Sam Donaldson is here, looking more like another candidate than a reporter as he is driven from Forbes event to Forbes event in the back of a dark blue Cadillac. And everywhere he goes Forbes is greeted by friendly crowds too large to count. The reporters from AP and Reuters do what they always do in these difficult situations when a candidate draws serious crowds. Each makes a rough guess of the number of people in the room. They then average these totals to create a fact for posterity.

If you had asked me who of all the rich men I had ever met was least likely to go courting the American voter, I would have given you Steve Forbes's name first. I have rarely encountered anyone so perfectly unhappy shaking hands and making small talk, so thoroughly uncomfortable in his skin. The sheer unease of his manners and conversation is a match for the most constipated English aristocrat. The reason is that he was raised in the manner of a constipated English aristocrat. The heir to the heir to the *Forbes* magazine fortune, he spent his boyhood on a horse farm in New Jersey. He attended Princeton in the late 1960s and, at the height of the antiestablishment sentiment, founded a magazine called *Business Today*. Somehow privilege and temperament conspired to make him a misfit.

And yet under the unwatchful gaze of the cameras something is happening. His deep unease is being transformed into a dignified reticence.

His reluctance to take any kind of conversational risk is being interpreted as a calculated display of political prudence. The television cameras flatten the landscape they seek to depict and, in the case of Forbes, make the strange seem simply ordinary. The cameras create the illusion that a candidate is being watched when in fact he is being hidden.

The most striking thing about the Forbes campaign is its repetitiveness. Spend a few hours stumping with Forbes in Iowa or New Hampshire and you've heard just about every word he will ever speak. Each of his speeches is not merely a reasonable approximation of the last but a near-perfect replica. All the other candidates have their favorite lines but try, with varying degrees of success, to find different ways to make the same points. With Forbes nothing is left to chance; it's the same every time, right down to the gestures and the taut grin he uses to punctuate his lines. He sets his wristwatch down on the podium together with his left hand and a single sheet of paper—though he never actually looks at his notes. Instead his eyes sweep across the crowd, left to right, with the same rhythmic efficiency as the carriage of a typewriter. I time his eye movements. Each sweep is almost exactly the same length, about eight seconds.

Offstage he is much the same as on. If he is unable to repeat himself he ducks. Shoulder to shoulder with journalists in his campaign van, bouncing over potholes at sixty miles an hour, he responds to questions not only in the same words but in the same *tone* as in his stump speech. "Why do you think the other candidates ganged up on you in Iowa?" I ask him. "They represent the politics of the past versus a vibrant vision of the future," he replies, automatically. Carving through the New Hampshire state assembly cafeteria en route to deliver his speech, he stops to converse with three ladies. It turns out that one of them has worked with the AFL-CIO. "Why aren't you going to keep the minimum wage?" she asks, a bit aggressively. "I worked closely with [former AFL-CIO president] Lane Kirkland at Radio Free Europe," says Forbes, apropos of nothing, and then bolts before the cameras have time to record the exchange.

I watch Forbes deliver the same speech half a dozen times before I get close enough to find evidence to support my hunch—or perhaps my hope—that a perfectly strict routine is not as straightforward as it appears. At the Chubb Life Insurance Company in Concord, New Hampshire, I find myself standing immediately behind him, waiting for his inner jukebox to produce the same tunes. I assumed that he read from the same written text but to my amazement see that he actually uses loose notes, as if he had just thought up his speech in the car on the way over. The notes are not even crisp and neatly typed, but a mess of slashes, signs, and keywords. They are the work not of a drone but of a man who is forever trying new things on for size, or at least thinks he is. The top few inches looks like this:

+ FRUSTRATE
XXXXXXX
+ GTR
– XXXXX
+ GROWTH
XXXX——

What the hell is *that* all about? I wonder but am interrupted by a second surprise: the microphone goes on the blink. There's a little crackle on the line that interferes with Forbes's speech. He looks up and spontaneously says, "That's Bob Dole." The room breaks up, and even Forbes himself can't quite believe it—he's made a joke. In the context of his performance that one little line is the equivalent of the invention of the microchip. An awkward smile of true, unexpected delight breaks sloppily across his face. A few years back there was a television commercial for the Special Olympics that concluded with a retarded boy bursting through the tape at the finish line and breaking into a joyous, heart-tugging smile. Forbes now wears exactly the same expression. He has a Special Olympics smile.

Suddenly I realize what I am watching: a man attempting to disprove what he is with what he says. Forbes is spending $35 million to ensure that every voter in Iowa and New Hampshire will hear the same commercial attacking Bob Dole something like forty times before Election Day. Its gist is that Dole is a dried-up old Washington hack while Forbes is a vital business giant who understands invention and entrepreneurship. Forbes is consumed by his faith that if you lower people's taxes you unleash their passions and inspire them to take all manner of risks. The flat tax is his Heloise, his Laura, his Dark Lady. And yet there he sits, astride a half-billion trust-fund dollars, unwilling to risk even a conversation or to stray from a single word in his memorized text. If I hadn't just watched Phil Gramm spending $20 million to persuade people that he alone knows the value of the dollar, I might have been shocked. But now

I understand that running seriously for president requires a man not to look too closely at himself.

JANUARY 21

The Rockingham County Republican Dinner. Everyone in New Hampshire who attends these banquets claims to hate government. Every ounce of being they have left over after pledging allegiance to the United States and singing the national anthem goes into despising the United States government. Yet the sort of people who turn up for New Hampshire Republican dinners are mainly professional Republicans—local officials, state representatives, congressmen's wives—and their friends and neighbors pressed into service. They show up at least in part because they think it will help their careers to be met and greeted by government higher-ups. That is, one purpose of these antigovernment rallies, from the point of view of those who pay one hundred bucks a plate to attend, is *to get ahead in government.*

One of the first people I see is Morry Taylor, hovering near the bar with a pair of ardent female supporters. He wants to know where I've been—as if following anyone other than him is a waste of time. When I tell him that I've been following Steve Forbes, he gets his grin on and says, "That must be *real* exciting." Of all the other candidates Forbes is the most ridiculous to Morry, and the media attention Forbes is attracting drives Morry to distraction. "That's not his money he's spending," Morry routinely informs audiences. "He didn't *make* that money. His gramps made it. And his daddy gave it to him. That's what's wrong with the newspaper business. They're so stupid they can't figure it out— having him speak for business!" What Morry fails to understand is that anyone who does not hold public office is granted equal commercial status in the Republican primary. Even Lamar Alexander, whose life has been a pursuit of political office, is allowed to describe himself as an entrepreneur. No distinction is made between an heir who presides over a magazine he inherited and a poor boy who built a manufacturing giant from scratch.

A sea of scribblers and one-eyed hairy monsters has turned out in force, but only for Forbes. While Morry stands alone and unnoticed in the corner of the banquet hall, Forbes is surrounded wherever he goes. I feel bad for Morry, but Forbes is the big story, and no one else—not

Steve Forbes: learning to wrestle, with a smile.

even Al D'Amato, who has turned up to speak out of the side of his mouth on Dole's behalf—commands more than passing attention. I ask a local worthy named Wally Stickney, who now endorses Forbes, why he is doing so well. "He's a real person, and he understands economics," says Stickney, neglecting to mention the $35 million ad campaign.

On his résumé Forbes claims truthfully to be the only person who has won four times "the prestigious Crystal Owl award." Tonight I bump into a journalist who competed against Forbes for the prize. The award was a publicity stunt for the U.S. Steel corporation, he says. Journalists were handed a list of questions and asked to guess such unknowable events as next year's rate of inflation. If there was a tie it was broken by guessing the Super Bowl score. Most journalists took it all as a great joke. Forbes took it seriously, pursued it fiercely, and won it repeatedly. Very WASP— like being good at croquet. But the prize now forms the cornerstone of his claim to economic literacy, together with his demeanor. There's no getting around the fact that Forbes looks and acts like the sort of person who *should* know all about economics. He calls to mind the WASP dad: the only subject on which you can even imagine having an intimate conversation with him is money, and, as a result, when talking about money you are often talking about something else.

In keeping with the classic WASP tradition Forbes has offered up his flat tax, and the economic prosperity that will supposedly ensue from it, as a cure for abortion, illiteracy, crime, and premarital sex. To have all these messy topics subsumed under a discussion of taxes clearly comes as both a relief to his fellow businessmen, who never were terribly interested in abortion, and as a face-saver for those abortion warriors who have grown weary of the war. Even though Forbes refuses to discuss abortion, he has won endorsements from professional pro-lifers such as former New Hampshire senator Gordon Humphrey. He has offered them an out from a fight they wished they'd never picked. His intense social discomfort merely amplifies the message. To raise abortion with Steve Forbes seems about as natural as telling your grandmother that you got laid last Saturday night.

At length this embodiment of the politics of repression rises and restates his claim that "there's no real distinction between values and economics," which is exactly the opposite of what a professional economist would tell you on the first day of class. He then furthers the gap between himself and the discipline he invokes by asserting the two spurious economic claims on which his successful campaign is founded. Here, in a nutshell, are the ideas that have captured the current presidential race:

1. "Every time we have lowered taxes in this country, government revenues have risen." Even I know that this is highly misleading. Nominal tax receipts have gone up every year—thanks to economic growth and inflation—but in general have risen less after taxes have been cut than after they have been raised. Forbes's mind has frozen around this assertion, however. His core belief is that the American people are caged animals; lowering taxes will have the same effect as letting the animal out of the cage. I am skeptical, as I always am of theories of human behavior that fail to explain the conduct of the theorists. I certainly would not work harder if Steve Forbes lowered my taxes, and I'll bet he wouldn't either.

2. "Cutting taxes leads to economic growth." The problem with this one is that the last big tax cut, during the Reagan administration, had no measurable impact on the economy's growth rate. And with tax rates now lower in the United States than any in the industrial world, it seems unlikely that they are the main drag, though of course you never really know.

Both of Forbes's economic beliefs date back to the early Reagan years, when a consultant named Arthur Laffer sketched a curve on a restaurant napkin. The Laffer curve showed that if the government raised tax rates from extremely high levels—say from 90 to 100 percent —it might actually suffer a decline in tax revenues. After all, if you had to give everything you earned to the government, who would bother to work? But the Laffer curve people have done this for so long that they have forgotten about the other end of their curve: by lowering tax rates from extremely low levels the government must at some point suffer a decline in revenues. The big question is where the curve bends. Forbes's flat tax implies that this occurs at a tax rate of about 17 percent.

On and on it goes until I realize it is one of those nights to find amusement wherever you can. Almost unnoticed as Forbes speaks, Dole's stand-in, Al D'Amato, slips away from the rostrum and heads to the men's room. En route he grabs a handsome young aide by the elbow and pulls him inside. I follow, on the hunch that I might be tracking to its source D'Amato's brave defense of gays in the military. I find them together—the aide standing a few steps behind D'Amato, who stands at the urinal barking instructions over his shoulder. But upon my entrance they fall silent.

I slip into the stall and hover beneath a defaced poster of Lamar Alexander, across which someone has scribbled, acutely, ANOTHER CLINTON: ALL TALK! and hope they'll forget I'm there, but they don't. Al finishes quickly and marches out to press the flesh and deliver his speech. He is introduced by a female Republican official with a cone-head hairdo as "the man who is pursuing the Whitewater hearings to pave the way for us to take back the White House in 1996." The crowd rises to its feet and cheers. Everyone within three tables of Forbes uses it as a chance to rubberneck. Just one look! Please!

JANUARY 22

A final journey into Steve Forbes Land: two factories, one chamber of commerce, and a Rotary Club. When you tour a factory with Morry Taylor you leave understanding how it works. When you tour a factory with Forbes you receive a high-school field trip lecture from its manager to which Forbes responds with little nods. He never asks a question or displays the slightest curiosity about or pleasure in how things work. His relation to the means of production is fully alienated.

The Rotary Club convenes for lunch at a family restaurant outside of

Portsmouth. Before Forbes rises again to proclaim his message of vibrant optimism, he must eat. Animal spirits! He follows the chief Rotarian to the buffet table and then through the line. He watches what the Rotarian does and mimics him exactly. Self-consciousness at the buffet table is only natural; we all find ourselves wondering whether we have taken too much of the sprightly roast beef and not enough of the withered lettuce. But Forbes takes the fine art of buffet repression to a ridiculous extreme. He takes precisely the same amount of everything as the Rotarian and arranges his plate so that it is identical—right down to the placement of the giant roll.

While the Rotarians move through the line Forbes sits down alone and digs in. He works through the plate the same way he always does—with no pleasure and perfect discipline. He begins with the rice and does not stop until he has finished off every last grain of it. Moving clockwise he polishes off the rest of his food in modules. First the chicken, then the salad, then the beans, and so on until nothing remains but a large cold bun. This is the only food he treats with interest. Disemboweling the soft doughy part from the harder shell, he rolls the shards into little wet bread balls. When the ball is perfectly smooth and round he pops it into his mouth. At the end of his lunch his plate is perfectly clean, save for a single slice of radish.

Of course he gives them exactly the same speech, decrying skeptics and naysayers and small-minded people who do not grasp the power of the animal spirits that will be unleashed by his tax cuts. But afterward, in the upstairs diner, a local TV interviewer, surrounded by the world's media, takes Forbes off to one side and attempts to do to him what he did to the bread roll. "We've heard a lot about your flat tax, but what kind of person is Steve Forbes?" he asks, reaching for the doughy part.

"He's forward looking, dynamic, optimistic," replies Forbes mechanically. The interviewer does not even know how to proceed. He gives up, and the press moves on, leaving a pair of bewildered diners, two women in their early thirties, who have witnessed the media frenzy. Such is the crush of the national press looking on that they were unable to see the candidate. They chat idly about the experience.

"Steve Forbes. He's the millionaire guy?"

"He's Malcolm Forbes's son."

"And he's ahead in the polls now?"

"I don't know."

"What's he look like?"

"He looks kinda average."

"Tony said the other day, 'So who you leaning towards?' I said, 'I dunno. Like who's the best-looking guy?' Are you gonna vote?"

"I dunno. Can I?"

But it is a rule of American politics that you cannot pass Go without collecting your share of personal abuse. Forbes's daily rise in the polls, which now show him ahead of Dole, has everyone aching for a scandal. As he exits the Rotary Club diner he runs smack into a giant ring of press people just like the ones you see in the movies. The idea seems to be that if you really want to figure out what lies inside a man you circle around him like a school of sharks with twenty cameras and fifty hostile faces and start hollering questions at him. Everyone but me seems to know when these circles are supposed to form; I am forever racing around the fringes trying to get in. On this occasion I happen to be standing just behind Forbes: I see them as he sees them. At the front are three pretty television reporters, two women and a man. They wear creepy, expectant smiles.

"When will you address questions about your personal life?" asks the most evil looking of the bunch.

"Ask me anything you want," says Forbes. His turtle eyes blink through his Coke-bottle lenses, and the TV hack looks confused. For the first time I think: This guy is tough. The shell formed over years of repression is built to resist. Anyone who tries to take his dignity away from him has got a war on his hands.

"What about your father's . . . personal life?" says the journalist, fishing for a total breakdown. Everyone knows that Malcolm Forbes liked the boys in the *Forbes* mail room. It's not even news. If his son can be goaded into anger about it, however, it's a headline.

The reporter is still smiling creepily in anticipation of Forbes's incipient anger or panic. I can't quite believe how repulsive this guy is; any ordinary person would have felt the urge to punch him in the mouth. His question is even more disgusting for being put in such a chickenshit way. "These people are evil," I say to the guy on my right, who, upon closer inspection, proves to be Bill Dal Col, Forbes's campaign manager. But he's smiling too: it's part of his game. "This is America," he says.

"My father is dead," says Forbes, now in full WASP mode. "I'll answer any questions about me."

All at once you can see the circle wilt. The people inside have no idea what to do or to say. Having persuaded themselves of their power to ruin not just candidacies but lives, they have worked themselves up into a collective frenzy. But the best they can do when faced with the candidate of repression, a man whose own wife probably does not know whether he wears boxers or briefs, is to ask him about his father. They can't even do *that* properly. Right then and there, between a strip mall and a Dunkin' Donuts, they just . . . back off. Within moments Forbes is again talking safely about money, and no one knows what else to ask him.

That night I flew on Forbes's plane with Forbes and Dal Col from New Hampshire to the candidate's home in the New Jersey suburbs. Not long after we boarded, Forbes reached behind his seat to retrieve a plate of chocolate-chip cookies. In the context of his character it seemed like a wanton act. He offered them around, and after the rest of us helped ourselves, he took one for himself. Then he carefully returned the plate to its shelf behind his seat. A few minutes later, however, he had the plate on his lap again and was giving the cookies a long once-over, trying to decide whether to go for the dark chocolate or the light fluffy kind. Suddenly he remembered us. Again he proffered the plate. This time we declined. For an awkward moment he sat there staring into the plate of cookies, wondering what to do.

Then it is as if he is seized by his old sense of proportion, or perhaps a resentment of his own desire: he won't have a cookie either. He returns the plate to the rear of the seat and answers my question about his tax plan.

FOUR

You're No Pig Farmer!

People are always saying that when you run for president you put your whole life under a microscope. The public view is not nearly so clear and accurate as that. It is true that you are subjected to public inspection, and that the process is pitiless, but in a different, more arbitrary way—as if you were being judged not through a magnifying lens but a prism. The distortive power of this prism is so great that through it Morry Taylor appears ridiculous and Steve Forbes looks almost as if he could be president.

This morning the first poll shows Forbes leading Dole in New Hampshire, 29–24. Word arrives in Des Moines that Pat Buchanan won the Alaska caucus yesterday with 33 percent of the vote, and that Forbes finished second, two points behind. The *Alaska* caucus? Until today no one ever mentioned that Alaska was holding a caucus, probably because the Dole campaign decided to pretend that it wasn't. Now the Dole people have the pleasure of watching Buchanan stage a press conference in the Hotel Fort Des Moines—the Dole campaign's hotel—to explain why he won and Dole finished a distant third, with just 17 percent of the vote. I know that Dole is meant to have a lock on the nomination, but it is hard to see why. People support him not because he lights a fire under them, but because they think he is going to win. The minute that changes, the Dole campaign collapses like a penny stock; everyone who wants to vote for, work for, or just be near a winner will go racing around looking for someone else to back.

. . .

As the Iowa caucus approaches, Des Moines is coming to resemble an especially ruthless debutante party, with the nine candidates doing whatever they can to attract the public eye. I have a friend who spent a couple of unhappy years living in Manhattan. Wherever he traveled outside of New York he asked himself: "Would I rather live here or in New York?" The answer was always "Here" until he got to Des Moines. But that was then, and this is now, and Des Moines is hopping. Each morning the willing journalist wakes up in Des Moines to find on his voice mail a fresh batch of invitations. Today I have a choice between spending the day with Bob Dole, or at any rate the busload of journalists that accompanies Dole to his rare, soporific campaign appearances, or with Expose the Right, the group of two dozen twenty-year-olds armed with state-of-the-art political weaponry who wreak havoc at every public event held by every candidate in Iowa and New Hampshire. They are heading to Mason City in northern Iowa, where Buddy Holly's last flight took off, and where Bob Dole's plane is soon meant to land.

Out on the trail these people are as strange as Martians—not because they are activists but because they are Democrats. Eighteen months ago the absence of the Democrats would have been unthinkable: everyone expected that Clinton would be out here shaking hands. But the man most famous for his ability to charm anyone within arm's reach has put himself distinctly out of arm's reach. Only later would anyone fully understand how and why he did this.

From the middle of 1995 the Clinton campaign ran a brutally efficient series of ads on local television. No one in Iowa or New Hampshire paid these much attention, but they were out there just the same, in the ether, wafting into the minds of the electorate. In roughly half the country the typical citizen saw an ad for Bill Clinton three to five times each week. Amazingly, for eighteen months leading up to the election the Clinton campaign shelled out to local television stations in battleground states— Ohio, New Mexico, Michigan—more than $100 million. The sums required panicked the most seasoned Democratic fund-raisers: these were Republican-sized numbers. The fund-raisers quickly learned that you don't raise more money than ever before without promising donors a sweeter bag of treats than ever before. The people who financed the $100-million advertising blitz were invited to sleep in the Lincoln bedroom, fly on Air Force One, attend state dinners, and chat directly with the president about their deepest concerns—all so that the president of the United States, who was able to command the attention of the world's

51

media, gratis, simply by strolling downstairs into his briefing room, could afford to address the American people in scripted television ads unvetted by critical, informed minds.

Political ads fall broadly into two categories: those designed to inflate the candidate's appeal and those intended to destroy the candidate's opponent. The Clinton ads, which the president himself helped to write, were mainly of the second type. The bulk of them were directed at the elderly and designed to prey on their natural fear of abandonment. The message they conveyed could be summarized in a sentence: If you are over sixty years old and the Republicans gain control of the White House, you will lose your health care. Vote for your life! It was a wild and wonderful distortion of the truth—no Republican in the race ever proposed gutting Medicare. But no Republican had the time, or the energy, or the money, to respond. Most of them didn't know what was happening until it was too late.

It was a great time to be president. It was also a great time to be Dick Morris, Clinton's chief strategist and the architect of the new strategy. Out of every dollar Clinton spent on ads, Morris and his team—they called themselves the "November 5 group"—pocketed twenty-five cents. Other Clinton advisers tried to drive him down; still, the November 5 group banked $6 million even before the Democratic convention. Anytime anyone questioned the effectiveness of the ads, Morris would take a poll proving the cynics wrong. The message was loud and clear, and America was listening! But the message in some ways was less interesting than its medium. Clinton, with Morris's help, was running maybe the first big-time Democratic campaign that avoided the so-called liberal media altogether. The ads remained conspicuously absent from Washington or New York or anyplace else where they might catch the attention of the national news media.

Morris claimed that the point of this omission—at least so far as he and the president were concerned—was precisely to avoid objective scrutiny. Clinton's chief fund-raiser, Harold Ickes, said that it was mainly an attempt to save money. Whatever the stated motive the effect was to end-run the usual fourth-estate referees of political speech. The press was no longer a vehicle for speaking to the people. The press was the enemy that muddied the message you were trying to deliver. Morris argued that all the old nostrums about needing the media no longer applied, that Americans were so cynical about everything that they no longer believed in anything as naïve as the Simple Truth. He believed, for instance, that voters did not distinguish in any meaningful way between paid ads and the free press. "I don't think people are any more cynical about ads than they are about the press," he said. "One is what the candidate wants you to know. The other is what the media want you to know."

Really, it was an extraordinary turn of strategic thinking, especially for a sitting Democratic president, who might rightfully expect a little help from his soul mates in the newsrooms and on the editorial boards. It was one thing to speak through political ads; it was another to speak only through political ads. But that is exactly what Morris proposed, and Clinton accepted. "Dick wanted to spend every goddamn dollar on ads," said Harold Ickes. "He thought TV was the only way to communicate." The more airtime Clinton bought, the less need he had to appear live before the cameras—and the more he could simply ignore the trail. With Morris's help Clinton created his own metaphysical trail. Right through to the Democratic convention and beyond, the Clinton campaign remained a specter, a flickering cathode ray in the suburbs of Albuquerque, New Mexico, and Toledo, Ohio.

And so the only vaguely Democratic presence this morning in Iowa and New Hampshire is this queer handful of twenty-year-olds, who don't yet know that all that matters is what is on the television set, and who are bent on making real live trouble for Bob Dole. To this end we set off at seven in two cars, one filled with an Expose the Right "truth squad," the other with me and a single twenty-four-year-old activist, to seek and destroy Dole. The sky rises clear and blue over a snowy Iowa landscape; no one in his right mind would imagine that disaster lies ahead. But an hour into the drive the wind starts whipping, and we're in the middle of a hellish whiteout. The sky above is still clear and blue, right down to the last ten feet of crisp air over the fields. Below that, all is chaos; we are unable to see more than a few feet in front of the windshield. Finally we roll up beside an aircraft hangar to discover a young Dole aide sleeping inside his car, waiting for any idiots who show up. Dole certainly isn't going to. And so we turn around and drive the three hours back to Des Moines, the enthusiasm of the activists strangely undimmed. Six hours of treacherous driving for nothing is for them merely business as usual. Activists are the fighting men of political campaigns. Their lives are long stretches of mind-numbing tedium punctuated by ferocious life-threatening encounters.

I first noticed the Expose the Right people at the first Iowa debate— a hundred people with bright orange signs and a chant, which they hollered over and over: "The right is wrong." I was in such a rush to find Morry Taylor that I didn't pay much attention to what they wanted at the time. I experienced the same sensation I always do upon encountering large groups of people chanting loudly and waving signs; that is, I was fairly certain that I was a part of whatever it was they were protesting. I steered clear of them, as I steer clear of the antivivisectionists on Madison Avenue.

So you can imagine my surprise when I discovered that Expose the Right consists of people who believe something I believe: that people who claim to speak for God pose the greatest danger to human liberty (and to God). Obviously the desire to chant exists independently of the desire to see any particular policy enacted or any set of attitudes adopted. Strangely, the initial effect of learning this was to make me feel more sympathetic toward the opposition. Now I know that someplace in the universe there is somebody who passionately opposes abortion and gun control but who feels uneasy about joining a group to chant about it; who senses, perhaps, that no matter what you chant you just end up boring everyone whom you don't anger.

It turns out that Expose the Right does more than chant, however. At least one Expose the Right activist armed with a carefully prepared question infiltrates the audience of every public political event in Iowa and New Hampshire. "We want people to be held accountable for their views," says Tom Andrews, the director of the project, a wholly owned subsidiary of People for the American Way. "They need to be able to answer a direct question in a direct way." Each answer is tape-recorded, transcribed, and stored in the Expose the Right files. If the candidate ducks, he is asked the same question over and over, pummeled into submission or, more commonly, humiliation. In the Expose the Right transcripts of the past few days, Bob Dole comes across as an unwilling pinball bouncing around inside a hostile machine. Here are two examples.

Three days ago at a press conference in Manchester, New Hampshire:

EXPOSE: Senator Dole, earlier today you said that you were opposed to discrimination.
DOLE: That's right, oh yeah, I'm opposed to discrimination.
EXPOSE: . . . Would you endorse legislation that would make it illegal to discriminate against gay men and women?
(He turns away.)

EXPOSE: Senator Dole . . .
DOLE: We're not having a press conference.

Yesterday in Marshalltown, Iowa:

EXPOSE: You told a People for the American Way member in New
    Hampshire that you were against dismissing someone because
    they were lesbian or gay.
DOLE: No, I think I said I didn't believe in discrimination.
EXPOSE: (Tries again to push with the question.)
DOLE: I don't believe in discrimination, and I know the question
    that . . . You people have been following me everywhere. We're
    very happy to have you in Iowa. Anybody else have a question?

Whatever else it is, Expose the Right is a brilliantly simple and cheap
(only about three hundred thousand dollars for both Iowa and New
Hampshire) technique for embarrassing any candidate who is either trying to fudge his views or simply does not have any. Relentless, systematic
questioning about homos and fetuses is exactly what most of the Republican candidates do not want. The lengths to which a candidate will go to
evade the Expose the Rightists is a measure of his discomfort in his political skin. Alan Keyes and Morry Taylor are the only two candidates in
the race who have had the nerve to engage Expose the Right directly. As
he entered the studio for the big Iowa debate, Keyes lunged into the
crowd of protesters and attacked them for their immorality. Morry, on
the other hand, just wondered who they were and what they were up to.
Apparently he spotted them idling in the corner of a banquet hall and
wandered over to tell them about the importance of working for a living.
    The candidate least comfortable answering questions is Bob Dole.
Dole is the only candidate, for instance, who has tossed Expose the Right
out of his events. He did this for the first time a week or so ago in the
Hotel Fort Des Moines, at an event staged by Pat Boone and Elizabeth
Dole called Families for Bob Dole. Just that morning Dole himself, ap-
pearing on *The Today Show,* had invited the entire population of Iowa to
his rally. But when the Dole people spotted the tiny orange cluster from
Expose the Right they forgot their manners. Henchmen muscled the
Rightists out of the room and called the hotel manager. They didn't even
let them keep warm in his lobby until a taxi came, but tossed them out
into the night with zero-degree temperatures and sixty-mile-an-hour

winds. Their foot-dragging caused the normally benign Dole man to become Rambo. "In ninety seconds I become your adversary," he told the
Expose the Rightists, absurdly. And Dole wasn't even there. He spoke to
his supporters over a phone.

In the past week the Dole camp has taken to disguising its movements—refusing to tell ordinary Iowans who call in to headquarters
where to find Dole on the trail for fear they may really be Expose the
Right sympathizers. It's a nice illustration of the way suspicion of one's
opponents leads inexorably to suspicion of the entire electorate. Maybe
that is why the most successful politicians insist on engaging with everyone, including perceived opponents.

JANUARY 31

This morning we finally catch up to Dole at the Iowa Pork Congress,
where he is speaking. The larger group of Expose the Right activists,
waving their bright orange signs, is arrested as members attempt to crash
the theater ropes; and I fear that once again they have been foiled. But
then I notice the leader of the truth squad wearing love beads, a fringed
leather vest, and a look of satisfaction. "We're in," she whispers. "We got
two people inside." "Are they disguised?" I ask. "There's no need," she
says, "because they are just ordinary Iowans. They blend in."

Down on the convention floor, beneath countless photographs of
swine, mingle young beauty queens with banners across their chests de-
noting distant corners of the pork empire. Upstairs in the lecture room
the crowd conforms to a surprising degree to a city boy's expectations
about pig farmers. Of the sixty people present, fifty-eight are middle-aged
men wearing serious expressions with their arms folded uncomfortably
over large bellies. Somewhere in their midst a pair of Expose the Right
activists lie poised once again to pounce on Dole with the gay rights
questions—but where? Then I spot the two young women. One wears a
mohair vest, the other a T-shirt that reads: NO WOMAN IS REQUIRED TO
BUILD THE WORLD BY DESTROYING HERSELF. These are no pig farmers,
I suspect, and wonder if Dole harbors the same suspicion.

Dole speaks for maybe twenty minutes and conveys little except how
badly he wants to win the Republican nomination. In that time he refers
to himself in the third person twenty-seven times. "Bob Dole keeps his
word." "If the farmers show up, Bob Dole'll win big time." "No one has

accused Bob Dole of going in for dramatics." I once had a Korean room-
mate whose English was a bit rough who did the same thing. When he
was tired he would say, "Kim Puk is tired." When he was hungry he
would say, "Kim Puk is very hungry." Is Bob Dole secretly Korean?

When Dole finishes, he agrees to take questions—and for the first
time I see firsthand why his campaign is keeping him hidden. The man
is obviously possessed by his self-destructive instincts. Rather than
choose a fellow who looks like he's spent his entire adult life farming pigs
—perhaps he suspects a ploy—Dole opts for the woman wearing the
T-shirt that says NO WOMAN IS REQUIRED TO BUILD THE WORLD
BY DESTROYING HERSELF. The minute she rises, however, Dole realizes what he has done and shifts his weight unhappily. As she speaks, his
mouth forms a perfect O, like a cartoon character expressing surprise.

> YOUNG WOMAN: Senator Dole, I'm from People for the American
> Way, and I want to know if you support legislation to prevent
> discrim—"
> DOLE: I answered that question.
> YOUNG WOMAN: Yes, but do you—
> DOLE (dismissively): I don't believe in discrimination—
> YOUNG WOMAN: . . . believe gays should—

"You're no pig farmer!" someone shouts from the back of the room,
and others soon join in. The young woman is shouted down. Dole is res-
cued by his ardent supporters. Poor Dole. The whole point of him is that
he isn't a fanatic. He doesn't believe in anything in the sense that, say, Pat
Buchanan does. Yet if this is the source of his appeal to the inert masses
it is the cause of his downfall in the Republican primary. People become
involved in primaries either for a cause or for their career. No one is passionately *for* Dole because Dole isn't passionately *for* anything. He's the
foil beside which the brilliantly distinctive characters around him shine.

For purposes of comparison I drive back to Mason City this evening
with my friend Joel Achenbach of the Washington *Post* to meet another
Expose the Right truth squad, there to needle Alan Keyes. Before the
event truth-squad leader Sasha convenes with the activists in a small
restaurant near the library where Keyes is scheduled to speak. The activists turn out to be a pair of intrepid high-school students from Des
Moines and an older woman from Mason City who lovingly lays upon the
table local newspaper stories about the candidates' movements in the

area. While the high-school students rehearse the question for Keyes ("Do you think it is fair to compare homosexuals to Satanists?"), she and Sasha agree that they will wave tiny orange signs in the foyer of the library.

Two hours later we find ourselves in a small-town library. Keyes arrives and takes the stage. The last time we met he was so enraged over Pat Buchanan's treatment of Native Americans that I was distracted from his unusual appearance. He is striking to look at: His face is coal black with gleaming white teeth and a beard that seems to grow out of his shirt and up around his throat until it diverges and reconnects on his upper lip. His arms are jerky, like a dictator's. But his most noticeable features are his long, slim feet, which form an unstable base for his round body, like a pair of flippers. (He's not much more than five seven, and his feet are size eleven and a half, AAA.) As he rocks back and forth on his flippers, waiting to be introduced, I brace myself for the madness sure to come. Then Keyes speaks.

His subject is of course the theme of his campaign: moral decay and the need to restore "the marriage-based two-parent family." According to Keyes, all our problems derive from the decline of the family, which was brought about by evil liberal policies of the last fifty years. All our solutions depend on re-creating the incentives for marriage by reforming welfare, education, and the tax code and, above all, restoring a sense of shame to the culture. "Our problems are not money problems," he says, "our problems are moral problems." Keyes is the mirror image of Steve Forbes. Forbes thinks the world can be explained—and controlled—by changing attitudes to the tax code. Keyes thinks the world can be explained—and controlled—by changing attitudes to abortion policy. Both are different from Dole, who doesn't believe the world can be either explained or controlled. "None of the Republican candidates are accidents, in my opinion," Keyes says. "They are all an answer to something." And it's true. But a roomful of liberal Harvard professors would mix more naturally with either wing of the Republican Party than the two wings mix with each other.

What Keyes says, however, is overwhelmed by how he says it. Even after that first time, when I assumed that he, like the other candidates, was working pretty much straight from memory, that he was just reproducing the same talk he had given a couple of hours before, I was struck dumb by the force of his eloquence. After the first twenty minutes I look up at Joel and find him looking back with the same stunned expression. "I don't know about you," he says, "but I'm about to go work for the guy."

When Keyes finishes speaking the audience does something I have never seen an audience do. It is so entranced that it actually forgets to applaud. And then, suddenly, as if it dawns on everyone at once that he, too, has a voice, the place erupts.

With the faintest trace of glee, Keyes takes questions. I have to remind myself that just a few hours earlier I was pitying a politician for the humiliation he suffered at the hands of his interrogators. Now I find myself pitying the interrogators for the humiliation they are about to suffer at the hands of a politician. The first high-school student receives a five-minute oration from Keyes on the evils of homosexuality that gets the crowd whooping and clapping; witnessing the terrible fallout, the second activist sinks low in his seat. He does not even bother to ask his question. Heckling Alan Keyes about homosexual rights is like heckling Martha Stewart about home interiors. Keyes is *delighted* to be questioned about his opinions because he is so clear in his own mind as to what he believes; the putative intolerance that Expose the Right is exposing is precisely what Keyes is selling. If they didn't already exist, and if Keyes weren't dead broke, he'd probably pay money to have a bunch of kids outside each event waving bright orange signs and shouting questions about homosexuals and fetuses. Keyes, like Buchanan—like all moralists—*thrives* on opposition. Despite misgivings about these views I can't help but admire how they are put: this is how politics should be conducted.

Tonight Mason City is paying homage to the gods of abstinence and self-restraint and not much else. But on the way out into the cold night air I pass the older activist—the lone survivor—still gamely waving her bright orange sign with one hand and clutching her newspaper clippings with the other. I can just make out the clipping on the top of her pile. It says:

> Meet Morry Taylor
> Republican candidate for president
> Dining and dancing at the Surf Club from 8 till 12
> Free food and beverage
> Plus a drawing for a free color TV

An entirely different value system is alive and well just a few miles down the road, in a town called Clear Lake, where Buddy Holly's plane crashed. It'll have to wait.

FIVE

The Messenger

We did not become the richest nation in the history of humankind because we didn't know how to handle money. Money is the one aspect of life we understand. But because we're good at dealing with money, what do we do? We try to make all our problems money problems. In America we don't have philosopher kings, we have businessmen.

— ALAN KEYES

JANUARY 31

After the speech I present myself at the front door of Keyes's rented Winnebago. A distinguished reporter from a big newspaper has told me that he had been trying to land an interview with Keyes for the past six months—phone calls, faxes, even e-mail messages, had gone unanswered. In six months Keyes was unable to spare him even thirty minutes of his time. I have been led to believe that getting to him was nearly impossible, and, before I heard him speak, that was fine by me. It turns out that this has less to do with the reticence of the candidate than the disorganization of his campaign; from moral certainty, it seems, follows logistical chaos. At any given time no one who works for him knows where Keyes is, only where he stands. But if in the middle of nowhere, in the middle of the night, a perfect stranger presents himself at the front door of the campaign Winnebago, Keyes will pull him up and in. And so sometime before midnight I ditch my rental car and take off on a thousand-mile tour of Alan Keyes's Iowa.

I can't help but think back to my initial reaction to the spectacle of Alan Keyes spewing moral outrage at various Republican gatherings: to wonder how this man ever got himself taken seriously. I doubted whether he was even capable of having an ordinary conversation—one in which he hears the other person out, considers his views, and in some way attempts to accommodate them. I soon learned that Keyes enjoyed the distinction of having been the only guest on *Crossfire* whose behavior was so outrageous that the producer apologized to the other guests after the show. I didn't think it possible to behave badly on *Crossfire*. Out of curiosity I requested a copy of the transcript. Sure enough, the show opened with Keyes vomiting vast paragraphs about the moral decay in America, barely punctuated by the attempts of the others to break in. Even on paper you could tell that Keyes shouted at the camera at the top of his lungs. When it became clear that someone else would be permitted to speak, he cut them off as soon as they opened their mouths by saying, "I

Alan Keyes: the power of passion.

61

listened while you spoke. Now let me finish the point I'm making." A brief excerpt can serve to give you some idea of the whole (we join the action after Keyes has spoken a few volumes on modern American morality):

MICHAEL KINSLEY: All right, Alan—
KEYES: How are we going to restore the moral identity and values that will finally—
KINSLEY: Alan, Alan, you've made your point—
KEYES: Back to those—
CLIFFORD ALEXANDER: I don't think it's going to be restored by you shouting at the rest of us.
KEYES: That is the—
ALEXANDER: If I may finish—
KEYES: The great—
ALEXANDER: Ten years ago—
KEYES: Wait a minute!

"Do you get points for loudness on this show?" a forlorn Alexander asks later.

Just a few hours ago I was dreading this moment, when I finally would have to hunt this man down and listen to him *for days*. And now . . . I'm hooked! Begging for more!

In the darkness of the cabin, Keyes offers a brief tour of his past. His father made a career of the army, which means Keyes was raised in about ten different places. His family has deep roots in Maryland, but unlike many black Marylanders was not Roman Catholic but Baptist, at least until Keyes's mother converted his father. Keyes studied political philosophy at Cornell with Allan Bloom, who is probably best known as the author of *The Closing of the American Mind*. He also left there with Bloom, mainly out of disenchantment with the Vietnam War protests on campus. With the teacher and a handful of other students Keyes passed a year in Paris before winding up at Harvard, where he won his doctorate. Along the way he became proficient in Greek, German, Spanish, Italian, and Russian. His Ph.D. thesis on Alexander Hamilton's thought dwelled on a speech that Hamilton gave to the Constitutional Convention that lasted for six hours and advanced the proposition of an electoral monarchy, rule by the elite, of which only the notes of the listeners survive. I am not sure which is more appealing to Keyes now, the substance of the address or the possibility of speaking for six hours without interruption.

Keyes discovered a talent for public speaking in schoolboy tournaments but became disenchanted with the skill upon leaving home for college. "Part of it is a natural gift, which has a certain effect apart from substance. What bothered me about that was that you could go on producing that effect as a kind of trick. This struck me as the worst kind of life. And so after high school, I stopped giving speeches for, oh, I think it was a good ten years." When at length he came back, he gave a Lincoln Day talk at Harvard's Dunster House. "I remember wanting them to be too struck by it to even think of applauding. The tribute I wanted for that speech was silence."

Since then he has been, in no particular order, State Department official, ambassador to the U.N. in the Reagan administration, president of Alabama A&M University, radio talk-show host, and candidate from Maryland for the U.S. Senate. Keyes ran for the Senate twice, weakly, faring even worse the second time than he did the first. Each time he left a trail of unpaid campaign debts in his wake and wound up with no visible means of support. His second Senate campaign wrote $20,000 in bad checks and somehow lost $38,000 from its treasury. Keyes paid himself a salary of $8,500 a month out of campaign funds, which, though not illegal, was unusual. In short, he is a kind of mirror image of the society he seeks to depict: his problems are not moral problems; his problems are money problems.

We stop for a few hours' sleep in a dingy motel, then rise in the dark and hit the road: a motel, two universities, and the community center of a savings bank. One Keyes event is much like another Keyes event. Keyes arrives late and delivers a clock-stopping thirty-minute oration followed by an even more glorious thirty-minute question-and-answer session. In these the answers occupy all but about forty seconds. After the standing ovation, but before the question period, a lone Keyes volunteer passes a collection basket and invites the audience to reach down deep to help the badly funded campaign. Along with the collection basket come these odd little cards. On them people are asked to check off one of six non-financial chores they might do for Keyes:

Be a church contact
Host a video party

Get five people to support Alan
Make telephone calls
Pray daily for Alan
Get twenty-five people to support Alan (and receive an autographed
  book)

They all do it. Everywhere you turn inside the Keyes campaign you see people acting—or seeming to act—against their immediate economic self-interest. Candidates usually entice people with handouts. Not on the scale of Morry Taylor, of course, but even the niggardly Dole campaign usually offers a table of cold cuts and free sodas to anyone who will listen to a Dole speech. The Keyes campaign asks people to *bring* food. In Cedar Rapids twelve hundred people turn up with a banquet. The miracle of the loaves and the fishes!

Political tastes are more easily identified during a primary than during a general election because more flavors are available. And the kind of people who turn out to buy what Keyes is selling represent a market not serviced by anyone exactly, though, of course, Buchanan is the closest substitute. A Keyes crowd is entirely white—in three days with Keyes I did not see a black person besides the candidate—but otherwise bears not the slightest resemblance to the crowds who come out for Dole and Forbes. With Dole and Forbes, you are always vaguely aware of what the people who show up do for a living. They wear suits; they carry cell phones; they network; they pig farm. With Keyes, there is never any visible means of support. Whoever his supporters are, they are not defined by their economic station but by their states of mind. They possess some phantom internal organ that releases religious passion at the sound of Keyes's voice—whole audiences with the spiritual equivalent of flipper feet. Entire families turn up, the howling of their babies extinguished by the man with the microphone. The appeal of Keyes's message to them is to confirm their choices in life, or perhaps the choices life has made for them. If the marriage-based family comprising God-fearing people is the ideal state of man, these people immediately are at the top of the heap. The pursed-lip expression that falls somewhere between pride and determination (like the one Clinton assumes whenever he has to salute a soldier) is what you see on a Keyes crowd at the end of the speech. Ask them for compassion, and you'll be amazed by how much they have to give; lend them money, and you'll regret it for the rest of your life.

But the main difference between the Keyes campaign and the others is Keyes himself. His message is always the same, but the language he deploys to convey it is so different as to constitute a new speech each time out. He takes his thesis statement and weaves these marvelous intricate kaleidoscopic word paintings around it. Commonly he finds a keynote—a phrase or a quote—and just runs off with it less like a public speaker than a musician. Maybe ten times, I hear him find his way back to Lincoln's famous description of America as "the last best hope of earth," but each time he follows it with a different fireworks display of sound and sense. Even then I think he is working from memory—that he just has in his mental warehouse an uncommonly large store of these wonderful riffs. But once, afterward, I ask him to repeat what he has just said. He looks at me like he doesn't know what I'm talking about. "I don't remember," he says.

FEBRUARY 2

A boat club on the banks of the Mississippi, two Best Westerns, and an American Legion Hall. Keyes is on fire—each speech is new and fresh. "There are times when I walk into a room and I know it is mine," he says at one point. "And it changes *everything*."

I wish I could be more dismissive of Keyes and confine him to the class of harmless lunatics, but that's not what he is. Saying exactly what he is is the problem—not just for me but for all the people who turn up to cheer him on and, I believe, even for him. He's not a viable presidential candidate; his campaign has reached the point where it has discovered the nobility of failure. It derives its strength and fervor from losing. What both he and his followers want is not to be elected but to be among the elect. "Those of us who believe in the existence of God," says Keyes, "have a certain advantage in making moral arguments," and he's right. By the end of a full day with him he has me persuaded of just about everything he believes right up until the moment I leave him for my own room in the Best Western. For the first time in my life I fear that we are in the midst of that crisis of character that will determine whether the Republic lives or dies. I worry that Keyes will think I am part of it. That is, I am not immune to the allure of the little status group he is creating; it's the only status group in sight.

But inevitably, just when I start thinking of Keyes as a boon companion and a reasonable person much like me and you, he goes and flies into a rage about some subject that heretofore he has evinced no interest in. Probably this is some sort of test—to see if I am a genuine follower or merely a pretender. Once every few hours I feel as the more skeptical disciples must have felt whenever Jesus lost his cool; for example, when he chased the money changers from the temple. Today the first flash point occurs when I ask Keyes why he, the most God-drenched candidate, didn't receive the support of the Iowa Christian Coalition; the second when he asks himself repeatedly why Pat Buchanan is making use of Michael New, the soldier in the U.S. Army who was court-martialed for refusing on constitutional grounds to wear U.N. blue. Keyes's point on the subject is extremely well taken: the president is commander in chief, and when a presidential candidate encourages soldiers to interpret the Constitution he undermines the authority of the office he is seeking to occupy. But he becomes furious, and disturbingly so, his arms jerking around and his voice becoming a megaphone. During a quiet moment when I ask him why he is getting so totally worked up, he says, "I surprise myself sometimes. I was surprised by that. *It offends* me. Maybe there's something else going on . . . ," but he drifts off into his own thoughts. I tell him he'd be more persuasive if he controlled his anger. "You're like my wife," he says. "My wife says I should *never* seem angry."

At the end of another long day—four long speeches and nearly four hundred miles on the road—we pull into our last Best Western for one final counterblast. We were due at seven o'clock; it is now past eight o'clock; and there is some doubt, in my mind at least, whether the citizens of Fort Madison, Iowa, will have lingered for Keyes, especially since the thermometer is predicted to plunge from zero to nearly forty below. We are met by an amazing sight: the conference room is not only still filled to the walls, but the 150 people inside are perfectly silent, rapt. They are watching a video of one of Alan Keyes's speeches, and they are so fixed upon it that they hardly notice when the man himself appears in the flesh. For any other candidate this would mean putting the crowd through the same speech twice. The only other candidate who would risk a TV at the front of the room would be Morry Taylor, and he would have it there to raffle off.

This morning before I leave Keyes his chief aide-de-camp tells me that Morry Taylor is the only other candidate Keyes ever bumps into on the campaign trail. Several of the other campaigns have noted Morry's tendency to be everywhere at once, but the Keyes aide attributes to Morry an almost mystical omnipresence. The last time it happened Morry was exiting a high school as Keyes was entering. The kids were chanting for Morry: "Cool! Cool! Cool!" "Yeah," Morry was shouting to them back over his shoulder, "and I drive a Viper."

Yesterday's *New York Times* suggests that there is little chance of Morry turning up today. He is storming through New Hampshire. The story on page 18 begins:

> The rich man's Presidential campaign of Maurice M. Taylor, the tire and wheel tycoon better known as Morry, blew into the New Hampshire legislature today, hurling blustery derision at fellow Republican contenders and startling the staid chamber with a studied informality. "Why don't you just say 'The Grizz is here,'" he instructed the sergeant-at-arms before striding into the House chamber.

But sure enough, on the way back to Des Moines from Alan Keyesville, I spot in the distance a pair of Land Yachts moving at speed toward me. I cut across the highway and find myself briefly back inside the Morry Taylor campaign.

Today's final stop on Morry's long itinerary is a Department of Agriculture building. It rises from the Iowa plain as a tribute to man's talent for complicating the simplest things, much like a modern presidential campaign. The point of these visits these days is not for the candidate to learn something about the country he seeks to govern, or even to solicit the votes of those he meets, but to create an interesting backdrop for the television cameras. But as usual there are no television cameras to record the Taylor for President campaign, just Morry, a couple of staffers, a local reporter, and me. As a result, the tone of the event is not the tone of a photo op but of an inspection by the boss.

After terrorizing the nervous manager of the facility ("I'm going to shut down the Ag Department in Washington," Morry says), the Grizz sets off on a tour. Soon he is gazing, incredulously, through a glass wall at a field of corn. Row upon row of tall green stalks swing gently inside a lab designed to reproduce the conditions of summer. Morry stares at it for what seems like minutes, then demands, "Why make it summer in the middle of winter in Iowa?"

A queasy look crosses the manager's face, and you can see him calculating the odds against a Taylor presidency.

"It's a waste of money," says Morry. "You ought to put this thing down in Florida where it *is* summer most of the time."

The manager mutters something about how they are studying that very idea, but before he can finish, Morry is preoccupied with the laboratory. With a rising sense that agricultural science is no more complicated than presidential politics, he dons a smock and marches into the lab. A wan technician in black-rimmed spectacles performs some intricate procedure with test tubes. From the rack in his hand, Morry selects one of the thin glass tubes and holds it up to the light for inspection.

"It looks dirty," he says.

"It was just baked to six hundred degrees," says the manager, a tad defensively. "To vaporize all the organic material inside."

Morry sticks his finger down inside the tube and swishes it around. "Isn't it contaminated?" he asks.

"It is now," says the manager.

Morry grunts, and moves on.

FEBRUARY 5 AND 6

Early this morning I leave Des Moines and fly to my hometown of New Orleans to witness the Louisiana caucus. Just a few weeks ago, before the Alaska caucus became front-page news, the Louisiana caucus seemed perfectly ignorable. But now Keyes, Buchanan, and Gramm are duking it out to see who goes on to Iowa. Tomorrow between four in the afternoon and eight o'clock the first votes will be cast. Either way it's bad news for Gramm, who as usual has spent millions. If he wins they'll say it was bought; if he loses they'll say he couldn't even buy a win. Buchanan is bigfooting across the state claiming total victory. Keyes, on the other hand, is saying that his campaign "is not about winning caucuses and primaries and things like that," which will come as news to everyone else in the race. Nevertheless, it is true. Keyes has set his sights on the hotter, deeper layers in men's minds where beliefs break down and re-form. He's not so much running as stumping on behalf of a candidate who will run fifty years from now.

On the morning of the caucus a small group of Keyes supporters gathers in a restaurant not far from the New Orleans airport and gets a whiff of what the Keyes campaign is about. What follows is about one-tenth of one answer to a question from the audience about his electoral hopes:

> We are in an era where I think some of the success that has been enjoyed by Christian political activism is having a little bit of a confusing effect. Because people have had success and they've come to leadership and all the media people say, "Well, the Christian Coalition is going to decide this, and this is going to decide that." And some people are sitting there and starting to think in a way that they didn't think when all of this started. Because the way to get into it is to finally realize that someone has got to bear witness pure and simply to what they think is right. So go for it, act on your heart, act on your conscience, act on your faith, and let the chips fall where they may. But *now* you start to enjoy a little success, and you look around and you say, "Yeah, well, if I follow this, I may enjoy a little more success. Well, yeah, well, okay, so that one is not really committed to these things, but he's going to win. And since he's going to win we need a place at the table, we need to be there" and so forth and so on. Now *that* is the calculation that starts to interfere with the judgment. And the judgment then becomes, "Yeah, he's saying all the things I believe, but I can't just act on what I believe anymore. That's unsophisticated, that's immature." Is it really? I thought that was why we got involved in this in the first place.

He knows exactly when an audience is about to burst into applause and tries to squelch it, redirect it, and husband it, rather than encourage it. Over and over again he raises his hand as if to say, "No wait, let me finish. What I have to say is too important for mere applause." He's a master at managing the crowd's emotions, bringing them right up to the brink of something, and then not letting them have it.

And then, for some inexplicable reason, Keyes becomes angry. He recalls the question I asked him about the Iowa Christian Coalition (why, in the wake of Dole's weakness, he didn't seek to win its support), and the rise in his voice causes everyone to jump in his seat. "I have never talked to or asked anyone for an endorsement at any time in this campaign. I have never even asked any one of the people like John who are working for me to come and work for me. Never! He cannot say that Alan Keyes ever came and said to him, 'John, work for me.' John, did I ever do this?" (He fixes John with a commanding stare.)

"No," says John.

"John didn't come here because Alan Keyes asked him to. I just present the message. If they care about it they come forward. I don't thank anybody. I don't care what their name is, what their background is, who *they think they are* for helping this campaign. Because I think this campaign has to rely on the strength of the message and the power of God, and we will get where we're supposed to get. If people feel that's right they'll come forward. If they don't think that's right they won't. I think what the person was suggesting was that I'd give the Christian Coalition a way out. Because now that Dole is sinking . . ."

He lets that thought hang for a moment, then continues:

You see, this must be a *terrible* feeling. You make a decision based on expediency, and it doesn't work. And then you are left without expediency and without principle. With nothing. This is sad. I never want to wake up the day after an election or anything else with that emptiness in me. Knowing I have given away the things that matter most for the sake of what I thought would win and finding that I have lost and have nothing. I have not said one word or done one thing with the principles that I believe in. And I *never* will. And knowing that, it doesn't matter how many times I lose because I'm not losing anything. I will carry it home right with me to the grave, till that moment when I look to see whether God approves. And that is all that really matters.

Afterward I recall the last evening in Iowa, when I asked him whether he did not suffer from messianic fantasies. In the front of the Winnebago, his two aides chuckled. At the time I thought they were laughing at the audacity of the suggestion. Now I think that they were laughing at its naïveté.

SIX

Animal Farm

By making off with 53 percent of the vote in Louisiana, Buchanan not only has ended Phil Gramm's campaign but has proved that he can win against a slick candidate with a lot of money. The victory knocked Gramm out of the race and left Buchanan mystified. Gramm poured huge sums of money and large numbers of people into Louisiana. Yet he barely showed up himself. While Gramm lingered in Iowa, Buchanan was tearing back and forth across Louisiana unopposed. Buchanan couldn't figure it out—until he saw the map of the caucus sites. It looked like a handful of freckles on the backside of an elephant. The Republican Party elite had made it so difficult for people to vote that Gramm could count on turnout being low. Low turnout meant almost certain victory, since Gramm had the money to bus his voters to the caucus sites. He hadn't expected Buchanan to light a fire under people.

In any case, the Republican field is now clearly stratified, with Buchanan, Dole, Alexander, and Forbes forming their own private layer of plausibility, and the others casting about for a reason to get out of bed in the morning. A losing political campaign must at some point cease to be about winning and start to be about something else: a moral crusade (Alan Keyes), a chance to blow your stack on C-Span (Bob Dornan), a fund-raiser for the next Senate election (Phil Gramm). In Morry Taylor's case that something else is fun. He has spent six months and nearly $6 million laying the groundwork for just this moment. His staffers have papered Iowa and New Hampshire with several hundred thousand questionnaires, ostensibly to determine what the voters think. But the cover sheet of the Morry poll captures the true spirit of the enterprise:

71

The other guys pay a pollster $25,000 to ask the opinions of just 600 people. I'm polling everybody, and I'm giving away $25,000 in a drawing.

Inside are ten questions (number 5: "Do you agree that we need an outsider to clean up the mess in Washington?") and, beneath each of these, two empty boxes. One is marked "You're right, Morry," the other "You're wrong, Morry." Anyone who checks the boxes is automatically included in one of five Iowa drawings for five grand, cash, one each night from now until the caucus.

This morning we have scarcely left the parking lot before the inside of the Land Yacht is hazy with cigar smoke. Morry leans back in his deck chair, indulgently responding to my questions about his future plans. He is perhaps the only presidential candidate in history to be overconfident while running eighth in a field of eight just four days before the Iowa caucus. On the off chance he loses, he says, he has no plans to run for anything else. He'll just go back to making tires and wheels. But then he pauses, exhales a cloud of smoke, and drops this bombshell: "I'm looking to buy a TV station."

"You got Rush [Limbaugh]," he continues, "but otherwise there's no one else out there. If I don't win this thing, the politicians are not going to like what I got planned for them. Fry 'em right up." As if to illustrate this point he produces a press release announcing the formal complaint he has filed with the Federal Election Commission against Lamar Alexander. Although Lamar claims he has spent only $170,928.95 in the state, the Concord *Monitor* revealed that he has blown $553,000 on local TV ads alone, far more than the legal limit.

The rest of the day is spent whipping back and forth across farmland, trying to scare up voters. Hardly anyone turns up for the scheduled events, and so we go jump-shooting large, unsuspecting groups of citizens: at conventions, in courthouses, in restaurants. Finally we arrive at the one event in Taylor's day guaranteed to attract a crowd large enough to make the candidate forget the obscurity of the past twelve hours, indeed large enough to shame every other man in the race. Last night the winner of Morry's five grand was a pig farmer in the southeast named Wilfred McCreedy, who, conveniently enough, hosts the Republican caucus in his township. Tonight a large basketball court teems with hopeful Iowans; stragglers are directed to the jogging track above, which soon fills up as well. At every table happy voters scramble to complete the Morry poll before the deadline.

The show begins. The lights go down, and on a giant screen at the front of the room, a picture of the White House goes up. THE LARGEST BUSINESS ON EARTH read the words over the picture. An eight-minute video glorifying Morry follows. At the end of the video the loudspeakers blare Morry's theme song, "Dancing in the Dark," until the man himself bursts into the room, assumes the stage, and recites his own version of Bruce Springsteen's lyrics.

> You need a spark
> To start a fire.
> And this gun's for hire . . .

"You don't see the senior partners from the big law firms running for office," says Morry, by way of summing up all of American politics. "Our country is being run by the *rejects* from the legal profession," and he's off on one of his tears. The five-thousand-dollar drawing gives the donor far more than five thousand dollars' worth of pleasure. Afterward, as we head for some airfield in eastern Iowa, Morry sounds intoxicated by the turnout. "Fifteen thousand votes will do it," he says. "You never know but we might—" He pauses. "Ah—you never know, people are funny. But I'll tell you what." He smiles his Cheshire Cat smile. "It's doable. It's doable." All in all, a nice illustration of a general rule: Any campaign, however moribund, can seem hot when you are inside of it.

At last we arrive at the airport. Waiting there are several vans and cars plastered with stickers for Lamar Alexander. Lamar is going places—the polls have him running a close third behind Buchanan and Dole—but as he rises he is coming under attack not only from Morry but from Steve Forbes, who has a new commercial explaining how Lamar, with help from political benefactors, turned a thousand bucks into $620,000. We pass the vans and enter the terminal to find a claque of clean-cut young men in suits clutching Lamar Alexander pamphlets. Lamar's jet is circling overhead! He's preparing to land! (Lamar does everything with exclamation points.) A few minutes later he does, in $25 million worth of jet, with LAMAR! emblazoned in red on its side.

Morry and his aides gather on the tarmac to watch the plane empty. The line is endless: first the security detail, then the camera crews, which, after Gramm's Louisiana disaster, have moved from him to Alexander. For the last four years Lamar has been raising money by telling people he is the only Republican in America who can beat Bill Clinton. He talks endlessly about his "vision." He squints as he does this; he sees it; the trouble is, no one else does. Some of the most expensive political consultants in America went to work for him. "His greatest strength is that he can be reshaped into anything," one of them explained to me. But though the money has rolled in, and the operatives have signed on, the Alexander campaign has gone nowhere. Until now.

Finally, the expensive political operatives emerge from the plane. They are smartly dressed and serious looking and old at heart, though young to look at. Among them is Mike Murphy, the legendary thirtysomething "media consultant" who, as it happens, grew up in Grosse Pointe, Michigan, next door to Morry Taylor. Whenever Morry wishes to drive home his point about the absurdity of professional campaign staff, he references Murphy. He tells his audiences about "a fat little kid from next door who didn't know anything you don't know and who is now making hundreds of thousands of dollars telling Lamar Alexander what you think."

Now, as Lamar's media director emerges from the plane, he is greeted by the terrible, improbable sight of Morry Taylor and network television crews with cameras at the ready to film Alexander's official arrival in Davenport, Iowa.

"Hey, Murphy!" Morry shouts up at him. "Look how fat *you* gettin'!"

Murphy blinks but says nothing.

"*You* eatin' too many doughnuts!" hollers Morry.

Murphy is now dizzy with confusion. He of course is the superior political force, Lamar Alexander's right-hand man. Lamar! But Morry is the big-shot businessman from next door who buys and sells people like him before breakfast. Rather than sort it out, Murphy flushes and races into the back of one of the waiting cars.

At length Alexander emerges and is surrounded by the cameras. You can see he is looking for some way to take advantage of the new camera crews. Spotting Morry, now lingering disinterestedly on the tarmac's fringe, Lamar strides over to shake hands. He offers Morry a phony smile and a line from his stump speech, "I just bought my mudboots for all of that negative advertising up in New Hampshire." The words turn to steam as soon as they leave his lips. Morry stares at Lamar for a few seconds, in the manner of a doctor preparing to deliver some bad news to his patient. "That's not negative advertising," he says. "They're just telling you the truth."

Lamar's happy face vanishes. Poof. A truly nightmarish sound bite has just occurred. The CBS cameras are rolling. The familiar fight-or-flight instinct takes over. Lamar doesn't wait around for more. He simply ends the conversation, turns, and racewalks away. "Gotta go!" he hollers over his shoulder as he disappears into the back of his car.

"That's what happens when you meet the *Grizz!*" Morry booms after him.

But the night is still young. Thrilled that they have captured on film a rare authentic moment (an unscripted exchange!) in American politics, the CBS crew newly assigned to Lamar phones New York. New York orders the crew to leave Alexander and to follow Morry wherever he goes next. Morry takes the crew on a tour around Alexander's jet, which looms massively beside Morry's own small plane. "Tell me what is wrong with this picture," I hear him saying. "Here you got a little plane made right here in America belonging to a guy who has made his own money. And over here you got a twenty-five-million-dollar Challenger *made in Canada* being used by a politician." Four or five carloads of Alexandrians gaze on helplessly.

Meanwhile, overhead, Bob Dole's jet is now circling. Unwisely it decides to land. There, on a tarmac in the middle of the night in the middle of nowhere, one-third of the Republican field has now assembled; even more astonishing, the one national news network filming the event is trailing around like a devoted puppy dog behind the surest loser. Dole's plane rolls inexorably toward Morry and CBS, oblivious to the danger. "And here," says Morry, "we have another politician."

He turns to address the camera, in the manner of a network reporter. "Has Dole ever made any real money?" he asks, rhetorically. "No. So what's he flying in? A *nineteen-million-dollar* Falcon. This one is made in France." The door to the plane opens, and Dole emerges. It appears that Morry will have one last chance to ask Dole about his $4 million government pension. But then, exhibiting a keen sense of self-preservation, the front-runner spots Morry, dives straight into his car, and beats Alexander to the airport exit. Morry shakes his head, sadly, like a small boy whose friends have just been called home by their mothers.

Soon the CBS camera has moved on, and we stand alone on the tar-

Lamar Alexander: the man Clinton feared most.

mac. It's then that I break the news to Morry that for the next few days he will be without media coverage. After today my editor forbids me to travel with Morry. "I didn't send you out to write Morry Taylor's biography," he said late last night. Like the network executives, he feels that Alexander is the man to watch, and that I should watch him. Also, he thinks I have become compromised, like other political reporters who have been granted exclusive access. Never mind that my access is exclusive only because no one else ever turns up to ask Morry questions. "I have to follow Lamar," I say.

"Well," says Morry, feigning indifference by turning away, "you gonna get enough vision to last you a lifetime."

I try to tell myself that our parting is all for the best. Just this morning, for instance, a local paper in New Hampshire published this disillusioning report:

> A class of middle-school students says GOP presidential hopeful Morry Taylor suggested cigar smoking and mimicked a girl's stuttering during a visit to their school. . . . When one pupil stuttered while asking a question Taylor told her "Sp-sp-spit it out of your mouth, girl," according to two students who published a letter to the editor Wednesday in *Foster's Daily Democrat*.

I haven't had the nerve to bring it up. I am sure that Morry would have an explanation. I am also sure that, whatever it is, it would only make things worse.

Ostensibly in search of Lamar Alexander I head out tonight to a church on the fringes of Des Moines that intends to celebrate heterosexual marriages and protest homosexual ones. Together with a crowd of maybe eight hundred people, Keyes, Gramm, and Pat Buchanan have all turned up to take their whacks. All the rest except Morry have agreed to sign some pledge to make homosexuals as miserable as possible. ("Who gives a shit?" Morry said when I asked him why he wasn't going. "If you want to be fruity-tooty, so what?")

Alexander's name is on the list of scheduled speakers, yet he fails to show. I discover that Lamar has a special gift for waiting until the last minute to see who is going to share his platform and then canceling if he doesn't like the looks of the event, or if something better comes along. Yesterday he told the local PBS station that his presence at a debate was "as good as done"; but then he canceled when he found out that Dole and Forbes weren't going to attend. A couple of days ago he passed out a schedule that said he would attend church services this Sunday; but then *This Week with David Brinkley* called, and God got stood up. In real life this sort of behavior is considered rude. Why not in politics?

The front of the room in which Lamar is scheduled to speak looks less like a political platform than a stage set on a children's television show. It is filled with props. In addition to the piano there is a red plaid shirt, a pair of L.L. Bean mudboots, three giant letter blocks (*A*, *B*, and *C*, which stand for "Alexander Beats Clinton"), and a big banner that says LAMAR! The Alexandrine taste for exclamation points—Come on Along! is his campaign slogan—suddenly makes perfect sense. Lamar has decided that the way to reach the American people is by treating them the way adults usually treat six-year-olds. Probably because he behaves so much like the authorities already in their lives, Alexander has just won by a landslide the straw poll of Iowa schoolchildren.

Lamar's wife serves as his warm-up act. "When I think of Lamar," she opens, "I think of Ivory Snow." She is called Honey (Honey!), though to watch her you would never guess it; indeed, I think that if Lamar Alexander ever wins the White House we shall finally appreciate the soft, yielding qualities of Hillary Clinton. Honey is tight as a coiled spring, all steel and no magnolia. "Make him number one in Boone," she concludes, grimly, "and then Lamar can be number one next November."

"Thank you very much, Honey," says the young man who moderates the event, eliciting a single sharp giggle from the front of the room.

Next comes Lamar himself, and you can see why he likes to lead with his wife. His soft, fuzzy, intensely understanding nature is nicely accentuated by his wife's hardness. The Alexanders have the same bad cop, good cop thing going as the Clintons and, for that matter, the Reagans. Is this the model for the modern American presidency?

As Alexander speaks, he leans forward tensely but pleasingly, like a schoolboy proffering an apple to the teacher. "We made a decision some time ago," he says, "that all of our advertising in Iowa would be positive." The applause this fetches is only slightly less enthusiastic than the applause Lamar gets when he subtly slides the knife into the competition. He attacks Dole's response to Clinton's State of the Union Address ("It was not a pretty picture"), Forbes's viability, and Clinton's mendacity ("We know what he will do. Someone will ask him a question. He'll move out from behind the podium to walk over to the questioner. He'll feel the questioner's pain . . ."). As he speaks I am overcome by the same creepy sensation I used to get whenever the preternaturally upbeat *Up with People* came on at halftime during football games. In my experience people who make a huge deal about being nice usually aren't, and Lamar is a case in point. He is insistently upbeat. And yet his campaign is the most negative operation around. It stands for nothing except what it isn't. Although Lamar is forever using the word "vision," his pitch is that he is *not* someone else—he's *not* Washington, he's *not* a negative advertiser, above all he's *not* Clinton. But of course he *is* Washington, he *is* negative, and, above all, he *is* Clinton, at least in his ability to tell everyone exactly what he wants to hear. Lamar is simply tapping into the cult of niceness to destroy his opponents. To which segment of the American population does this appeal? Usually a candidate shares something important with his followers: Dole attracts veterans, cynics, and the chronically risk averse;

Buchanan attracts the angry rabble; Keyes attracts moralists. I could only conclude that Alexander attracts people who use niceness to get what they want.

A day with Lamar, and I start to appreciate the virtues of negative advertising. The standards of honesty are higher in negative ads than in positive ones, just as the standards of accuracy are higher in negative pieces of journalism than in positive ones. (Steve Forbes's ads are far more honest than the replies they have elicited.) Lamar's glowing tributes to himself contain all sorts of distortions, particularly about his financial life, that no one bothers to correct because they offend nothing but the truth. A negative ad that shades the truth in this way would cause the victim to leap into action and discredit his attacker.

FEBRUARY 12

When I phoned Wilfred McCreedy, the winner of Morry's five-thousand-dollar drawing, to ask if I could observe the Iowa caucus on his farm, I was barely able to hear his response over the squealing of pigs. Upon my dropping of Morry's name he said, "That Morry Taylor, he has it exactly right." I was in.

At noon I wheel into the farm—a big white house on the side of a narrow road backed by several hundred acres of golden-brown fields. Waiting for me is a hearty middle-aged couple, a wonderful concoction of meat and vegetables, a glass of milk, and a brief family history. The McCreedys have been farming the same land in the middle of nowhere for 128 years. "I was at the top of my class in school," McCreedy says. "He was also at the bottom," says Mrs. McCreedy, "because he was the only one there." They've both traveled some—in the army in the late fifties McCreedy went to New York, and he was back as recently as 1986, after which visit he concluded that "the country is going to hell." But it's been ten years since the McCreedys took a vacation, and their farm hours make investment banking seem like a walk in the park. They are walking demonstrations of true independence. Unlike their neighbors—and just about everyone else in Iowa—the McCreedys do not accept any federal subsidies for their produce.

Before long the talk drifts to politics. On the phone McCreedy became a bit worked up about the marriage rally at the church in Des Moines. "Those gays and lesbians are going to *protest* that meeting," he said in a tone of utter disbelief. "Goddamn, that makes me angry!" He said he would have driven the two and a half hours to Des Moines to throw his support behind the straights, but his sows were pigging. Now once again he says how angry the gays made him, but in the flesh his anger comes across differently.

"You put a group of all-female pigs out there, and they won't become homosexuals and lesbians," he says. At some level he may be angry, but his prejudice seems mainly to give him pleasure. As he lays into Clinton, homosexuals, and the U.S. government, his real emotion is more like delight—the delight of a good fan rooting for his team. Go straights!

"Is it true that Forbes owns a Mapplethorpe photograph?" he asks.

I say it is, or at any rate that Forbes has not denied the reports.

"Dat gumit!" he says.

"Oh, Wilfred, what does that matter?" asks Mrs. McCreedy.

"That man took pornographic photographs of homosexuals!" bellows Mr. McCreedy, at which point Mrs. McCreedy just rolls her eyes back toward the long row of miniature porcelain pigs on her mantelpiece.

I have tried to make myself as agreeable as possible, but it's only a matter of time before I have to come clean with my associations. After all, the McCreedys are clearly very conservative and I write for what is widely viewed to be a liberal publication. The tension builds as Mr. Mc-Creedy stakes out a political position on the other end of the spectrum from my employer. But it's nearly two hours before I discover that the McCreedys have no idea where I am from or what I do—only that I am a friend of Morry Taylor's. "You're not from PETA, are you?" asks Mrs. McCreedy, finally.

I have no idea what she's talking about. "People for the Ethical Treatment of Animals," she explains. "You just never know when they are going to interrupt. Lately they've gone to our schools dressed up as carrots to tell the kids not to eat meat."

It's truly astonishing: as far as these people know, I am some protester who has come to disrupt their lives, and yet they still fed me and humored me before venturing to ask. One of the few things I recall from a Greek literature course in college is Homer's insistence that kindness to strangers is the mark of a civilized person. Nestor and his sons feed Telemachus first, then ask questions later; the Cyclops questions Odysseus first, then attempts to eat him. The McCreedys have the gift of kindness to strangers. I put PETA on the list of things to be against.

But now there is no getting around it: I must explain what the hell I'm doing in their kitchen. I mention *The New Republic* and hold my breath.

"Is that Fred Barnes's place?" asks McCreedy. (Barnes appears weekly on the political show *The McLaughlin Group*. He plays the conservative to Eleanor Clift's liberal, Morton Kondracke's moderate, and John McLaughlin's celebrity. At *The New Republic* Fred was regarded, politically speaking, as the freak who voted for Bush.)

I say that until very recently it was.

"Oh, man!" says McCreedy. "I *love* that guy. Really? Fred Barnes?"

It is true.

"He's my man," says Mr. McCreedy, slapping me on the shoulder. It's all very Japanese. Neither of us wants to put a fine point on political disagreement, and so I've been granted the status of conservative by association.

After a bit Mr. McCreedy announces that it's time to "go chorin'."

On the way over in the car he gives me an idea what it's like to host a caucus. In the past couple of days Gramm has called six times, Buchanan twice, and Keyes once. Alexander has sent McCreedy two books and a videotape about himself. Pollsters call the McCreedys eight times a day, roughly. On the way down the driveway McCreedy spots a blue-and-orange FedEx package poking out from his mailbox. "Maybe it's one of those shirts from Alexander," he says, laughing. It is. Or at least it's a collection of Alexandriana. At length I ask him who he's for. "I'm undecided," he says. "A week ago I was for Forbes. Then I got my check—I was for Morry Taylor. Now I don't know—you gotta find me one who's gonna beat Bill Clinton. Which one you think?"

"None of them," I say.

"Damn!" he says, slamming his hand on the steering wheel. But he's a good sport about it. He's unhappy for about four seconds, and then he's rueful.

Soon we arrive at the pig sheds, long, low-slung buildings lined with six-by-five-foot metal troughs filled to the brim with oinkers. McCreedy opens the first door; I recoil and gag. The blast of odor is the most moving thing I've experienced on the campaign trail since I last heard Alan Keyes speak.

"If you want to be a *billionaire*," says McCreedy, "you figure out how to take the smell outta hog shit—you'll be a billionaire."

While I choke in the corner of his office, McCreedy marches through the pens unfazed, checking to see that the pigs have food and that none of them are dead.

"I don't understand," he hollers out over the noise of the pigs. "When that McLaughlin hollers out, *'Fred Beetlebum Barnes.'* What is that Beetlebum business? What's that about?"

I have no idea.

A pig shed is organized like a college alumni parade—as you walk the length the pigs get younger until you arrive at the end and find the ones that have just been weaned. The shed I eventually toss feed into is filled with nursing piglets and sows about to give birth. At the sight of the large white feed pail they crowd together and screech for their dinner, oblivious to their impending doom. In the first week of each piglet's short life Wilfred takes a pair of steel clippers and cuts its eyeteeth. "I'd like to do that to Eleanor Clift!" he booms out as I make my way down the row. "Clip her eyeteeth! Get Fred Barnes to hold her!"

A few hours later, at around seven o'clock, twenty-five voters arrive in the McCreedys' living room to discuss the candidates. Only three are even mentioned: Dole, Keyes, and Richard Lugar. From the sounds of their talk, the people in the room are divided between Keyes and Dole. But while the Keyes supporters are devoted to their man, the Dole supporters are all frustrated supporters of other candidates who believe that Dole is the only Republican capable of beating Clinton. Mixed in are a few people who have bought Senator Lugar's line that he is the last refuge of common decency. Lugar supporters are a bit like Alexander supporters: they have persuaded themselves of the essential corruption of the other candidates. Keyes supporters, whom you might expect to be that way, are not. That, I suppose, is the difference between genuine moral conviction and polite moral disapproval.

Just before eight o'clock Mr. McCreedy passes around a pad of yellow Post-its. Two men then collect the votes in a silver pot and adjourn to the dining-room table. Quietly, they add the totals: Dole 11, Keyes 7, Alexander 4, Lugar 3. I ask Mr. McCreedy whom he went for, and he laughs and says, "Guess." When the tally is announced to the room and it dawns on everyone at once that no one voted for Morry Taylor, there is a murmur, and then someone shouts, "Wilfred, does that mean you got to give the five thousand dollars back?" It's clear they all think that Morry was a fool: he spent five grand on the guy, and he couldn't even buy his vote. I prefer to see it another way. Who else but Morry Taylor could give a guy five grand and still leave him free in his heart to vote for whom he pleases?

SEVEN

Strong Thermal

Sometime after I leave the pig farm the results from Iowa trickle in through the car radio. In the end they come to this:

Dole: 25,738 (28 percent)
Buchanan: 22,512 (23 percent)
Alexander: 17,003 (18 percent)
Forbes: 9,816 (10 percent)
Gramm: 9,001 (9 percent)
Keyes: 7,179 (7 percent)
Lugar: 3,576 (4 percent)
Taylor: 1,380 (1 percent)
Dornan: 131 (0 percent)

Dole took 37 percent of the Iowa vote in 1988 in his losing battle with George Bush. Iowa was meant to go to Dole in a landslide, and on the radio Buchanan sounds elated. Had Keyes not run, Buchanan thinks but does not say, he would have won. And beating Dole on his home turf in the Midwest might well have driven him from the race. For his part, Dole sounds unnerved, frayed, a loser in the making, and thus, for the first time, worth paying attention to. Until now he's done nothing but steal the more successful ideas of the other major candidates. Forbes got him talking about the flat tax and abolishing the Internal Revenue Service. Buchanan has him talking about the North American Free Trade Agreement as if he had nothing to do with it when he had a great deal to do with it indeed. But tonight Dole hits a new bottom. He steals Morry Taylor's trademark line.

"I'm a doer," he says. "Not a talker."

It's a sign, I decide. I disregard orders from above and set out to find Morry. At length I track him down in Des Moines, where I find him inside one of the Land Yachts shouting at Lenny, his piss-boy. That in itself isn't unusual. What is unusual is that he is shouting about the sort of thing an ordinary politician might shout about: some local journalist has dug into his past and found a story worth writing.

My first reaction, coming as this does on the heels of such devastating results for the Taylor campaign, is to be slightly saddened that this man who breaks all the rules of presidential politics obeys this one: Morry Taylor has something to hide. Sure enough, when he sees me, the candidate stops shouting and starts whispering. This, too, is unusual. All the other candidates and all the other political operatives are forever clustered together whispering their secrets. But with Morry and his piss-boys life is lived right out in the open. The Taylor campaign is not very good at this game of keeping the truth from the journalists, however, for the minute Morry storms out of the Land Yacht the secret comes tumbling out of the piss-boy. Here is Morry's secret:

A couple of years ago Morry was on a business trip in Des Moines when he came across a sad article in the local paper. A local black high-school student—a football star and an honor student—had been shot while on vacation in Chicago. The bullet left him paralyzed from the waist down, and his family with financial problems. His parents remodeled their home to accommodate the boy's wheelchair but in the end came up short nineteen thousand dollars. The newspaper story Morry had read explained how the family was being forced to sell their home. Morry sent over the nineteen grand to the family the next day, anonymously, through a lawyer. Soon after that the newspapers wrote up the story about how an anonymous benefactor had come to the rescue.

And that was that, except that now Morry is running for president. He has become something of a public figure in Iowa, what with his name recognition running up around 80 percent. The newspaper has heard that he was the benefactor and is planning to expose his good deed. That was what I had walked in on: Morry had just been told that some local journalist was preparing to run with this story. Apparently, Morry feels that the last thing the family needs is to feel indebted to some rich guy who is now running for president; and that is why he's become so angry. He doesn't want to be exposed.

That is the skeleton in the candidate's closet. It bears the same relation to ordinary political skeletons as the candidate does to ordinary
politicians. It is something worth thinking about on the way to New
Hampshire.

FEBRUARY 15

It's an hour before the final New Hampshire debate. By arriving early at
the television studio I thought I might sneak into the back with the Dole
campaign or, at any rate, avoid the room where they stuff the journalists.
Wherever the journalists are stuffed you can be sure nothing interesting
will happen; that's the point of stuffing them there. But it appears I am
out of luck. Already, the candidates are safely inside, the police arrest in-
terlopers, a phalanx of guards blocks the front door of the ABC affiliate,
and Morry Taylor's Land Yachts hog all available parking. From the dark
snowdrifts on either side of the walkways leading up to the station, wild
beasts howl. Upon inspection they are not wild beasts at all but a few
hundred young demonstrators baying for fiscal austerity and holding
signs that say BALANCE THE BUDGET.

The first rule of Campaign Journalism is to look as if you belong
where you don't. When they hand you the press badge, I now know, the
best thing to do is stuff it away in your pocket. Summoning a false sense
of entitlement I stride through the glass doors of the television station.
Within seconds I am surrounded by the Manchester police, who haul me
before the authorities. A man with a wire coming out of his ear demands
to know what I think I'm doing; a woman holding a clipboard stands
ready to check whatever I say. Clearly I have to tell them something, so
I tell them the only thing that pops to mind: "I have an urgent message
for Morry Taylor."

At just that moment, before the police have time to throw me back
out into the snow, the doors behind us swing open. New Hampshire senator Bob Smith marches through, together with Jim Courtovitch, Phil
Gramm's campaign manager, last seen explaining how Gramm would
take New Hampshire. But Gramm has just held his press conference announcing that he will quit the race and endorse Dole, whom he spent the
past year describing as unfit for the presidency. Jim might spend more
time mourning the event, he cheerily explains, but he is swimming in job
offers from the other candidates. In this and many other ways politics is

85

not like business. Go bankrupt in business, and you are a pariah. Go belly-up in politics, and you are hot property. The cops let Jim pass.

In the meantime something has happened. Having seen me shaking hands with Gramm's campaign manager, the woman with the clipboard is more curious who I am. A single brief exchange with the political insider alters my status. We chat, and I can see she wants badly to be helpful. Each candidate is allowed only five staffers, she explains sadly. If Morry Taylor has reached his quota I am out of luck, no matter how urgent my message for him. Morry came with only four, I say—to assist her in her helpfulness—he's waiting for me. She checks the guest list. Amazingly, I'm right.

Upstairs is indeed the inner sanctum of Republican presidential politics: the candidates, their aides, and a handful of ABC's biggest clients. The only two journalists present are Tim Russert of *Meet the Press* and Howard Fineman of *Newsweek,* both of whom have the air of men who have been invited. (Howard wasn't; he's just learned the tricks.) The candidates are enclosed with their advisers in glass offices. Lugar is composing his remarks in longhand; Alexander is pacing back and forth and being quizzed by Mike Murphy; Morry is drinking a glass of red wine and reciting an attack on politics as we know it into a dull beige wall. An aide interrupts him to break the news that the Keyes campaign, which has been staying in the same New Hampshire hotel as the Taylor campaign, has left.

"So what?" says Morry.

"So . . . uh, they told the manager that we'd pay their bill," says the aide, uneasily.

"Jesus," says Morry's campaign manager.

"That's right," says Morry. "Jesus told Alan it was okay."

As usual Bob Dole has the biggest space and the special privileges: all the political big shots who have endorsed him—Governors Weld, Merrill, Branstad, et al.—have been let in with their guests, too. The Dole people try to create a sanctum within the sanctuary. They rope themselves off from the other candidates.

The debate lasts ninety minutes, and while it is no doubt tedious to anyone who hasn't followed the eight remaining candidates, it is the highest entertainment for those few of us who have. It's like watching a B movie: everyone remains perfectly inside his narrow character. Bouncing up and down like a Puerto Rican shortstop, Lamar lashes into Dole while at the same time decrying negative advertising. Forbes lashes into

Lamar about his personal finances, prompting Lamar to lash back. Buchanan lashes into "Mr. Greenspan and Mr. Rubin," thus creating job opportunities for anti-anti-Semites. Morry lashes into the English language. All manner of strange linguistic events occur in the interstices of Morry's synapses: "practicality" becomes "pracality," "frustrated" becomes "flustrated," "Strom Thurmond" becomes "Strong Thermal." It is its own kind of poetry, an improvement on the clichés of life and politics. In the space of five minutes the man is capable of referring to himself as a "country pumpkin," or claiming that he bought his wife a "Norman Mailer dress." (It turns out to be a Nicole Miller dress.) But Morry's poetry has no place in politics.

The debate produces one memorable moment, when Dole waves a few snapshots and tries to make a joke of Steve Forbes's endless advertising aimed at him. "They didn't even use a good picture of me," Dole says, "so Steve, I brought some pictures. So if you are going to use negative ads—"

"Senator, no pretty picture can get around what you've done on taxes," replies Forbes.

"Yeah, yeah. I know your problem," says Dole. "You've got a lot of money. You're trying to buy this election."

The joke's gone sour because Dole's gone sour. There is an awkward moment when Dole fumbles the snapshots with his left hand to Bob Dornan on his right, who passes them on to Forbes, who doesn't even bother to look at them. The biggest winner is B-1 Bob Dornan, who now somehow produces a foot-high blowup of himself holding his grandchild. The timing is so perfect that it looks planned, but it is a stroke of pure luck—Dornan had no idea Dole was going to turn up with snapshots. Like all the luck in this campaign, it isn't Dole's. You know you have hit bottom when you are successfully parodied by Bob Dornan.

Other than that, Dole simply mutters disconnected phrases in response to the attacks on him from all sides. He treats the debate as he treats the press and the voters—as an undignified distraction from his lifelong quest for the White House. "It's an abomination," a Dole aide later tells me, "that Bob Dole has to share a platform with Morry Taylor." But it's worse than that: Dole has arrived at the point where he needs Morry to defend him. "Senator Dole," Morry says, exhibiting his typical unwillingness to join in with any mob, "he's been a champion, a good old warhorse for the Republican Party. He's taken all the blows they whack at him tonight." Good old Morry.

As the debate winds down, we the elect are led downstairs to the studio, together with George Stephanopoulos, who is on hand to speak for Clinton. We enter the room with the candidates as the final insults hurtle through the air. Amid the confusion there is a brief chance to see these people for who they are rather than who they pretend to be. The most striking sight is the alacrity of the Alexander staffers. They rush in like an Indy 500 pit crew, clean away the notes Alexander has taken at the podium, and sweep him away in a concerned flutter. Another point of interest is the stuff the candidates left behind on their desks; even the Alexander people permit a piece of paper on which their candidate had scribbled notes to flutter to the ground. It reads: Let people decide Best ever Forb dull. As if in retaliation, Forbes left behind a war of chicken scratches, which read in part: Taxes—flat. Confidence Flat tax. Alex-s Flat tax—business Alexander # tax.

Which about sums up their jousting war for third place. But as Stephanopoulos smiles innocently and prepares to tell the world that Bill Clinton is not complacent about the race, that the president is taking the Republican primary very seriously, I notice the Dole photographs. They lie stacked on the shelf of Forbes's lectern. They are originals, curled and soiled, as if they have been sitting in some shoe box for years until Dole stumbled across them late one night while he was worrying about how to retaliate against Steve Forbes in the big debate. Two are color: a bad one of his wife, Liddy, stunning in the flesh, looking tired and plain; a better one of Dole's dog, Leader, rubbing noses with a yellow lab. The third is a black-and-white shot of Dole smiling broadly and holding a baby. In the photograph he looks twenty years younger. The black pen he clutches to keep his right arm in place juts up and is set off by the baby's white gown. Dole is looking at the camera; the baby is looking at Dole's gnarled, wounded hand. And then I remember: Dole is not like the others in this respect. One of his great campaign fears that he's lived with since he first ran for office thirty-eight years ago is that he'll be handed a baby to kiss. He's afraid that he might drop it.

FEBRUARY 16–18

By the time I catch up to the Dole campaign it has lost interest in disseminating the Dole family photo album. I ask five different Dole aides the identity of the baby held by Dole. It seems an innocent enough query—after all, this was the picture Dole had selected for publication. I get no answer. The basic pose of the Dole campaign is, the less anyone finds out about its candidate the better. You can spot the Dole office in the row of glass boxes on the ground floor of the Manchester Holiday Inn: it's the one with newspaper taped up on the glass to prevent people from looking in. Dole himself remains largely out of sight. He makes two or three very brief, formal appearances each day and is otherwise unavailable for interviews.

Dole's speeches add nothing to the general blank picture. The act is always the same. The announcer shouts the names of all the state politicians who have endorsed Dole; they race out onto the stage one at a time like ballplayers before a game. Dole waits in the background until the crowd reaches a low fever pitch. When he comes out he stands at the podium with his left foot and left side jutted forward, though he is right-handed, and his crippled right hand resting on the podium. Almost always he starts in with something self-deprecating: "That's a lot better than the speech is going to be," something like that. It is the clearest remark Dole will ever utter. The few words he speaks worth hearing are words he didn't intend to speak. Gaffes. A gaffe, the journalist Michael Kinsley has said, is when a politician tells the truth. "We didn't plan it this way," Dole gaffes one morning, inside a New Hampshire factory. "I didn't realize jobs and trade and what makes America work would become important in the last few days."

A dozen times I listen to his talk, pen poised idly over paper. Nothing. Not a thought, not an image, not a quote. It takes me a while to figure out why this is, but then it strikes me: Bob Dole isn't running for president. The *concept* of Bob Dole is running. The man himself has subcontracted out all the dirty work to people who make their careers managing reality for politicians. That is why he is referring to himself in the third person. He isn't there, at least not in any meaningful sense. Every Dole speech leaves me feeling that a man like this runs for the presidency not because he thinks he should be president. He thinks no one else should be president, so it might as well be him.

Everything that I or any other citizen will discover about Bob Dole is discovered by accident. I stalk him through the snow at the world dogsledding championship and watch him meet and greet the pooches. A schoolgirl approaches him as he's about to leave and, after nabbing a photo, asks him if he's had fun. "You learn a lot out here campaigning," Dole says, motioning to a sled of twenty dogs. "They're all nice dogs, too.

Bob Dole at home as he never could be on the trail.

Not like the Congress." He thinks no one is listening. He said it just for the fun of it. I catch him in a back room before a speech to a Rotary Club. He thinks no one is looking. He checks out his reflection in the mirror furtively—his hair is sprayed and dyed—and then whips out of his pocket a tiny canister and squirts two quick blasts of breath spray into his mouth. A few years ago in an interview with *60 Minutes* he broke down in sobs while explaining that one of the consequences of his war wound is a reluctance to look at himself squarely in the mirror, which just goes to show that insistently not looking in the mirror is itself a form of vanity.

A campaign, like a fish, rots from the head, though perhaps it does so more quickly. The Dole campaign consists of slick young men in blue suits forever whispering to each other in dark corners, from campaign manager Scott Reed and press secretary Nelson Warfield right on down to the guy who carries the extra cell phones. "Rented strangers" is what conservative columnist George Will calls these people, and their prominence around Dole says a lot about the nature of our politics. The more the two parties agree on policy, the less their battles are waged along lines of principle, the more they become a game of tactics, and the more "serious" candidates like Dole depend on their rented strangers to think up putatively clever strategies. The Dole campaign pays top dollar for everything, and I get the feeling that the many rented strangers who work for it have a big personal financial stake in Dole's soldiering on, that they'll be the last to tell him that really he shouldn't be doing this again. One of their favorite techniques in New Hampshire has been to hire telemarketing firms to call Buchanan supporters and, in the guise of pollsters, relate damning untruths. (Why not? It worked on Forbes in Iowa.) In response to Buchanan's complaints, Dole's rented strangers tell reporters that Buchanan is doing the calling to a few of his supporters to tar Dole. It takes a special sort of credulity to believe them.*

I stop half a dozen people carrying Buchanan signs who tell the same stories of strange phone calls in the night. After a day with the Dole campaign I take off for the steam room at the Manchester YMCA to purge myself of the dreadful feeling coming over me. A few minutes later an extremely fat old man waddles in, spies me, drops his towel, and sits on a plastic stool right next to me. "You're a new face," he says, "I always notice a new face." I say that's nice, grab for a towel, and tell him I came for the campaign. He shifts on his stool and says, "I'm a Buchanan man, myself." (Buchanan men are the kind of guys who can sidle up to other guys

---

*After the primaries, the Dole campaign's Federal Election Commission filings revealed that Dole had spent millions on this effort, but by then of course it was too late to matter. One of the firms that did the calling, Campaign Tel of New York, supplied *The Wall Street Journal* with a sample script: "My name is ——— and I'm calling with a special message from Iowa's farm families. Iowa's farm bureau has adopted a resolution that opposes the flat tax like the one offered by candidate Steve Forbes. Under the Forbes flat tax, Iowa's farmers would pay an average of $5,000 more in taxes."

in steam rooms without the slightest fear of being thought gay.) Moments later he's complaining about the calls he's been getting at home. Here, roughly, is what he said:

> A guy calls. He says, "Hi, my name is William, are you aware that Pat Buchanan is an extremist?" And I say: "Whaddya mean?" And he says, "Pat wants to give nuclear weapons to South Korea and Japan." So I ask him: "Where does this information come from?" He says he doesn't know. So I ask him: "What does Bob Dole think about that?" And this kid doesn't know that either. He knows absolutely nothing about Bob Dole. So I ask: "Who *are* you anyway?" And he says he's with an organization called the National Research Institute in Houston. So I ask him for his phone number. And he says he can't give it to me. Then he hangs up.

There is, of course, no listing in Houston for the National Research Institute.

The Dole campaign, in short, resembles what many people suspect the Buchanan campaign is: closed, secretive, nasty, a bit smug. Maybe that's what happens when you lose once too often: you stop trusting the voters. By contrast, the Buchanan campaign is open, honest, friendly, and helpful. Buchanan has campaigned with a decent respect for the process. He has put himself before the press and the people and been very open about what he believes. On the other hand, you can only afford to campaign dirty if no one expects you to.

Still, I'll bet Dole is the guy in the race that people most want to like but can't quite figure out how to do it. Much as I loathe his approach to getting elected, I, too, want to like him. Every night after a day with Dole I return home and recall a pair of mental pictures that the day has badly blemished. The first is the one of Dole recuperating from his war wounds as described by the author Richard Ben Cramer: hanging from a pole by his bad right arm and trying to straighten it out until he was sweating and crying from the pain.

The second is a windy afternoon in June 1994 in a graveyard on the French coast, a few days after Dole says he realized he had to run for president one last time. I had traveled to Normandy on Clinton's plane to witness the D-Day celebrations, but about halfway through, the rawness of the thing killed any interest I had in trying to whip off some copy about it, and so I stopped being a journalist and just started watching.

Just before Clinton addressed the veterans of the invasion, I found my-self walking alone through the rows of white crosses until I reached a place where there was no one else but a pair of old soldiers. They seemed ancient, though, of course, they could not have been much older than Bob Dole. They were trembling and leaning on each other as they looked down on a cross, and at first I thought it was just from the strains of age. Then I saw the name and place on the cross: Stenson (I'll say) from Mis-sissippi. The dates on the cross explained that the boy had died at the age of nineteen on the first day of the invasion. The old men wore name tags, too: Stenson from Mississippi. Two of three brothers had survived that day. They were crying without tears.

That's Dole, I would like to believe. He has the emotions, or at least you can sense them lurking inside him, but he has no idea how to give them proper expression. He is crying without tears.

FEBRUARY 19

I drive out from Manchester to a rally in Milford on the eve of what may be Dole's final New Hampshire primary. A large crowd has gathered out-side the redbrick fort, but, as usual, half of it consists of journalists and Buchanan supporters there to dance on Dole's grave. This evening the local fire marshal, who has somehow gotten involved, is allowing only a relative handful into the hall to hear Dole speak in person. The rest will have to stand in the snow and the dark and stare into the bluff facade of the town hall, from which Dole's voice is piped. But just when they shut the thick wooden doors for the last time and say no one else will be ad-mitted, a pair of bigfooting journalists cuts through the crowd. *Crossfire* star Robert Novak climbs the steps with *Newsweek's* senior editor Jonathan Alter right behind. The crowd and the fire marshal part for Novak, and the door swings open for just long enough to let him through. Then, bam! The gates of paradise shut fast in Alter's face.

"What are you doing?!" wails Alter. "Bob Novak and I were together."

The fire marshal stonewalls him.

"I'm from *Newsweek!*" shouts Alter.

The marshal seems even less impressed, but Alter wants to get in more than the marshal wants to keep him out. Invoking *Newsweek* and Novak he finally pushes his way through the door . . . and then out again. Every nerve in his journalist's body told him that he had to be *on the scene.* But like every other journalist here he took one look at Dole and remembered that there was nothing to be gained from watching Dole in the flesh.

Presently the voice of Dole emanates from the town hall's facade. It's not so much a speech as a series of disconnected phrases uttered in an elegiac tone, some of which cause the people around me to break out into giggles. ("Like everyone else in this room I was born.") A Dole speech sounds like the sort of thing a redbrick building would say if a redbrick building could speak. He pulls the rhythms of his One America refrain up short just as it starts to flow:

> We're not rich, we're not poor
> We're not urban, we're not rural
> We're not black, we're not white
> Uh—you can go on and on and on and on.

I have a dream, kind of. And gentlemen in England now abed . . . well . . . I dunno . . . maybe they should get up.

It is more like the Cliffs Notes of a Great Speech than the speech itself. The only lines Dole can deliver with any kind of strength sound like they were cribbed from *Robert's Rules of Order:* "Start the hearings. Go through the process. Do it in an orderly way." The whole time Dole is speaking, it is as if he were saying: *This is the speech I would give you if I was the sort of person who gives speeches.* I'm not sure whether Dole is actually modest or simply embarrassed by immodesty.

At some point in the middle of it all, he has lost even his most ardent supporters, and the crowd outside in the snow gets to talking. A pair of old men wearing Dole stickers want to know what I think of their man, whom they view as a genuine American hero.

Now, normally I don't argue with the supporters. There's no point—their views are their identity. Nothing you can tell even the most phlegmatic follower of Dick Lugar will shake his faith in his man; it will only make him think worse of you. And so I should have known better than to open my trap at the back of a crowd in Milford. But I was tired, the hour was late. "If Clinton had been nineteen in 1941 he would have been a war hero, too," I say, carelessly. "And if Dole had been nineteen in 1969 he would have found a way to avoid the war." What had been until then a pleasant conversation turned sour. There was no place here for a heretic; but if not here and now, where and when?

In a silent and futile protest against the qualities apparently required of a front-runner I skip out to finish the New Hampshire primary with Pat Buchanan.

With a pair of fellow scribes I whip out of the parking lot in my Nissan Pathfinder in search of Pat Buchanan and immediately come upon a mini-van parked in an alleyway. Through the open passenger window a strangely familiar hand karate chops the air. Buchanan. He's making some point to an enterprising British journalist who has caught him ducking out of the back of the hotel. "Is it true that you said that Hitler was a man of courage?" shouts the British journalist. Buchanan just breaks out into delighted laughter at this transparent attempt to gin up a caricature. We start out right on his tail, but soon there are about six other cars filled with TV crews and photographers speeding past us in the emergency lane, competing to suck Buchanan's exhaust. Crazy people, willing to risk life and limb on the off chance that Buchanan stops at Dunkin' Donuts.

Buchanan is meant to tour the Timco lumber mill an hour or so north of Manchester, but the bubble prevents it from happening. The swarming, yammering crowd of journalists makes it impossible for Buchanan to tour the factory, and so after about five minutes everyone ends up standing and shivering in the snow outside while Buchanan answers the questions posed by the pushiest journalists. There are no voters here, of course, but just about everyone who ever appeared on a Sunday-morning political talk show is fighting for a glimpse of a man who makes his living on Sunday-morning political talk shows. *Capital Gang* satellites circle the fringe of the crowd while their star shines. Margaret Carlson. Robert Novak. Arianna Stassinopoulos Huffington. A millionairess. Inside a lumber mill!

But maybe the strangest sight is the half-dozen Japanese and Koreans perched on piles of logs craning to overcome their height disadvantage and get a clean shot of the man who plans to stick a wrench in global trade. Alone, off to one side of the logs, stands a South Korean version of Sam Donaldson, reciting to himself what he is about to say to the camera. "Did you know," I ask him, after introducing myself, "that Pat Buchanan wants to give South Korea nuclear weapons?" I want to test the reach of Dole's push polls, but the man looks surprised. "For free?" he asks. So far as I know, I say. He turns excitedly and tells it to his camera: Tomorrow South Korea will know, too.

When finally it becomes too late for anything else I stop in at the Taylor for President campaign headquarters to watch the returns. I enter to find a huge crowd and Morry onstage raffling his final five thousand dollars. At the back of the room a poster declares the early returns, which by the end of the night will come to read:

Buchanan: 56,982 (27 percent)
Dole: 54,508 (26 percent)
Alexander: 47,224 (23 percent)
Forbes: 25,482 (12 percent)
Lugar: 10,811 (5 percent)
Keyes: 5,610 (3 percent)
Taylor: 2,976 (1 percent)
Gramm: 754 (1 percent)
Dornan: 515 (1 percent)

The landslide crashing down upon him fails to dent Morry's spirit, even though the Taylor campaign strategy had hinged entirely on Morry's winning either Iowa or New Hampshire. "I want to thank all of you—this is a great country," he says to loud cheers, as he hands over the five grand to the lucky winner.

Then he makes his final pitch. Up until now Morry has said that if elected he'll only serve one four-year term. Now he offers New Hampshire a better deal: "It only takes me two years—then I'm gone," he says in his best money-back-guarantee tone. In his heart, however, he knows it's all over. When he spots me looking on sadly, he comes over and says, "Go with Buchanan, you'll have more fun."

FEBRUARY 20

It is nearing midnight when I walk across the New Hampshire tarmac alone with Scott Mackenzie, the treasurer of the Buchanan campaign. We are both early for the flight to South Carolina, where, on March 2, there happens to be another primary. There is something strange: the plane is big. Coming out of Iowa, after Buchanan shocked everyone, he had with him only about twenty journalists. Back then he flew commercial because the campaign didn't have the money to charter a plane. Yet here waiting on the tarmac is a 124-seater, bought and paid for. Not a runner-up plane; it is a winner plane. I ask the obvious question.

"We've known our numbers all along," says Mackenzie. "We knew we were going to win Alaska. We knew we were going to win in Louisiana. We knew we were going to finish close in Iowa." I wonder aloud how he could know Buchanan was going to win in New Hampshire when the margin of victory was so slight. "We didn't think it was going to be so close," he says. "But we had some very good numbers." But where did the numbers come from? I ask. Only the slickest and most expensive campaigns can afford the sort of precise tracking polls that can predict results. Mackenzie smiles. "The Dole campaign leaks like a sieve," he says.

All along the Dole campaign people have gone to the greatest lengths to seem discreet. They grant few interviews. They speak in whispers. They tape newspaper over the glass walls of their offices to prevent outsiders from looking in. But all along, it turns out, they have been passing their most valuable proprietary information—their tracking polls—directly to the enemy. It puts secrecy in a different light. The point of the suspicious behavior was not to keep the enemy from looking in. The point was to keep themselves from spilling out.

EIGHT

The Mouth of the Old South

In a democracy you never know who the messenger will be.

—STANLEY CROUCH

FEBRUARY 21

There are about sixty other journalists on board when Buchanan's plane takes off from Manchester, New Hampshire, for somewhere in South Carolina, where the campaign now moves. It is past midnight, and everyone at once is crashing from overdoses of politics and caffeine. Buchanan and his wife, Shelley, sit in the front row, backed by six rows of staffers and a new, heavily armed Secret Service detail. The candidate barely moves or speaks but sits quietly, staring straight ahead, turning over in his mind the phrases that will take him through the South Carolina of his imagination. The nostalgia salesman is on his way to a place where the craving for nostalgia runs higher than anywhere else in America, and God knows where it will all end. Just an hour ago Buchanan bore into the eyes of fifty television cameras and the hearts of his success-crazed southern followers—"peasants with pitchforks," he called them. "Do not wait for me to come to you," he said, "saddle up and ride to the sound of the guns."

Whatever else it is, the New Hampshire primary is a turning point in the relationship between politicians and people. No longer will the candidates pretend to be speaking to individual Americans. Instead they speak abstractly to "America," which, depending on how you look at it, means either everyone or no one. New Hampshire also marks a shift in the relationship between politicians and journalists. From now on, a journalist can no longer set himself up in a hotel in Iowa or New Hamp-

shire and know that all the candidates sooner or later must appear. Now
he must attach himself to a single candidate as he jets back and forth
across the country and depend upon him entirely for his food, his planes,
his buses, and his hotel rooms.

Two hours after we leave, we land in Columbia, South Carolina, and
set off for our hotels. Buchanan and his closest aides clamber into cars
and head in one direction; the rest of us walk down a long tarmac to a bus
and head in another. Only we don't. The Buchanan campaign is only
semi-prepared to go national. While it had the foresight to rent a big
plane, it has no clue what to do with the journalists inside. The young
Buchananites on the ground in South Carolina cannot remember the
name of the hotel in which they have reserved rooms, or whether they
have reserved rooms at all. They argue about who said what to whom
until two-thirty in the morning, and then, clearly desperate to announce
something, announce this: Although Pat Buchanan will not leave Columbia until noon, we must all be in our hotel lobby with our luggage at
five-thirty sharp—that is, assuming we find a hotel.

"Jesus Christ, that's three hours from now!" a cameraman shouts from
the back of the bus.

"What the fuck is going on here?" shrieks a radio guy.

Who would have thought that the rise of Buchanan would leave the
American media longing for a strongman? The news that they will be
lucky to get three hours in their hotel rooms leads the TV camera crews
in the back of the bus to scream insults at the Buchanan aides in the front
for the next five minutes. This, in turn, leads the lone Secret Service man
assigned to us to leap into action. Unfortunately, he asks *me* what he
should do. I have no idea, of course, and advise him to lie low. The next
twenty minutes is more of the same: journalists screaming bloody murder inside the dark and musty bus while the Buchanan aides bicker
among themselves, until, at length, a particularly large network cameraman shouts "Get this fucking bus *moving*" into the bus driver's ear, and
the driver hits the gas. It's nearing three in the morning. Somewhere in
Columbia, South Carolina, Pat Buchanan sleeps.

We drive for maybe thirty minutes to a motel on an interstate highway. The man behind the desk has never heard of Pat Buchanan. We
climb back onto the bus and drive for another ten minutes to another
motel. Again, no luck, except this time the poor guy working the midnight shift makes the mistake of announcing he has twelve empty rooms.
Everyone at once thinks the same renegade thought: Why not go it

alone? The aggressive-aggressive journalists attack the guy behind the desk as if he were harboring state secrets; the passive-aggressive ones strike out across country, where, it is rumored, there are other motels, other rooms. Soon the interstate highway outside Columbia resembles a scene from a World War I film. Everywhere, journalists are going over the top: clambering over large mud dunes in the predawn mist, vaulting over highway medians, racing up to the door of Fairfield Inns. The same energy directed at the emptiness of the Dole and Clinton campaigns would change the course of American history. When the discovery is made that Fairfield has only nine rooms, dejection sweeps the ranks until a voice from on down the highway punctuates the sullen mist: "There's a Ramada!" And all the roomless wonders go sprinting madly over the South Carolina mud dunes. It's four in the morning, and the Buchanan aides have lost control of the press pack.

I am one of the lucky ones—so I believe. By 4:30 a.m. I am safely inside my room at the Ramada Inn and, after a few phone calls, secure that the Buchanan aides will fetch me in six hours. I am even pleased that the young Buchanan aide who promised to deliver my bags fails to do so, for it permits me to skip the 5:30 baggage call. For the next six hours I don't sleep of course but try to write down what just happened over the past twenty-four hours. As I do I find, among other things, that I have developed genuine affection for Buchanan and his campaign. One reason, despite disagreeing with Buchanan on just about everything, is that he has been ganged up on by a self-righteous elite whose sense of itself is bound up in its belief that he is worse than he is. Buchanan to his credit tries to say exactly what he thinks—he does not speak in code. Nevertheless people are forever reading between the lines of his speeches or his books to demonstrate that he is evil, because what he actually says is insufficient proof. Former Nixon speechwriter William Safire is now saying that, on the spectrum of anti-Semitism, if most Americans are a 1 and Hitler a 10, Buchanan is a 4 or a 5. Compare this to Safire's blurb on the cover of Buchanan's 1988 memoir, *Right from the Beginning:* "My old friend from the Nixon White House days has written a crackerjack book with humor, wit, poignancy, and, perhaps, prophecy." Some of my best friends are anti-Semites.

At 11:00 a.m. I wander back down to the lobby. It is empty. I remind myself that two Buchanan aides and one Secret Service man separately assured me six different times that they would collect me at 11:15. The deal could not have been more explicit. I had gone so far as to ask, perhaps rudely, "You aren't going to change this on me an hour from now, like you've changed everything else?" They promised that Pat's plans were firm. Yet somehow between 4:30 a.m. and 10:30 a.m. Pat's plans changed. A few dozen phone calls and thirty minutes later I locate Pat's hotel and discover why I feel so oddly alone: Pat Buchanan has checked out. He's left South Carolina. He is on his way to North Dakota. He wants to give a speech at the base of Mount Rushmore. I receive this news standing at a bank of pay phones populated by traveling salesmen. Suddenly I realize: I have no luggage. Pat Buchanan has stolen it.

Just six hours earlier I had almost felt important. There I sat, a mere seven rows behind the winner of the New Hampshire primary, poised to write the first draft of history. Now I stand alone in a motel outside Columbia, South Carolina, in the same clothes I wore forty-eight hours ago, stinking so badly that I can smell myself. I am no stranger to logistical chaos; if on some level you don't positively enjoy being stranded in the middle of an Iowa whiteout you should never get into this racket. Twice I've checked out of my hotel room from airplanes (the maids dump your stuff in a trash bag). Three times I've returned rental cars by phoning the company and giving it directions to its abandoned vehicle. But this is new ground . . . standing on the median of an interstate highway in a place I've never been, have never wanted to be, have no business whatsoever being. I envy the people whizzing past me at sixty miles an hour. At least they have a ride home.

FEBRUARY 28

Downtown Atlanta: I retrieve my long-lost luggage from a pile of flotsam in the lobby of the Marriott and hop into a van behind Buchanan and half of Atlanta's police force. Our driver, a local peasant taking time off from his pitchfork, is laconic about the fuss. "I'm not used to driving with the police in front of me," he says. "I'm used to them being behind me." We follow Buchanan through red lights over to the CNN studios, which are, in the Buchanan story, the equivalent of Dr. Frankenstein's laboratory. There I squeeze into the elevator with the candidate, his aides, four Secret Service agents, and a bone to pick. During the past week the Buchanan campaign has lost and found my luggage four separate times.

While waiting for my possessions to appear simultaneously with Buchanan I have missed both the Delaware and Arizona primaries.

"Well, look what the cat dragged in," says Buchanan when he spots me.

"You ditched me seven days ago in South Carolina," I say. "You left me in a second-rate hotel. You stole my bags." Buchanan is wearing a wrinkled dark suit, white shirt, red tie. His face looks tired and puffy— he didn't get to sleep until after one and rose at four to speak on the radio. He's just lost two close primaries. Perhaps it isn't the best time to pick a fight. Still, he seems to consider my complaint. "In the Nixon era," he says, finally, "we used to leave you guys behind deliberately. But this time it was probably a mistake."

The word is that Pat is crushed by the Arizona results—he threw all his ferocious energy into a state he was meant to win and wound up third, behind Forbes and Dole. One of the reasons he wound up third, it seems, was that he stirred up more trouble than anyone has seen in a long time. He is maybe the first presidential candidate who tossed away a white cowboy hat at the O.K. Corral and donned a black one. But my own immediate impression is that Buchanan is more at one with himself now, since, like all romantics, he is more deeply attracted to failure than to success. He hasn't the first idea how to behave when he wins. Among the first things he said when he climbed aboard the plane after *each* of his three victories—Alaska, Louisiana, and New Hampshire—was "this is the first election I've ever won." Certainly no historian who gazes back over the newsreels of Buchanan's Arizona campaign—grabbing for the black hats, brandishing machine guns over his head—will argue that it was designed actually to seize power. Buchanan has no real interest in getting his hands on power. He's only secondarily interested in having his views written into the Republican Party platform: the moment that happens he'll have lost his purpose in life. That purpose is to remain an outsider, an agitator, a sore loser.

FEBRUARY 29

I arrive at the Sheraton on the outskirts of Columbia, South Carolina, about a half hour before the four most successful candidates— Buchanan, Dole, Forbes, and Alexander—are scheduled to collide in something called the Business and Industry Trade Association debate.

Waiting for the candidates just outside the hotel, a small lily-white crowd waves Dole signs; beside the highway just off the hotel's property a slightly larger crowd of young black protesters raises hell. Every now and then a black person wanders onto Sheraton turf and is removed by police officers. Order reigns, at least for a moment. But then suddenly there is a commotion at the hotel's front door, and a oval black man with flipper-sized feet is propelled into the sunlight. "These money-grubbing interests are trying to exclude my message from the agenda," he shouts to two or three people who happen to be standing around.

Keyes! He is staging a hunger strike, he says. Until he's allowed to debate he will not eat.

I follow him as he makes his way alone down to the strip of land along the highway where the black kids march with signs. His arms and legs are jerking here and there; he looks as if his joints could use a few squirts of WD-40. It occurs to me that it is the first time I have seen Keyes with other blacks. They instantly recognize him and gather around. A pair of television cameras turns up, and Keyes lets fly. "I have now been excluded from the debate arbitrarily," he explains. "Arbitrarily and without justification. Because I'm doing well they want to keep me out."

"Is this racism?" a reporter asks. The kids start to chant: "E-rase—racism—e-rase—racism!"

"I frankly do not know what it represents," says Keyes, generously.

"What do you think of the Confederate flag?" asks one of the black kids. Keyes couldn't care less about the Confederate flag. In one of his many wonderful stump riffs he argues that people and groups who focus on symbolic slights tend to win a lot of meaningless, symbolic battles. But he looks into the crowd and knows that it isn't the time to go into what he believes.

"I feel that the Rebel flag is an inappropriate symbol of what I believe in," says Keyes, and the kids go wild. They start up a chant.

"Brother on the move! Brother on the move! Brother on the move!"

No black man staging a protest against white men ever looked less like a brother on the move. As he flaps on down the highway on his flipper feet, I suddenly recall something Morry Taylor said about him after the final New Hampshire debate. "Keyes has got that look in his eye," said Morry. "I seen it with other guys. He's just gone up and up and up, and now he's out of the universe. He's never coming back." Morry was right—Keyes has crossed the invisible line into fanaticism. He's no longer subject to the thousand little restraints on his behavior that gov-

103

ern a man with conventional ambition. He's Gandhi after South Africa, Saint Simeon Stylites after his pillar years.

The debate pales by comparison. In the event Keyes's exclusion merely helps Buchanan, who is now the only remaining moralist. Buchanan, for his part, shrewdly claims that he is outraged that Keyes is not included. The sight of Buchanan defending Keyes—who spends about a third of his life lacerating Buchanan—reminds me of the only other thing I can think of that the two men have in common: a lack of self-control in the presence of food. Buchanan cannot pass a Dunkin' Donuts without a twitching in his soul; I once made three stops with him there in one day. Keyes is, if anything, even less continent. One morning in Iowa I watched him pay a call on McDonald's just as the menu was seguing from breakfast to lunch. Keyes bought an Egg McMuffin, a sack of Chicken McNuggets, a Quarter Pounder with cheese, and a large fries. Back on the road he made quick work of the McNuggets and the Egg McMuffin and then tried to put the burger aside. Five minutes later, however, he announced that he might as well eat his lunch with his breakfast and polished off the rest.

And now: a hunger strike!

MARCH 1

I drive down to Charleston from Columbia in the early morning darkness so that I can be waiting for Buchanan when he arrives at the Citadel for what promises to be high theater. Not long after I arrive I find a cadet who offers me a tour of the campus. This now includes a lecture on the feminist writer Susan Faludi, who has just published a long, unsympathetic article about the school, and a visit to the room where the first female cadet, Shannon Faulkner, spent one night before dropping out. On Faludi the cadets are in full *Backlash* mode. One cadet who helped her with her article tells me that "she came and said she was writing a book about women trying to get into male institutions, and the next thing you know we're wife beaters and homosexuals." If the cadets didn't have problems with women before, they do now.

Faulkner's room is still wired with special electronics, including a panic button and a pair of video monitors. On the wall of the entrance to her barracks are two plaques, which, had Faulkner remained, she would have been required to polish:

104

DUTY, THEN, IS THE SUBLIMEST WORD IN THE ENGLISH LANGUAGE—Robert E. Lee.

A CADET DOES NOT LIE, CHEAT OR STEAL NOR TOLERATE THOSE WHO DO.

A cadet named Mike Murphy tells me that he traveled to Washington during the Faulkner episode to solicit the support of Republicans in keeping women out of the Citadel. He met with fifty congressmen and twenty-five senators. "Every last one of them said they supported us," he says, "and not one of them ever did anything." Buchanan, on the other hand, devoted several newspaper columns to their defense, and everywhere there are signs of the bond this has created. "He stood with us when no one stood with us," one cadet says.

After the tour we head out to meet Buchanan and find that the main gates to the campus are being locked, for the first time in five years, the cadet tells me. The school claims it is closing the gates for Buchanan's protection, but it is hard to see how: the gate is not a bulletproof wall but a row of thin black iron bars. More likely, the school is terrified that Buchanan will walk on campus and make the six o'clock news. The Citadel has a better sense of survival than Buchanan, but then institutions generally do have keener instincts of self-preservation than individuals. It's an unpleasant chilly morning, drizzling just insistently enough that the crowd seeks protection under a tent. Alone in the cold rain stand the cadets, who are dressed for war in a rain forest and seem to enjoy the downpour. The 200 or so cadets who have come to cheer Buchanan had to skip classes to do so. (For their transgression they will be punished with ten hours of solitary confinement.) The rain beads harmlessly on their shiny black waxed shoes and their matted black hats. A young man with a buzz cut—a former cadet, as it turns out—is hurriedly transcribing a line from a book that he feels is appropriate to use in introducing Buchanan: *To move swiftly, strike vigorously, and secure the fruits of victory is the secret of a successful war.* (It never gets used.) Of the 1,700 cadets in the corps, I ask him, how many would have turned up if they had been let out of class by their teachers? "Just to be conservative," he says without a trace of irony, "one hundred percent." What, I wonder, would be his liberal estimate? That the buildings would have come, too?

Buchanan drives up with his new entourage, but before he emerges from his car the traveling press, the aides, and the Secret Service must find their places beneath the large white tents. The gang's all here: *Time,*

Newsweek, ABC, NBC, CBS, CNN, the Washington *Post, The New York Times,* half a dozen daily papers. A man who looks distinctly like Al Franken, the *Saturday Night Live* comedian, stands alone in the rain, talking to a pair of cadets. It *is* Al Franken. He's been sent here by *Newsweek* to satirize the Buchanan campaign. Tough job. The cadets fail to recognize him, however, and, seizing the opportunity, Franken goes to work on them. He berates a pair of cadets for skipping classes to see Buchanan. "I'm a taxpayer," he says. "Why am I paying my money for you to go to school to skip classes?"

One of the cadets looks uneasy. "We're taking the consequences, sir," he says, seriously. But Franken presses. "What class are you missing right now?" he asks, in a genuinely bullying tone. "History of Western Civilization," says the cadet, stiff as a rod. "Good thing to know about, son," mutters Franken, "Western civilization."

The cadets, who still don't recognize him, are growing tenser by the moment. They do their best to conceal their rising anger; they try to reason with the comedian. "Sir," asks one, "did you ever go to college?" Franken says he didn't just go to college; he went to Harvard. "Didn't you ever miss class?" asks the cadet. "I'm the journalist here," shouts Franken, then claims that the question is irrelevant since Harvard is a private school, and he paid his own way. "Yes, sir," says the cadet, po-faced. "I understand about private schools. But you still get federal funding." Franken wheels on Sidney Blumenthal of *The New Yorker.* "Help me out here," he says. "Does Harvard get federal funding?"

As a discussion ensues, a crowd of fifty cadets becomes involved, and you can see some of them starting to recognize the celebrity—though his two tense victims remain oblivious.

"That's Al Franken," shouts someone.

"How do I get on *Saturday Night Live?*" shouts another cadet.

"You want to know how you get on a show like that?" says Franken. "You study. You think I missed a comedy class even once?"

The two hapless cadets now have sick little expressions on their faces. "Oh, God," says one, "I knew that guy looked like Stuart Smalley" (Franken's twelve-step character best known from his role in the therapeutic film *Stuart Saves His Family*). "That's Stuart Smalley." "Who else here is from *Saturday Night Live?*" asks the other. For a delicious moment the cadets think that Buchanan isn't coming at all, that the long dark sedan that Buchanan is reputed to be sitting inside of is a hoax, that they have been set up by *Saturday Night Live,* that they are no more than an Al Franken vehicle. And you realize: Buchanan at the Citadel borders on farce.

"A *disgrace!*" Franken is shouting into a horde of cadets from under his giant red-and-white umbrella. "A *disgrace! For the Citadel. For the state.*"

"Cancel *Saturday Night Live,*" a cadet shouts back. "It's dead. Kill it!"

Now Buchanan steps out of his car, to complete the picture. In the sky overhead cadets lean out of their windows to catch a glimpse of their lone political patron; on the ground below cadets cheer wildly. They care intensely about a small part of what he has to say, as is true of almost all of Buchanan's supporters. The churchgoers who go berserk when he flays liberal Supreme Court justices barely applaud when he talks trade; the unemployed textile workers who seem rather indifferent to abortion go nuts when he flays Japanese corporations. The cadets at the Citadel don't care about either economics or abortion but about Buchanan's rousing defense of southern tradition. And who can blame them: all they have is their peculiar reverence for the past, and they have been told by everyone else that it is bad. Buchanan tells them it is noble. Nothing else matters, or seems to. Except that when it is over he shakes hands with the cadets through the bars of closed gates. "The barons and knights are heading to the castle," he says of the Dole forces. "We're just seeing if we can get over the wall."

At the end of the day I stop by an Alexander rally in Charleston. LAMAR! is painted in big red letters behind the stage, but the event has a dispirited Salvation Army band feel to it. The effable Lamar brings on-stage Alfred E. Brumley Jr. to lead the crowd in singing "Jesus Hold My Hand," but no one knows the words. Not five minutes into the event the familiar uncharitable sensation I will forever associate with Alexander rises like bile in my throat. "I fought for a long time to value our traditions," Lamar says, in his best New South manner, "but it's time to move on ahead." Lamar shows that there is no ready New South substitute for Old South feeling.

Lamar also shows how stressful it is to seem relaxed when you are not. He has finally stopped hopping up and down when he speaks, but he retains his other nervous tics. He has a habit, for instance, of staring into the crowd on his right but, every now and then, glancing quickly back to his left, like a driver checking his rearview mirror. There is no one behind

him anymore, however. All that he will see in his mirror is his own trademark, all that is left of his campaign, suspended in the air, like the smile
of the Cheshire Cat:

!

MARCH 2

I spend Election Day fetching rental cars around the state and returning
them to their respective companies. In eight hours of driving, the only
indication that the future of the Republican Party is at stake are a pair of
Dole signs and, at nearly six in the evening, an hour before the polls
close, a radio spot that features Steve Forbes explaining why South Car-
olinians should not vote for Dole. The voters don't listen, however. The
state goes for Dole in a landslide, as has been forecasted by Buchanan's
demeanor since Tuesday. Dole wins 45 percent of the vote next to
Buchanan's 29 percent. Morry Taylor, theoretically still a presidential
candidate, gets ninety-one votes, or about three-hundredths of 1 percent
of the total.

I finish the day—after returning the third and final rental car—at the
private air terminal in Columbia. As I'm waiting for Dole's plane to drop
out of the sky I am gradually surrounded by Republican pooh-bahs. First
to arrive is Arizona senator John McCain. I am strangely pleased to meet
a war hero who is shorter than I am. For the next twenty minutes it's just
the two of us in the private air terminal, and for about the twenty-fifth
time I experience a little shudder of improbability. This business of constantly bumping into the history makers in strange out-of-the-way places
is leading me to develop a gift for acting more nonchalant (less chalant?)
than I feel. I still am floored by the idea that a senator will take the time
to talk to me, even when he has no one else to talk to. I am amazed that
any reporter in this situation can bring himself to ask a difficult question.
Certainly I cannot.

This is unfortunate, as McCain is especially blunt. Indeed, for the
first time since I began my political journey an important politician is
simply speaking his mind, or seems to be. The effect could not be more
unnerving than if I had just met a giraffe with no neck. The senator appears to commit indiscretions by the score. But I have no idea whether
these are indiscretions everyone has already heard, and thus part of

108

McCain's political persona, or true gaffes that will get him in trouble and make me famous for my reportorial skills. Is it shocking that while every elected official in America is busy sucking up to Ross Perot, McCain not only describes Perot as "nutty" but also tells me that Perot calls him constantly to whine about even mild criticism? Should I stop the presses when he says that Buchanan drew more people to rallies in Arizona than he ever could? I don't know, and I'm not even sure I want to.

Most of the traits I'd just assumed came with the species *Homo politicus* are missing in McCain. He has with him no rented strangers in blue suits, and, at the mention of Dole's campaign staffers, he rolls his eyes conspicuously. His eyes do not dart around the room in search of the bigger, better deal. He does not lower his voice exactly one octave to convey sincerity when he especially wants you to believe what he is saying. For that matter he doesn't seem especially to care whether you believe what he is saying. He just talks. I have no idea how to respond, and so, for the purposes of campaign journalism, the conversation vanishes like steam as soon as it has ended. But from McCain I do collect another curious Dole anecdote. During the five and a half years McCain spent as a Vietnam POW, Dole wore a POW bracelet with McCain's name on it. "And I never knew it," says McCain. "He never said a word about it until it came up in a speech a few years ago." McCain still backed Gramm at first, however: "I thought he was a better politician than Dole. Shows what I know."

At length a handful of Dole's local campaign staff arrive, followed by former South Carolina governor Carroll Campbell, followed by current South Carolina governor David Beasley, followed by South Carolina senator Strom Thurmond. When Thurmond walks in, his gray suit bagging at his ankles, the terminal goes quiet. The ninety-five-year-old senator shuffles down the receiving line shaking hands until he arrives at the lone young woman. "That pretty girl's hands are cold," he says, going back for more. "Let an old man warm them up." As he makes feeble love to her I notice that the hands of the other men bear Citadel rings. The cadets may have gone for Buchanan, they tell me, but their fathers went for Dole. There, in a nutshell, was Buchanan's southern problem: once the authorities rallied behind Dole, the troops were bound to follow. People trained to follow orders make poor rebels indeed. Under fire, the Citadel will always close its gates. Its passion was overcome by its love of order and discipline—and by the jobs for its graduates created by the brand-new Michelin factory just down the road. "Did you see that half the

Christian Coalition went with Dole?" McCain asks one of the Citadel graduates. "The half that works at the BMW plant," he replies.

And so Bob Dole was right: the Republican nomination would be handed to him after all. He didn't need to know why he should be president. He could give himself over to the rented strangers, and they would take care of the rest. They would lose no luggage; they would take no stands; they would leave no Republican governor unexploited. But the passion they so abhor is an inconvenient thing; when it is no longer wanted it will not simply slink away into the night. It must find other ways to express itself. It will channel itself into quixotic third-party movements, into the hatred of authority, into a thousand soul-stirring speeches. The only place you can be sure it will not channel itself is into the White House.

At Dole's victory rally tonight the stage is filled with the many governors and senators who have just given Dole the biggest win of his political career. You can see them up there rowed and happy, reassuring themselves that Forbes and Alexander and Buchanan will now have to drop from the race and the Republican Party will soon return to normal. Sure it will. Look at it: a fanatic with a Special Olympics smile and a half-billion-dollar trust fund buying anti-Dole ads by the bushel, a potato-faced rabble-rouser out in front of a mob of 10 million justly outraged peasants, and one very angry black man bent on starving himself who has now, somehow, disappeared.

NINE

Losers

Lead had scored its old time victory over steel; the heroic had broken its great heart against the commonplace. There are those who say that it is sometimes otherwise.

—AMBROSE BIERCE,
What I Saw at Shiloh

MARCH 7

Two days ago Dole swept the other southern primaries, including Georgia's. Yesterday Lugar and Alexander dropped from the race and endorsed Dole, surprising no one except those who had forgotten that Alexander and Lugar were even in the race. And yet today Pat Buchanan behaves as if it is the first day of the rest of his life. Today is the first and only day of what began in Buchanan's romantic imagination as a full-week bus tour through the Old South. The *Pitchfork Express*, he called it, then further announced to anyone who would listen, "I'm gonna look like something out of *Deliverance* getting off that bus with my pitchfork." I was fully prepared to squeal like a pig. But, save for a glorious moment when a Buchanan aide asks if we would like to watch one of his creationist tapes on the bus monitors, the *Pitchfork Express* rolls along pretty much like any other political bus tour of Tennessee. The trouble with a long, slow, winding journey is that there is too much space to cover and too little time to cover it; and in any case the media prefer a series of two-minute interviews to a documentary film. The Republican primary isn't really designed for populism.

The man is, however. Not five minutes into his first speech in the school gym of Knoxville's Christian Academy Buchanan has the crowd of

111

creamy-skinned teenagers stomping on the bleachers, waving signs about trade and taxes they couldn't possibly have thought up themselves, and screaming at full blast, "Go! Pat! Go!" and "Get the pitchforks!" Then in a rare moment of silence, a voice from the crowd shrieks out: "Don't support the nominee!"

Buchanan looks up. You can see him revving the engine, feeling the strength of the machine beneath him. Then he lets out the clutch. "Here's what we do," he says. "We go to San Diego. We break the doors open to the party. We take it over!"

I'm almost sure he didn't plan to say it; it's Fort Sumter all over again. Immediately after the morning speech the reporters pick up their cell phones and call their counterparts on the Dole campaign. They, in turn, inform Dole that Buchanan plans to take over the party in San Diego. Dole snaps back to his reporters that Buchanan is fracturing the Republican Party. This is relayed back to Buchanan, who says, "I don't need a lecture from Bob Dole about what it means to be a loyal Republican." In a matter of hours the two camps are rent beautifully by a process designed to fuel strife and discontent. Buchanan refuses to return calls from Republican Party big shots (when he is in a giving vein he has his sister, Bay, return them on his behalf), but he is happy to mix it up through intermediaries. By the end of the week he will have bought himself a mechanical parrot—a bird with a battery pack—that he will take onstage with him to squawk back at him his best lines about trade and the culture war. Bob the Parrot, he calls it.

Toward the end of the day, as the sun is setting over the brown foothills, I receive an urgent message from the Taylor campaign: Morry is pulling out tomorrow morning and endorsing Dole. It was never clear where Morry would concede defeat. He owns homes in Illinois, Michigan, and Florida; he has his campaign headquarters in Iowa; and he has factories in Tennessee, California, Ireland, Italy, and God knows where else. Now we know: the candidate will concede in Detroit.

MARCH 8

I fly to Detroit at the crack of dawn. There is no sign of life in the lobby of the Holiday Inn when I arrive. I find Morry on the board of special events, misspelled in white plastic letters, between a pair of sales conferences: MORREY TAYLOR EVENT. He is in the Jefferson Room.

Of the twenty-five chairs in the room, nineteen are empty. The only witnesses to the end of the Taylor campaign are Morry's wife, Michelle, a Dole man, a pair of local photographers, and two reporters, one from the Detroit *Free Press,* the other from a local radio station. Modest as Morry's press coverage appears, he now has one more reporter than witnessed the one thousand delegates from United We Stand storm his hospitality suite in Dallas. Morry stands rakishly before his audience with his arm draped over the podium, a cup of steaming coffee in his hand. He nods grimly when I walk in. He is still angry, and rightly so, about the fallacious story I had picked up from *The New York Times,* which had picked it up in turn from the Associated Press, which had taken it from *Foster's Daily Democrat,* in New Hampshire. It was the story about his poking fun at a girl who stuttered.

Even though there were three journalists on hand, no word of the event appeared until five days after it supposedly occurred. Then, prodded by their teachers, the children wrote a letter to *Foster's Daily Democrat* complaining about Morry. The letter was transformed into a story in the paper about the girl with the stutter. (The paper later conceded, too late, that the girl didn't stutter.) Within a week CNN was asking Morry about it on the air. And so here, in microcosm, lies one of the main problems of campaign journalism. It is all done on the fly by people who don't have time to double-check anything, and so once a mistake is made it gets repeated over and over again. In my experience almost every defining moment is in some way distorted in the retelling. The truth becomes lost in the myth that grows up around it.

All I could say to Morry when he called to shout at me for repeating the story was that "I ap-ap-ap-apologize." Now I can see that it isn't enough because as I arrive Morry is ripping into journalists in a way that he didn't used to; he sounds almost like a normal candidate. "They write whole editorials, and they never even met you," he says to the reporter from the Detroit *Free Press.* "They can be just running off with something someone else has said. And it could be *totally* wrong." He finds me in the back of the room and fixes me with a stare.

"There's a perfect example," he says. "Sitting right there. Michael Lewis."

"I didn't treat you so badly," I say, uneasily. Thinking: I flew to Detroit at six in the morning for this?

"You see," he says, scornfully, "there he goes again—trying to defend himself." He pauses and takes a breath. "I don't have nothing against the press," he says, to the possible astonishment of the other two journalists in the room. "I feel sorry for the press. Think of how many people just don't read them." But soon enough Morry moves on to his endorsement of Dole, and it is a curious thing. It is unlike the endorsements from Lugar and Alexander, for example, as Morry expects nothing in exchange, whereas Lugar wants Dole to appoint him secretary of state, and Alexander wants to be indulged by the Republican Party when he runs for president again four years from now. Maybe because Morry is simply a free man saying what he thinks, his speech doesn't come across as the Dole people had hoped.

The Dole campaign—which is really not much more than a series of these endorsements—had said only that there would be a big announcement today in Michigan, leaving it to the press to assume that Dole would be endorsed by Governor John Engler. The Michigan polls were showing Buchanan running close, largely because his views on trade resonate in the Rust Belt. The Dole people had wanted the world to see Morry attacking Buchanan on trade in front of an Engler-sized crowd of journalists. But one of Morry's people mistakenly told a reporter the truth—that Morry, not Engler, would be doing the endorsing—and, instead of Morry banging on Buchanan in front of the nation's media, the Dole people got me and two other reporters watching Morry talk about whatever he wanted to. They were lucky to have that. Morry's views on trade are closer to Buchanan's than to Dole's—he advocates erecting a customhouse in the middle of Nebraska through which all Japanese goods must be cleared. Like all of Morry's decisions, his Dole endorsement is driven by his instincts rather than his analysis. He likes Buchanan, but he likes Dole more.

As Morry rambles on, not about trade but about the various problems that beset an ordinary titan of commerce when he runs for president, it emerges that he spoke with Dole onstage before the big debate in Iowa. While every other candidate had joined in the lynch mob, and was doing whatever he could to destroy Bob Dole, Morry leaned over and tried to make Dole feel better. Today in the Jefferson Room of the Holiday Inn, for the benefit of no one, Morry recalls the moment: "At that time, the senator said to me, 'You know, Morry, when I was out here at the straw poll in Ames last summer all I seen was Gramm signs and your signs. I had no Dole signs.' And I said to the senator, 'Yeah, but I'll tell you something, Senator. You remember that man that stood up in the front row, cheering you on, and wanted to shake your hand when you first got down here? That was my father. He served in World War Two. And so you had one supporter. He would vote for me, but he was more excited to see you.' And so that's what I told the senator. Then I told him he'd get my endorsement."

We all have a fantasy, and it is profitably exploited by Hollywood, that if only an honest and genuinely free man with a heart of gold ran for president, everything in the world would be put aright. Well, now we know what happens when an honest and genuinely free man with a heart of gold runs for president. He spends $6.5 million and gets seven thousand votes. "I probably got more bang for my dollar than all of them combined," Morry concludes. "Except Dornan. The mad bomber. He spent nothing."

Then he pauses, and his Cheshire Cat smile reappears. "But I beat him."

MARCH 11

The press has vanished to the point where Buchanan can't afford to charter a plane. Buchanan had sixty journalists with him when he left New Hampshire and maybe forty-five last week in Georgia. Now there are only twenty-three, and twelve of them are the obligatory crews from the networks and CNN. And six of *those* say they'll be gone by Wednesday. The strange thing is that the crowds keep turning up, with almost no help from the Buchanan campaign: twelve hundred in Dallas, one thousand in Houston, fourteen hundred in Memphis. Dole attracts journalists, but not people; Buchanan attracts people, but not journalists. It is maybe the strangest moment of this strange campaign, when the journalists are abandoning the candidate who offers not only the best entertainment value but who also, not coincidentally, is most likely to reshape the world in his image. Tonight, in the church of the Christian Heritage Academy in Oklahoma City, there are somewhere north of two thousand people, every one a fanatical loyalist; and once again Buchanan demonstrates that joy and anger are closer to each other than either of them is to indifference. The crowd knows all of its hero's best lines and responds to them on cue, like the audience of *The Rocky Horror Picture Show*.

"You know what the Founding Fathers would have said?" Pat asks.

"Lock and load!" they scream back at him.

"Lock and load," he says, more like a teacher concurring with an excellent pupil than a candidate.

I am beginning to feel at these Buchanan rallies as I imagine Cézanne must occasionally have felt when he stared up at Mont Saint-Victoire in the morning: How many different ways can you paint the same mountain? But as Cézanne knew deep down in his obsessive heart, there is no end of ways you can see if you just keep on looking. As always, Buchanan attracts a surprisingly prosperous and ordinary crowd; if you close your ears to their roiling enthusiasm you might think you are at a Dole event. But you're not. The central fact about the Buchanan supporters is their panicky feeling of powerlessness. Some part of this feeling is no doubt the response of a psychotic mind to the complications of modern life. But another part of it is perfectly legitimate and endemic to minority life in a democracy. The people don't rule. The majority does. It's for just this reason—that, ultimately, they won't win—that groups of people whose interests are not remotely similar can afford to join together into a single political movement. It's only when such a movement comes close to actual power that it experiences the ordinary pressures to fracture. The evangelical Christian in the tweed jacket with the Buchanan sign looks first to his right, where he sees a raving lunatic, and then to his left, where he finds an unemployed worker, and asks: Do I want *him* to have his finger on the button?

Between rallies Buchanan makes a brief stop at a tall glass tower in downtown Oklahoma City, a few miles from where the bomb exploded. The Secret Service men are especially secretive here, and within a few moments they have lost the few journalists who have bothered to follow. I hop onto an elevator, start pressing buttons, and soon find myself standing inside a smaller version of a *Geraldo* set, a large empty well facing a few dozen chairs nailed dutifully to the floor. But in the middle of the well sits a desk, and at the desk, with his feet crossed beneath his chair, sits Pat Buchanan. He's facing away from where the audience would be and looking up at the top of the wall. There, under three harsh spotlights, is the minuscule black eye of a camera—more like a monitor at a convenience store than a television camera. In the next hour Buchanan delivers maybe twenty rapid interviews into the black eye, which beams them via satellite to more than one thousand television stations. Every few minutes one interview ends and another begins.

What's odd about all this is that we can see nothing except the black

116

eye high on the wall. Buchanan alone can hear the questions, through his earpiece. The other four people in the room—Shelley and three slumbering journalists who came in with her—sit listening to Pat, amid pregnant pauses. My game is to try to guess what he has been asked. It is not difficult.

"This murder was on a massive scale," he is saying when I arrive. "Certainly anyone who knows as much as I do about Treblinka knows that."

(Do you really believe that the number of Jews killed in Treblinka has been overstated?)

Pause . . .

"Uh-huh, uh-huh . . ."

Pause . . .

"Colin Powell has only been a Republican for three months. He's declared he would not support me."

(Would you support Colin Powell as a vice-presidential candidate?)

Pause . . .

"If he does that, he's going to have the fight of his life on his hands in San Diego."

(Do you think Dole will abandon the pro-life plank in the platform?)

Pause . . .

"I'm driving a good old American Cadillac."

(Is it true that despite your protectionist trade position you drive a Mercedes?)

At this point he swivels and looks at me and says, "Well, look who's turned up again," offering an opening to ask him the shortest question about his past performances I can think of: " 'The ashes of our fathers and the temples of our Gods'—where did that phrase come from?"

"Macaulay," he says. "Men do battle against fearful odds for the ashes of our fathers and the temples of our Gods." Then he pauses all by himself. "A great phrase. Yes, sir. I'll think of the whole quatrain in a minute."

"Hello. Who we got here?"

Pause . . .

"Walter? Hello, Walter."

Pause . . .

"Is that you, Walter?"

Pause . . .

"No one has approached me or even talked to me about stepping out of this race. My sister got one call from someone at the Dole campaign

117

asking if we wanted to have lunch. We said we're not doing lunch right now; we're campaigning."

Pause . . .

"Walter! Walter! Use your head, Walter! Look, how can a speech by a defeated candidate on a night where the approval rating of the nominee jumped ten percent be said to hurt the nominee?"

Pause . . .

"Rally behind what, Walter? What ideas, Walter? What vision, Walter? And what agenda? What exactly does Bob Dole stand for? The Republican Party, Mr. Dole says, is in a battle for its heart and soul. He is right. We have ideas, vision, we got a broad agenda of issues. From campaign finance reform, judicial reform, term limits, protective orders, a new America First foreign policy, no more unfair trade deals. What about going and debating these all out in San Diego, and, if we are a party of ideas, why not have a debate on ideas and unify it behind a broad conservative agenda? We are *eight months* before the election, and people are saying that if Pat Buchanan runs for two more weeks the Republican Party is in trouble. Is it that *weak* an institution that it can't stand two more weeks of debate? What would Senator Dole have been doing now if we'd *won* in Georgia? Demand we get out for party unity? I mean, if I had been demanding after New Hampshire, 'Look, I'm the front-runner, get out, Mr. Dole, you're dividing the party,' people would have laughed. He doesn't have a majority of the delegates right now. He won't and can't, I believe, until after California, which is two weeks from now. Let's take a look at the situation then. But I think we're going to go to that convention, I know we are, and fight for what we believe in. That's what people voted for us for. They voted for us not simply to give us the nomination 'cause they wanted us to have it. But also to fight to represent them. And we're going to do that."

Pause . . .

I think to myself: Ever since South Carolina, when it became certain—or nearly so—that Dole would bag the nomination, the main question that is asked of the others is, Why on earth are you still in it? But this emphasis on who wins is a form of madness. In the first place, politics is not like the stock market, where an ordinary person can make money by correctly guessing a winner; in the second, the winner in this case has had no effect whatsoever on the debate. The debate has been framed entirely by the losers, especially Buchanan. I don't know whether this is the way American politics has always worked; maybe we just live in times when the fear of losing is so all-consuming that winners live their lives too scared to do much of anything. Maybe you have to be scared to win.

"Dallas live?"

There is no other sign that Walter is gone except that Buchanan turns to me and recites:

> How can men die better
> Than facing fearful odds
> For the ashes of their fathers
> And the temple of their Gods?

TEN

Blue-Collar Blues

Forbes dropped out of the race yesterday and followed up his $37 million televised attack on Dole with a ringing endorsement, leaving Buchanan as the only surviving heretic. But while Dole seems content to let the governors and the senators do his bidding, Buchanan is actually out talking to people; not coincidentally Buchanan is the only one actually learning something about the country he seeks to govern and thus the only candidate in a position to teach me something I don't already know. All by himself he has inspired *The New York Times* to run a seven-part series on "downsizing." "There's cordite on the ground out there," he tells me, when I ask him what he thinks he is up to. "All we have to do is put a match to it." Here in Michigan that means searching out workers who have been maltreated by the free market, and whose anger has driven them into politics. Pat Buchanan, former staffer to Richard Nixon and Ronald Reagan, is at war with the market on behalf of the American worker.

As a rule, you can judge the strength and depth of a political movement by how long it takes you to stumble upon its ringleaders at one of their events. Within about thirty seconds of arriving at a gathering of Detroit autoworkers who support Pat Buchanan—Citizens for Better Government, they call themselves—I find myself at a restaurant table with the two men who run the show. They are the only two autoworkers who have turned up, at least for the moment. The first one, named Gordon, hands me a flyer headlined "UAW Rank and File behind Buchanan" that lists the names of the thirteen autoworkers who have "endorsed" Buchanan. The second one, Henry, turns out to be the real leader of this cryptic force. He's a huge, pale man, maybe fifty-five years old, who sits across from me and glares as if I'm the enemy, which I slowly become. "How many people are involved in this movement?" I ask him.

"We don't discuss that," he says. "It's national."

"Well," I say, "who is the head of it, nationally?"

"We don't discuss that," he says.

"What trades do the members belong to?"

"We don't discuss that."

At that point I drop my grilled lamb hoagie onto the plate and say, "Well, look, what's the point of organizing into a political movement if you won't discuss it?" He blinks for a moment and then says, "We don't discuss that either."

The force of Henry's view of the world as a conspiracy against him and his fellows is such that I have to close my eyes and remind myself that I'm not interviewing a militiaman. "Does any of your movement favor Ross Perot?" I ask, on a hunch. "The true grassroots people abandoned Ross Perot," says Henry, angrily emerging from his shell. "It's the opportunists and the gullibles that stayed with him."

An hour into the ceremony Buchanan arrives and shakes hands with his blue-collar following. He doesn't give them much of a speech, maybe because there aren't a whole lot of them to talk to; but he does offer up a version of the passage that he has worked into his routine to appeal to the politically self-conscious workingman. It is a curious thing to hear, coming as it does from the lips of a Republican:

> Someone has got to stand up for the workingmen and -women of America who don't have no representatives at these trade negotiations where they decide what industries are going to live and what are gonna die. It is wrong to negotiate trade deals for the benefit of transnational corporations that encourage them to shut down their plants in Toledo and Youngstown and to open up a plant in Singapore or China because that takes away jobs from American workers and hollows out our manufacturing base. Look, we won World War Two. You know why? We had great generals like MacArthur and Patton. And admirals like Nimitz. We had great soldiers, great American soldiers. But we also had this great industrial heartland of America. The productive capacity of this nation. And it is being gutted and hollowed out. We went up to Youngstown, Ohio. We went up along that river, the Mahoning Valley. Steel mills. Factories. *Gone. Dead.* Shut down for fifteen

years. Take a look. Take a look at what we were and what we are. Those are the dying husks of what almost appears to be a dying civilization.

A few years ago I found myself seated across the table from Buchanan on his television show, *Crossfire.* He attacked me for what he perceived to be my ambivalence toward capitalism when all I was trying to say was that the market does not always deliver morally pleasing results. But even then you could see that, like all social conservatives, he didn't know quite which way to jump in the marketplace. The two biggest ambitions of the social conservative are to prevent change and to rein in human desire. The market is uniquely designed to facilitate change and to satisfy desire. On the one hand, Buchanan couldn't bear to believe that the economic policies and attitudes promoted by his beloved Ronald Reagan had led to anything but good. On the other hand, he was clearly disturbed by the corporate upheaval orchestrated by Wall Street financiers, by the massive layoffs that accompany economic change, and by the stagnant real wages in the manufacturing sector. It was only a matter of time before he was forced to choose. Now he has.

After the rally, if you could call it that, I drive down the road past the prison to Flint, to the GM truck and bus assembly plant, which is busy shutting down in response to a big strike in Ohio. Every fifteen minutes or so, seemingly gleeful workers come sprinting out the side door, like kids let out of school early, and race to their cars and pickup trucks. I make my way to the UAW local across the street, number 659. Inside the beige-brick building I find two men with rakish pompadours chewing the fat over a desk. The pompadour behind the desk insists that under no circumstances will he grant me an interview. I tell him where I've just been and with whom.

"They're not part of the UAW," he says.

"Oh yes they are," I say and show him the flyer listing their names and union affiliation to prove it.

"Not if they support Pat Buchanan, they're not," he says. "Or if they are, they are mentally deranged. Got to see a psychiatrist." His buddy chuckles and adds, "Maybe their medical will cover it."

I exit by the front door past the sign that says WELCOME TO THE UAW LOCAL and walk around the back to the parking lot. There on the wall of the building is a sign. It reads: THE PARKING OF ANY FOREIGN MADE AUTOS ON LOCAL 659 PROPERTY IS ABSOLUTELY PROHIB-

ITED. VIOLATORS WILL HAVE THEIR AUTOS TOWED AT THEIR OWN PERSONAL EXPENSE—JOINT COUNCIL. Obviously there must be all sorts of people who live in the Rust Belt who don't care about how Americans are competing against foreigners just as there must be all sorts of people who live in Dallas who don't care about the Cowboys. But you'd never guess it from watching a presidential campaign pass through.

That evening I drive north out of Detroit away from the American workingman and toward the upper one-half of 1 percent of Americans who are doing better than ever. Just when you think that houses could not possibly grow bigger and that people could not possibly grow richer you reach a gated enclave in Grosse Pointe Farms, between the hunt club and the country club, where the Fords and the Strohs have settled into their gorgeous ruts. The address I have for Morry Taylor—number 260—does not appear to exist, so I pick the biggest pile of bricks I can find and roll up the driveway. But as I leave the car and approach the door a voice from behind pulls me up short.

"Wrong house, Speed!"

I turn to find first a large bronze sculpture of a grizzly bear and, behind that, the chief executive officer of Titan Wheel International freshly returned to private citizenship. He's standing on his ample porch in a polo shirt with a glass of red wine in one hand and a cigar in the other. Normally when a man stops running for president he loses a certain aura. But, at first glance at least, Morry is unchanged by his public demotion. "That looks too small to be yours," I say, pointing at the impressive piece of real estate behind him. "Yeah," he shouts, "but I got three of them." Then he disappears inside leaving me to confirm the truth of the claim: two big ones on the road and a smaller one at the back of the property, which houses the gym and the racquetball court.

I am here in part because I somehow cannot stay away (once you've found your candidate it's hard to give him up, I'm told) but also because Morry's business interests have magically intersected with the Buchanan campaign. Every time Buchanan opens a newspaper in the Midwest he finds new evidence to support his theory of American decline. His most recent piece of evidence is not the GM strike—which he is choosing to ignore—but the announcement that McLouth Steel of Detroit is on the brink of bankruptcy. Thirteen hundred manufacturing jobs are about to go up in smoke, and Buchanan will soon be hammering away at McLouth as an example of what is wrong with America. "I went out and looked into those mighty steel mills," he will say, "and they have vanished. All the way from Willow Run to McLouth Steel." But if you read to the end of the stories about McLouth Steel you see that there is still some small possibility of a future for the company. Morry Taylor is trying to buy it.

His swift exit from politics has only increased Morry's contempt for politicians and people who write about them. He is quick to explain to me, for instance, why I stand no chance whatsoever of understanding the American worker. "If you want to know what they think," he says, "you have to go spend half a day on the production line. At first they'll only tell you all the good things—they don't tell you their problems. Then you hear what they're gonna spend their money on when they get a raise— how they're really gonna buy them a nice pair a tennis shoes. Or maybe they're gonna take their kids to the county fair. Things that if you had to do them you would think: I gotta do this boring thing?"

Why he is after McLouth is unclear. His chief financial backer told him that buying it "took more guts than brains," and his chief strategist has sent him a memo that concludes, "it is not a wise decision to buy McLouth Steel." He takes both as a good sign—if everyone says that it is as bad as all that, maybe it's good. A lot of people had tried to dissuade him from running for president, but Morry had not regretted *that* decision for a moment. At any rate, he has just spoken with McLouth's creditors, who have told him that the company, which has been operating under Chapter 11 bankruptcy protection, has just enough cash to keep on making steel. But after he met with the creditors he met with the union, which was not so sanguine.

MARCH 16

I wake up in a deep goose-down bed in one of the Taylor homes, aware that in the past few weeks I have gone from being Morry Taylor's Boswell to Pat Buchanan's Leni Riefenstahl, and back again. But what can you do when you are faced with a choice between a nominee doing his best to avoid engaging with anyone outside of the U.S. Senate and a pair of losers who are busy grappling with the billion-footed beast? The beast is already up this morning and stalking about on the top of the front page of the Detroit *Free Press:* MCLOUTH STEEL IS BROKE AND CLOSING, it reads in the sort of big, bold letters normally reserved for acts of war. "It means they gotta move real fast," says Morry, shedding his gaudy bathrobe on his way up the stairs. Then he adds, "I'm a lucky guy."

A few minutes later he's tossed on his Lucky's Grizzly Beer pullover with the head of a snarling grizzly bear on the back, and we're off to the factory at speed. After a quick stop for cigars, we are soon on a stretch of road overlooking an industrial wasteland—belching smokestacks and slumbering rail yards as far as the eye can see. A few miles later, we come upon a lovely aqua stretch of the Detroit River and beside it McLouth Steel. It is as if some enterprising capitalist had bought the most wretched Soviet factory and transported it piece by piece to Detroit, as an example of how not to structure an economy. The windows are busted out of the side of the mill, and the scrap yard is a moonscape of desolation. But the outside is the best of it. Unlike, say, an investment bank, where a casual visitor would fail to detect even the most dire financial problems, a bankrupt factory *looks bankrupt.*

"It's like going into a big swamp," explains Morry, helpfully, while chomping on the spit-bright butt of his cigar. "And you find this woman who has been in the swamp a long time. You just need a little imagination—wash off the twigs, the mud, and everything, get her all spiffed up. By looking at the outline you might think you have a pretty trim figure underneath. Then again, you might not. Then you need a plastic surgeon." As I sort that one out we enter the gates of the mill and are stopped by a phalanx of guards. "If I buy this thing I'll be here for the next six months," Morry stage-whispers. "I'll get my motorbike with the all-terrain tires. I'll be all over this place. They'll all be saying, 'Fucker was just here a minute ago; don't know where he's at now.'"

Soon enough Morry talks his way past the guardhouse and into the redbrick building beside the mill that houses management, when management isn't kicking back in its fancier building down the road. On the bulletin board beside the beleaguered-looking office is a memo to the workers, imploring them to work harder: 8 HOURS WORK FOR 8 HOURS PAY, it says, only someone has scratched out the second "8" and replaced it with a "4." Morry marches in to conduct a not-entirely-pleasant interview with the current chief executive—who sustains false hopes of keeping his job. I take off for the mill.

Immediately upon entering I sense that I have walked into a place where I do not belong and that if I take a wrong step some mobile machine or flying steel beam will correct me. But the moment the workers discover I came with Morry Taylor ("I'll vote for him if he buys the place," one shouts over the din), I cease to be a nuisance and become a celebrity. They find me a hard hat and start asking me what's going to happen to them—next week will be their first without a paycheck. Though it quickly becomes clear that I have no idea, a small group of them, led by a man named Jim, takes me by the hand to show me what's left of a company that once employed nearly six thousand workers. Jim wears a red-and-white skullcap over his Medusa hair, which grows down into an equally unruly beard. He has a hacking cough, and his face is flushed pink with overexposure. From tip to toe he is covered with grime in a way he wasn't ten years back, he says, when McLouth had the money to keep the mill clean. A few months ago he broke his foot, he says, and he waited for a bit to go into the hospital because "I was ashamed by what the nurses would think when they saw me." He has worked for McLouth for thirty-seven years.

His tour starts in the lunchroom—a metal cell in the center of the mill, which, though perfectly disgusting with grime, is at least quiet. The inside of a steel mill—or at any rate this steel mill—looks like an aircraft hangar into which someone has randomly dumped a lot of big, greasy, outdated machinery. In the summer it is hotter than the air outside; in winter, because of the wind tunnel that it creates, it is colder. When the machinery is working—as it was when I entered—it creates enough noise that if you want to be heard by your neighbor you have to shout into his ear. Any luck that befalls the man who works with these machines is bad luck. In his thirty-seven years Jim has seen more than thirty workers killed, and he starts to list the most common causes of death: crushed by machinery, gassed, electrocuted, burned to death by hydraulic fuel. Still, these are the heavy-industry, good jobs every politician says he wants to create—and that Jim wants to keep.

The tour proceeds to the men's room: a ten-by-twelve cesspool with two inches of mucky water on the floor in which swim rubber gloves, shards of sandwiches, rusty nails, and coils of steel. There are no doors on the two stalls, no seats on the two toilets and no handles on the two faucets—a problem solved by running the water constantly. Nothing would be functional inside the plant itself, Jim tells me, if the machinery were not so simple. As it is he has spent the better part of the past ten years cannibalizing working machines for parts to keep other machines going. "We're in here scrounging for nuts and bolts," he says, "and they're out there building a new office building for themselves."

126

If ever there was a place where Pat Buchanan's message would be heard, here it is. But how in this context do you drag anyone's thoughts toward politics? Who has the spirit for it? Jim reads *Time* and *Newsweek* and knows something about the election. But he hasn't thought twice about how national politics might relate to his immediate predicament. Why should he? With a weary sense of duty, I ask a question about Buchanan. And with a weary sense of duty, Jim says that "there are probably a couple of guys here who'll go vote for Buchanan, but I don't know who they are."

An hour or so later a security guard rushes breathlessly into the grease pit where we stand and explains, more or less, that Morry has been ejected. I find him waiting for me in his automobile, with his Cheshire Cat grin on. Once he had finished hounding the management he sneaked off for a peek at the mills and was nabbed. On the way back home I ask him a bit stupidly what happens to the workers once McLouth Steel shuts down. "They'll sit around," he says. "There will be more divorce. Some kids'll get the hell kicked out of 'em. Some women will get the hell kicked out of 'em. Some of them will get jobs—the skilled guys. But in the next round of layoffs they'll be the first to be let go. It creates a tragedy."

He pauses. "Go ask the Christian Coalition what should be done right now."

MARCH 17

The South Side Chicago St. Patrick's Day parade is yet another political event to which I would normally be dragged kicking and screaming, but that now seems mandatory. The chance to march beside Pat Buchanan clad in a union jacket proves irresistible. Buchanan was initially blocked from participating in the parade, but then Local 150, Union of Operating Engineers—the guys behind the wheel of cranes and forklifts—stepped in and invited him to march alongside them. Why they did this depends on whom you ask. The portly plumber who glowers at Pat at the start of the parade says that it was a publicity stunt for Bill Dugan, the union president, who in exchange is permitted to march alongside Pat and be interviewed by about two hundred journalists. Dugan says it was because Buchanan is "the only guy who has the guts to stand up and talk about our issues." Whatever the case, Buchanan is resplendent in his shamrock-green turtleneck, Jackie Stewart checkered racing cap, and black jacket with PAT stenciled across the pocket and the union logo. LABOR OMNIA VINCIT, it says. As he starts marching down the black asphalt beneath the clover-strewn lampposts it is easy to overlook his pin-striped slacks and black wing tips.

It is never very dignified trailing around behind one of these people, but today marks a new low for the Buchanan journalists. Six parade volunteers use a thin rope to shepherd the press pool and keep the journalists out in front of, but not too close to, Buchanan. The effect is similar to the running of the bulls in Pamplona. The journalists tease the rope, trying to get as close as possible without being knocked over. The rope, for its part, is unpredictable and forever changing speed. One moment there is something like a stationary press conference with Buchanan on one side and the journalists on the other; the next the rope is moving full speed ahead, and fat cameramen are tumbling to the earth and being trampled by union officials, Pat at their center. A few minutes into the parade I am ushered onto Pat's side of the rope. There I'm able to observe the process with amused detachment rather than mortal terror, at least until I see the faces in the crowd as Buchanan sees them.

God knows how he does it. Even though no one knew Buchanan would be here until yesterday, all sorts of people came prepared, with insults as well as with cheers. A Brueghel of two hundred thousand drunken bleacher bums seems to be screaming at us all at once. "Go! Pat! Go!" is in places drowned out by "You! Suck! Meat!" One woman runs alongside the parade and shrieks penetrating moral instruction. ("You should be ashamed of yourself!" "Women have rights, too!") "Looks like we're the story here," Buchanan says, mildly, about midway through the half-mile march, and we are. The boos are nearly as loud as the cheers, but almost everyone seems to have an opinion. As we pass a final balcony overflowing with drunken twenty-five-year-olds flipping the bird and screaming at the top of their lungs, "Up yours, Pat!" I look over to Buchanan on my left and see that he's laughing and waving to them with an enthusiasm most political candidates reserve for their ardent supporters.

"Are you actually *enjoying* this?" I finally ask him.

"Sure!" he says, with great gusto. "Aren't you?"

I shrug.

"What would you rather be doing?" he says. "*Crossfire?*"

"Fuck you, Buchanan!" someone screams.

"Yo! Hitler!" shouts someone else.

To which Buchanan responds with another hearty laugh and a friendly wave. Only at the end of the parade, where the people are too drunk to take much of an interest in anything, does Buchanan's interest flag. In those rare moments when there is neither an enemy nor a friend in sight, he's as lost as a normal person.

Later this evening, after a rally in which he dismisses Dole as "Beltway Bob of the Business Roundtable" and the Dole campaign as "the bland leading the bland," Buchanan appears at my side in the Marriott restaurant. I suddenly remember there was something I was supposed to ask him. "Titan Wheel has a board seat open, and Morry Taylor tells me it's yours if you want it," I say, the first and probably the last time I will ever be in a position to hand out a seat on a corporate board. It's Pat's chance to play an active role in sorting out McLouth Steel. He blinks for a moment and then says, "Morry Taylor is a very nice guy. But I'm not a corporate board guy." He has worked himself into such a frenzy that he seems actually to believe this.

MARCH 18

I go to see Bill Dugan, the union leader who invited Buchanan to march in the parade. Dugan's office is in a building on a stretch of single-lane highway. He keeps me waiting for ten minutes or so, which gives me a chance to look around. In the lobby there is a toy model of a large crane, the pictures of the six union presidents since the local was founded in 1928, and a letter of complaint sent to Bill Clinton by Frank Hanley, the *capo di tutti capi* of all Operating Engineers. At length Dugan sends his pretty secretary out to fetch me.

Union leaders seem to have a more efficiently self-interested way about them than union members; they are more naturally predators than prey. Dugan's office is decorated wall to wall with mounted rifles and the heads of maybe fifteen dead animals: wild boar, wildebeest, antelope, outrageously large heads with outrageously large horns. Off in one corner stands the head of a giraffe that Dugan shot in Botswana, and if you ever wondered how you mount a head of a giraffe here is the answer. You chop it off just above the torso and stand eight feet of neck on the floor. Still, it seems rather unsporting of him, and I ask him if he shot them all. "If I hadn't they wouldn't be on the wall, would they?" he replies curtly.

129

None of the beasts died in America, however. He would never shoot an American animal, Dugan says, planted and glowering from behind his gargantuan wooden desk.

It turns out that Dugan doesn't much care either for liberals or for journalists. Surprise! The coverage of yesterday's event merely confirmed his prejudices. The newspapers stressed the crowd's hostility to Buchanan; Dugan feels that this is merely one more distortion by the liberal press of the one candidate who has the guts to talk about the important issues. He grabs for a handful of telephone message slips, every one from a supporter pleased with the event. "By God, Bill, we're proud of you" is a typical response.

Then I notice the fawn. On the wall beneath the wildebeest, curled up in a ball, is a tiny white-speckled fawn, not much larger than an alley cat. Bambi. Dugan explains that he was driving down the road a few years ago when the car in front of him hit a deer. Both cars stopped, and Dugan negotiated to take the animal and skin it before the meat spoiled. He tossed the carcass in his boat, which happened to be hitched to the back of his truck. When he got home and cut into the animal he found a pair of fawns. The deer was days away from birthing. One of the fawns he stuck in his deep freeze, where it resides to this day. The other he had mounted in this sweet little display.

Consider the career of this animal. There it lay, awaiting its own birth, when its mother chanced to be at the wrong place at the wrong time. Dying before birth, it was then cut unknowingly from the womb, then eviscerated. Its carcass, or what remained of it, was tacked to a slab of wood, which was then affixed to the wall of a man. The fawn went straight from the womb to a wall mount in Bill Dugan's office, where it now lies curled, peaceful and seemingly content—a testament to the undying truth that the more innocent your life, the less you have to say about your fate.

APRIL 1

The Dole campaign has run out of money to spend on television ads, leaving the Clinton campaign to paint whatever picture of Dole it wishes. And that, sadly, is the extent of the campaign.

California was over before it began, and with his win in California Dole won the nomination. The primaries were so tightly stacked that there was no time after New Hampshire for Buchanan to campaign. That was lucky for Dole, who collapsed whenever there was anything like an open contest. When it became clear to Buchanan that the race was over he diverted his quixotic campaign away from the new trail and onto the old one. We drove past the Reagans' house; we stayed in the hotel where the Nixons were married; we stopped at San Clemente and spent the night in the rooms Buchanan used to occupy on his visits to his old boss.

Buchanan has lost. But he has not conceded, much less endorsed Dole. He just up and flew back home from California to Virginia. "What are you going to do now?" I asked one of his twenty-two-year-old aides on the flight back to Washington, fully expecting him to put on the crookedly straight face of the newly unemployed campaign staffer and say that he's already started negotiating for a job with the opposition. But instead he said, "We're going up into the hills until August. Then we're going to come back down in San Diego and take over the party." He was quoting Buchanan word for word. Except that while Buchanan spoke the lines with a trace of dramatic irony his young aide was perfectly serious.

I have no such romantic consolation. The passion has dispersed and headed for the hills; all free men have gone back to their free lives. But I am stuck for the moment with the two men who are considered electable, and whatever their virtues they are fairly insistent about being ignorable. Bill Clinton, who won the Democratic nomination without ever announcing his candidacy, is holed up in the White House with his chief strategist, Dick Morris, devising ever more expensive television advertisements. Dole, who won the Republican nomination without getting wet, is holed up down the street in the Senate. Neither can afford to be honest or to say anything of interest, unless someone else says it first. As neither seems to have any particular reason for wanting to be president, the race has an even greater than usual private, egotistical flavor. Both men want to be president *very, very much,* which is to say that neither is willing to lose for a cause. They don't mean any harm by their hollowness, and so I try not to hold it against them. They just want to win; and in this climate hollowness is, apparently, an advantage.

The trick, I decide, is not to give in to their terrible lot of the winner's life—pretending that black is white and white is black, avoiding risk and adventure—but to find the sort of people who can help me to find another way. Happily, I do this on a beach in Florida, where resolutions come easy. A few yards down the road from the sterile skyscraper in Bal Harbour that houses Bob Dole's condominium, I take time off and search through my notes from the past few months. I figure that somewhere on the trail there must be other people like me, who dread the prospect of watching the shadows of Clinton and Dole creep through their peculiar world for the next seven months. Surely politics cannot be useful, or even educational, unless someone is willing to take a risk, or say something that might get him in trouble.

Two weeks later I return to Washington. I pick up the phone and call Senator John McCain.

ELEVEN

Surrogates

I leave my hotel earlier than I need to and walk down from the Washington Monument to the Vietnam Veterans Memorial. Even at 7:30 a.m. the Mall is nearly deserted, the Lincoln Memorial empty. The Vietnam Veterans Memorial, on the other hand, is teeming with people who appear to have been up for hours, walking slowly along the length of the black marble slab bearing the names of the dead. For the next twenty minutes I sit on a bench dodging bird droppings and waiting for McCain, who has agreed to meet me here to talk about why successful political campaigns are the way they are. In my attempts to spot him at a distance I can't help but notice how differently ordinary people behave from politicians. Maybe fifty likely candidates pass through my line of vision, and not one of them could pass for a U.S. senator at one hundred paces. They comb their hair in public, scratch themselves, hold hands.

At eight on the button McCain appears at my side, looking very senatorial except for a pair of outrageously wide black aviator sunglasses with some undignified name—Hobbie? Hippo?—stenciled on the earpiece. He takes the seat on the bench beside me, and for a brief moment I feel I am in one of those movies about Washington in which the clueless protagonist gleans some crucial piece of information from the terrified insider, who is constantly glancing over his shoulder. Except that there is no single piece of information I know enough to seek, and McCain long ago decided he was going to be seen with whomever he pleases.

The campaign has moved back to Washington at least until early summer. Except for a handful of tactical speeches and photos, the candidates will shape public opinion of themselves on the job, in the Senate and the

John McCain: exploring the heroic possibilities of American politics.

White House. The net effect of this is to turn up the heat on Capitol Hill, and senators with nerve are going to exploit the moment. In a couple of weeks, I've just learned, McCain himself plans to rise on the Senate floor and attach his campaign finance reform bill to some unrelated piece of legislation. This will embarrass just about every other senator, since many of them have spent their careers calling for campaign finance reform while at the same time doing everything they can to stop it from happening. Bob Dole is a prime example of this phenomenon. Probably McCain's bill will require Dole to embarrass himself explaining why he is *for* big money in politics.

What makes this so interesting is that McCain suddenly finds himself at the heart of the Dole campaign. Since he appeared at his side on the stage in South Carolina, McCain has been the Dole surrogate most demanded, both by Dole himself and by audiences who want to see someone speak out on Dole's behalf—and it's not hard to see why. Few Republicans seem to care about the differences between the two men—though they might soon care more. For the moment what matters most to the people who wish to see McCain speak for Dole is the formative experience that the two senators ostensibly share: both nearly died in a war; both endured indescribable pain and suffering. Dole's ordeal is at the hollow center of his national campaign—to some extent it is his campaign. McCain's trials are less known. On October 26, 1967, when he ejected out of his navy jet and into a North Vietnamese mob, McCain suffered two broken arms, a shattered knee and shoulder, and bayonet wounds in his ankle and groin. Robert Timberg's gripping book, *The Nightingale's Song*, depicts McCain two months later, in his first prison cell:

> McCain weighed less than one hundred pounds. His hair, flecked with gray since high school, was nearly snow-white. Clots of food clung to his face, neck, hair and beard. His cheeks were sunken, his neck chickenlike, his legs atrophied. His knee bore a fresh surgical slash, his ankle an angry scar from the bayonet wound. His right arm, little more than skin and bone, protruded like a stick. But it was McCain's eyes that riveted [his cell mate George] Day. "His eyes, I'll never forget, were just burning bright. They were bug-eyed like you see in those pictures from the Jewish concentration camps. His eyes were real pop-eyed like that. I said, 'The gooks have dumped this guy on us so they can blame us for killing him,' because I didn't think he was going to live out the day."

McCain survived in captivity without medical treatment for the next five years, enduring torture so exquisite that even to read about it causes sweat to pop out on your brow: his captors would hang him by his broken arms from dangling ropes for hours on end, for instance. But the aston-

135

ishing part of McCain's experience was its voluntary aspect. McCain is the third generation of a distinguished military family. His father was an admiral during the Vietnam War. The North Vietnamese hoped that this famous prisoner of war would violate U.S. military policy, which dictated that prisoners be returned in the order they arrived. In accepting their offer of freedom McCain would testify to the demoralization of American troops. For five and a half years his captors tried to torture him into going home. For five and a half years he refused to go.

As McCain reminisces, I realize I have made a tactical mistake. I am in the wrong place at the wrong time. I had hoped to talk to McCain about how Dole might react to McCain's plans to saddle Dole with a campaign finance reform bill. I had hoped to find out why it was that a man ostensibly so brave is frightened of his own shadow when forced to appeal directly to people for their votes. But it feels obscene to talk about such things in such places. My blunder is what the financial speculator George Soros calls a fertile fallacy, however. All by himself McCain is leading the conversation in a direction well worth following, toward one of the peculiar fault lines in our culture that guides American politics, almost without our knowing it.

We walk alongside the black granite slab against the oncoming traffic, then back again. The tourists pass us, stopping to get the feel of the place and to read the names. One sign of the memorial's success is that it has followed a path similar to those it seeks to commemorate. Like the veterans themselves, it has gone from being feared and loathed to being widely revered. The Park Service says the memorial has become the second most frequently visited site in Washington, after the Capitol. McCain admits that at first he found it depressing and even faintly antagonistic. But one day he was passing through on his own—he visits often by himself—and discovered a couple of veterans running their hands across the inscribed names. Clearly the two men had never met before, but they had fallen into conversation, swapped war stories, and in a few minutes were clutching each other and weeping. "If that kind of healing goes on," says McCain, "well, then it's a good thing."

Someone once said that an explanation is where the mind comes to rest. There is a feeling about McCain—one that seems lacking in Dole—that he has somehow explained his own experience to himself. He has assimilated his trauma differently than the candidate he's behind. "This is the McCain theory—and I think it's valid," he says. "I was an adult when I was shot down—thirty-one years old. I'd had a whole life.

He was nineteen. What were you like when you were nineteen? I believe that everything Bob Dole has done since the war was dictated by that experience." The Vietnam veteran has achieved the kind of equanimity that is supposed to be available only to veterans of good wars. When Clinton arrived at the White House, for instance, McCain sent him a note saying that anytime the president wished to walk down to the Vietnam Veterans Memorial the senator from Arizona would be glad to walk alongside him. Clinton sent back a nice note.

Recalling this exchange causes McCain to break his rhythm. We are walking back toward the bench, and McCain is limping slightly, like a high-school football star. He is remembering something else. "Back in the mid-1980s," he begins, "a guy who protested the war came into my office. He said his name was David Ifshin."

In December 1970 David Ifshin had led a group of American students to Hanoi, where he delivered an antiwar radio address to American soldiers engaged in attacks on North Vietnam. Like other anti-American propaganda, his program was piped into McCain's prison cell from six in the morning until nine at night. But McCain, who can generate anger in a heartbeat, shows not the faintest trace of resentment. "Ifshin stood in my office," he explains, "and he said, 'I came here to tell you that I made a mistake. I was wrong, and I'm sorry.' And I said to him, 'Look, I accept your apology. We'll be friends. But more important, I want you to forget it. Go on with your life. You cannot look back.'" Here he pauses, and I figure he's finished. But he's groping behind his aviator sunglasses for the point of his anecdote—that forgiveness is ultimately less self-destructive than the bitter desire for revenge. Or perhaps that there is no such thing as revenge, in the sense that it never actually offsets the original grievance. Five months ago Ifshin was diagnosed with cancer. The cancer has proved untreatable and has spread rapidly. Ifshin is now dying. He is forty-seven years old and has a wife and three young children. "When I heard about it," says McCain, "it did pass through my mind: Suppose I had told David Ifshin to get the hell out of my office. How would I feel about myself now?"

APRIL 23

I'm walking out the door of my Washington apartment on my way to find David Ifshin when John McCain calls. I've made the mistake of telling his press secretary what I'm up to, and she's passed it along to the senator, who is seriously concerned. "Look, I don't mean to insult you," he says, "but be careful with this. If you wrote anything that hurt David or Gail or the kids—the Ifshins have three young children—I'd never forgive myself. I'd forgive you, but I wouldn't forgive myself."

It's a half-hour drive out of Washington to the Ifshins' house in the Maryland suburbs, where I find a gaunt bearded man stretched out on a patio lounge chair, attended by his wife, Gail. The cancer has carved deep, dark trenches into his cheeks. This afternoon he is tired, and his voice is barely audible as he sketches his political career.

The cover of *Life* magazine of April 23, 1971, shows David Ifshin, age twenty-two, at a war rally, wearing a collegiate goatee. He's standing directly behind Jane Fonda, who has her fist raised. After his war protests he worked on a kibbutz; but when he returned to America he also returned to national politics. He went on to work, to a storm of protest, on the Mondale presidential campaign. He spent ten years as general counsel to AIPAC, the Israel lobby. He had met Bill Clinton briefly in 1972 in the heat of the antiwar movement; twenty years later, when Clinton ran for president, Ifshin became general counsel for his campaign. Before he accepted the job, however, he told Clinton that each time he'd joined a presidential campaign he'd been attacked for his war record. He felt a perpetual political embarrassment to his employers. "I brought it up with Clinton deliberately," he says, "and he said he knew what I had done and admired it then. And that he still admired it now."

But the past is especially stubborn these days. Ifshin's work with Clinton is still landing him in the news. He makes an important cameo appearance in *Blood Sport,* for instance, James B. Stewart's book about the Whitewater scandal. "Get the facts, get them out, and get it over in a single day," he tells Mickey Kantor on page 210, when the story first breaks in *The New York Times.* Kantor first agrees to send a team of lawyers down to Little Rock and get to the bottom of the thing. But later—presumably after speaking with the Clintons—Kantor changes his mind. "If you don't level with them," Ifshin tells Kantor prophetically, "you'll wind up with a special prosecutor."

Having eventually broken with the Clinton campaign, Ifshin is now back in touch with Clinton himself, who calls Ifshin two or three times each week, even when he's traveling. Last month the entire Ifshin family spent the night in the Lincoln bedroom. In the pictures of Clinton playing with the children the president's ruddy good health seems almost obscene beside Ifshin's drawn face. Yet, when I called him, Ifshin did not hesitate to rise to the occasion. "I'm very proud of this story," he says, "and it's never been written." I ask him about his feelings toward McCain. "One of our true political heroes," he says. "He's a giant."

Ifshin's version of their story differs from McCain's in its important details and in its spirit. The way McCain tells it, Ifshin is the hero: he decided he'd made a mistake and bravely took responsibility for his actions. The way Ifshin tells it, McCain is the hero. As I listen to him I realize that this is the reverse of the usual Washington investigation, in which the reporter visits each interested party to collect the dirt on the adversary. Here is a case where each is needed to explain the other's nobility of spirit. I have never heard two political allies, much less two political opponents, cast each other in a more flattering light.

"I had always wanted to apologize," Ifshin begins, "but did not know who to apologize to." His moment to act, he decided, came at an AIPAC meeting around 1986 at the Washington Hilton. Ifshin spotted McCain at a distance and decided that he was the man who deserved the apology. "I hoisted my courage up and went over to him," recalls Ifshin, "and before I could get a word out [McCain] said, 'I owe you an apology.'" A couple of years earlier, during the 1984 presidential campaign, McCain had given a speech in which he attacked Ifshin's war record. "Basically someone had handed him a script to read," said Ifshin, "and he read it. He was sorry he did it and said he wouldn't do that kind of thing again. Then he asked me to stop by his office, which I did. And normally wouldn't do. It was blind fate, I told him at that time. I said, 'I owed you an apology, and you robbed me of the chance to make it'—and he was characteristically modest and humble about it." Later that year McCain and Ifshin, together with a Vietnamese émigré named Doan Van Toai, established the Institute for Democracy in Vietnam.

Ifshin shifts painfully in his lawn chair and stops to catch his breath. It was at the Vietnam Veterans Memorial that what he calls "the second half of the story" with McCain began. On Memorial Day 1993 Clinton spoke at the site. Both McCain and Ifshin were present. Clinton was cheered loudly. He was also heckled. And one of the hecklers waved a sign that said TELL US ABOUT IFSHIN.

Four weeks later Ifshin found himself on a flight to Washington with McCain, who motioned for him to take the seat beside him. "He asked why I hadn't taken a job in the administration. I said this and that. We played twenty questions until finally he said, 'It's because of that stupid sign, isn't it?' And I said, 'Yes, partly, it was.' And he said, 'Come to my office tomorrow morning and we'll settle this thing once and for all.'"

The next day, June 30, 1993, David Ifshin turned up in McCain's wood-paneled office in the Russell Senate Office Building to find that the senator had drafted a letter, which he entered later that day in the *Congressional Record*. It began by praising Clinton's Memorial Day address on behalf of Vietnam's veterans. The veterans, McCain wrote, "were very impressed by [Clinton's] determination to offer an eloquent tribute to their service when it would have been far easier for him to have avoided the event altogether." He decried the behavior of the protesters. Then he moved on:

> Among the demonstrators that day, one individual held a sign which asked the president to explain his association with a person known to many of our colleagues, Mr. David Ifshin. "Tell us about Ifshin," it read. My other purpose in speaking today is to do just that: I want to talk about David Ifshin. David Ifshin is my friend. . . .

David Ifshin died on April 30. At the funeral, on May 2, John McCain succumbed to his great grief before he finished his prepared remarks. President Clinton also spoke. But that is a small thing compared to what he did for Ifshin the past few months. As Ifshin lay dying Clinton called him often while he worked—from the Oval Office, from *Air Force One*—and made his old political ally feel as if he were alive and engaged rather than drifting inexorably out of the world. He didn't have to do that, you know; presidents are very good at getting out of things they do not want to do. We grow so used to suspecting our leaders of bad faith that we ignore their deeper humanity; that is what enables us to hate them so blindly.

Sometime after the funeral I had a letter from Gail Ifshin, David's widow:

> I don't believe I mentioned this important aspect of our overnight at the White House. Our presence there was obviously not an unalloyed pleasure; David knew the President was saying good-bye. As a result, through much of our visit David and I were somewhat

subdued. But the President was magnificent. He focussed on our children. Through much of our dinner, then later in jeans in the Lincoln bedroom with us (the kids were in their pajamas), and then even later until past midnight in his study down the hall from our bedroom, he talked to the children. He asked questions, he listened to their answers, and he talked and talked about history, about President Lincoln, about all the historical objects in his study, on and on, and the children were riveted. In that way, the President gave a wonderful gift to our children. He gave them the memory of a unique and intimate experience in the White House with the President, and it was all a tribute to David.

TWELVE

The Normal Person of Tomorrow

APRIL 27

A few weeks in Washington and you feel the same letdown as if you opened *Gone with the Wind* and found instead the collected audits of Arthur Andersen. The city is a great romance that has been gutted by quotidian concerns. The wide boulevards and grand monuments were created when America was an idea, before anyone had any idea what sort of people would live here, or what they would do for a living, or how frightened they would be as they did it. The setting creates expectations that go unmet, and even unconsidered, by the people who live in official Washington. And so, in a way, Washington is an apt setting for the presidential campaign.

I have moved back to Washington with the two campaigns, and set aside the day to visit them in person. Unfortunately, this is not as easy as you might think. The Dole campaign, which invited me to visit its offices just last week, now is uneasy. "Call back at the end of the week," I'm told by one of the rented strangers. "With the judges it's a little crazy around here." "The judges" refers to a speech that Dole now intends to give decrying the insidious behavior of liberal judges, an issue that originated this election cycle with Buchanan in New Hampshire. All I want is a peek at the lobby, I plead, but to no avail. Soon enough an explanation for the change of heart emerges—from the Clinton campaign. The Dole campaign has spent all its money defending itself against Steve Forbes and Pat Buchanan. To cut costs it has moved all but a handful of its staffers off its payroll and onto the payroll of the Republican National Committee. At this very moment temporary walls are rising inside the Dole campaign headquarters to create the illusion that the people behind them are not in fact still working for the Dole campaign, and that the ads they are buying are not to promote Dole but to sell ideas.* The directors don't want the reviewers to watch the stage set going up.

The White House—where the stage set comes ready-made—proves easier to penetrate. A friend who works inside sneaks me into the building late tonight, after the last tourist has stuck the last wad of bubble gum beneath the last coffee table. Theater ropes block the entrance to the Oval Office, but still I am able to step inside and look around for a minute or so, though I don't quite have time to rifle the drawers. The books behind Clinton's desk, fat biographies of Franklin Delano Roosevelt and Harry Truman, are clearly props rather than live reading material. The desktop is cluttered with more props—Russian dolls and Chinese party poppers and other official souvenirs of the president's foreign policy. The office seems designed to disguise the true personality of the occupant, which, of course, doesn't mean that the occupant has something to hide. It is a way of keeping visitors at a distance. Important people often do.

Outside the Oval Office runs a short, narrow corridor carpeted in a dusty blue. It passes on a tangent to the president, swings around a bend, and dead-ends into a wall next to the national security adviser—Power Alley, as it is known around the White House, even though it looks more like the hallway of a bed-and-breakfast in Vermont. Strung out along it are the offices of the president's closest advisers. The nearer you get to power, the tighter the space: everyone wants access, or, at least, the appearance of access. No one cares how big his office is, or what he can see through his window. All anyone cares about is how close he is to the president. Or so I am told.

It is here that you can see the most important fault line in politics at this quiet moment in American history. It isn't the ideological one between Democrats and Republicans. It's the temperamental one between Insiders and Outsiders. Insiders of both parties agree on pretty much all the important issues at this point—which is why watching them compete is about as satisfying as watching a pair of heavyweight boxers locked in a clinch. They quibble over welfare, but most everyone agrees it needs to be reformed. They dispute a few billion dollars in defense spending, but most everyone agrees on the need to maintain a massive force much

*Financing laws permit political parties to spend unlimited sums on "issue-based" ads, but place strict spending limits on ads supporting a specific candidate.

greater than our obvious needs. Occasionally tensions flare over the economic inequality spawned by the free marketplace, but most everyone believes in principle that the government should stay out of it and let the market take its course. Even on those issues on which Insiders appear to disagree—abortion, say, or gun control—they have reached a kind of truce. Above all there is a similarity of temperament. To be a part of the Insider culture a person must appear to be discreet, stable, and risk averse. The most damning criticism you can level at an Insider is that he is "imprudent." One of the greatest Insiders of all time, George Bush, made a fetish of the phrase "wouldn't be prudent."

The Outsiders—the agitators, the troublemakers, the champions of lost causes—are temperamentally unsuited to treating politics as if it were a rigged fight. The Outsider is by nature indiscreet, unstable, and risk loving and as a result will rarely land himself a seat in Power Alley. (Pat Buchanan's drift from Insider to Outsider mirrors the drift in American politics away from large-bore crisis management and toward small-bore career management.) Occasionally the Outsider may call himself a Democrat or a Republican, but he can't be contained by either party, because his enemy is not the other party but the entire system. He has a taste for the structural issues: campaign finance reform, global trade. The current crop of Outsiders—Buchanan on the right, Perot in the center, Jesse Jackson on the left—stood together against the North American Free Trade Agreement, for instance, and for campaign finance reform. Each in his own way speaks to the dissatisfaction with politics that 70 percent of Americans claim to feel. Each in his own way is guided by some mythic view of the past. And each in his own way addresses the central problem of politics: that an awful lot lies beyond its reach. To succeed, an Outsider must grab for what he knows he cannot have. He'll probably never get it, but he might knock it loose so that someone else will, one day.

After a few minutes I tiptoe back out the way I came in and head for home. There I find Ralph Nader. Nader made his name as a consumer activist who himself eschews consumption, or seems to. Nader has lived in Washington for nearly forty years, and still no one knows where he sleeps at night. His friends say he lives in a rathole near the offices of his nonprofit organization, Public Citizen. His enemies claim that he lives in a mansion in Woodley Park. But no one can say for sure because when the sun goes down Ralph . . . vanishes. But tonight on my television he's being interviewed by Tim Russert, comparing the Democrats and the Republicans to a duopoly—like Coke and Pepsi—engaged in "protective imitation." That was interesting enough, I suppose. But it was the following exchange that pulled me up short:

> RUSSERT: It wouldn't bother you if you woke up in November 1996 and Bill Clinton was not reelected because he lost the state of California to Bob Dole, and the reason was that Ralph Nader siphoned off six percent of the vote?
>
> NADER: If that happens to Clinton it's because he refuses to adapt and he deserves it.

Ralph Nader is running for president?

APRIL 29

He is, it turns out. Last November Nader let it slip in an interview that he was thinking of having his name placed on the California ballot by the Green Party. In the year leading up to the primaries his was the only protest directed at Clinton from the left; all the other likely candidates joined the conspiracy of silence. Nader—like Morry Taylor—had never run for anything in his life. What triggered his sudden desire to come forward was . . . the speed limit! With each passing day he'd grown more upset by Clinton's decision not to veto any of the Republican legislation deregulating the economy. But what finally drove him around the bend and into the race was Clinton's decision not to preserve the mandatory fifty-five-mile-per-hour speed limit that Nader himself had helped to pass into law. "It's just as if he's a Republican, so what's the point?" Nader told Rogers Worthington of the Chicago *Tribune*.

Once the word spread, the Green Party responded with an enthusiasm unmatched by anything in politics last fall since Morry Taylor spoke to the People in Dallas. A few weeks later Nader officially entered the race, though what that means is hard to say, since he's not taking a lot of trouble to explain or even to be seen. He says that five thousand dollars should suffice to pay for his presidential campaign, which, oddly enough, is his annual household budget.

Nader, in short, is different from other presidential candidates. The

145

literature on him is endless, even though he has never stood for office. It runs from Nader's own books on corporate wrongdoing to books by the young people who go to work for him—Nader's Raiders, he calls them—on all manner of social ills to miles of congressional testimony to children's books about Nader, complete with drawings of little Ralph. There is a book called *Me & Ralph: Is Nader Unsafe for America?* written twenty years ago by a former managing editor of *The New Republic* named David Sanford. Over 135 blistering pages it details how the author, who edited Nader's articles for *The New Republic*, came to loathe Nader—and fear he would run for president. There is another book, called *Ralph Nader Will You Marry Me?* by Amy Deveraux, a minister in the Movement of Spiritual Inner Awareness in California, who spent twelve years chasing after Nader and writing him poems, letters, songs, and even a stage play. ("I was so happy to see him," she writes, of her most intimate encounter with Ralph, "that I beamed up at him and started singing my solar energy song. Ralph tried to cut me off by gruffly saying he had already heard it, and his secretary grabbed me by the shoulders and muscled me down the hall.") This man whose career has

Ralph Nader: a silent scream from the American left.

been devoted to tightening the nuts and bolts of consumer safety evokes strong and unruly passions.

Maybe that's why Nader is harder to find than other candidates—though when you finally do, he is accessible in a way even obscure candidates are not. The first few times I called him he failed to respond. On my fourth try, however, I heard back from him immediately. He seemed to have all the time in the world. "This is not like the other presidential campaigns, you know," he warned me, with an unnerving little chuckle. "I don't intend to go up in the state of California waving signs and shouting and all that." But before he hung up he agreed to take me along the next time he hit the road in the name of the Green Party.

Then he vanished. Completely. Over the next two weeks I called him a dozen times—to no avail. No one I asked about him seemed to have any idea where he lived or even what he did in his spare time. But then one evening last week he called out of the blue to ask if I would like to attend a lecture he was giving at Gettysburg College, in Pennsylvania. He told me to be in front of the Dupont Plaza Hotel at three o'clock sharp. He didn't want to keep me waiting, he said.

But he has. At 3:20 I am still shifting my weight back and forth on the pavement. I pass the time reading a yellowing transcript of the congressional hearings about the lurid General Motors investigation of Nader. The story that led to the hearings was broken exactly thirty years ago by James Ridgeway in *The New Republic:* "The Dick," it was called. But it was the hearings held by Senator Abraham Ribicoff ten days later that transformed Nader from an obscure Washington lawyer into a national celebrity. The transcripts still make good reading. They open with the president of General Motors offering a predictably lame defense. Then the car company's private detective, Mr. Vincent Gillen of Garden City, New York, has his say. Gillen was Nader's godsend; before he testified, the Dick had used a miniature camera to snap photographs of the senators and other witnesses; during the testimony he confessed that he traveled the country at GM's behest and, on the pretext of conducting an employment background check, asked Nader's old friends about his sexual and financial behavior. The rest is history.

By three-thirty I am starting to worry that maybe I am, too. I call Nader's office. "Don't worry," says the woman who always answers the phone. "Ralph's always thirty minutes late." I return to the transcript. There I read, for the first time, Nader's original testimony. Thus an American legend was born:

Mr. Chairman, [Nader began], I owe you a deep apology for being late this morning. I ought to explain it briefly to you and to anyone else in the room. I usually take no more than twelve minutes to come down from my residence to the Capitol by cab. In this instance I gave myself twenty minutes. And I waited and waited and waited to get a cab, and as my frustration mounted, I almost felt like going out and buying a Chevrolet. . . .

Exactly thirty-five minutes after he was scheduled to arrive, Nader pulls up to the Dupont Plaza Hotel in the passenger seat of a midsized Ford. I squeeze myself into the backseat directly behind him and alongside a pair of Gettysburg College students, and we're off. For the next hour and a half I watch the back of Nader's head, an unruly salt-and-pepper tangle that tumbles down over the exposed white tags on his shambolic windbreaker. He alternates between scratching out his speech with a number 2 pencil and responding to my questions until he grows weary of them and starts asking his own. Nader is interested in just about everything political. He wants to know, for example, if the oddball third-party candidates that he encountered in New Hampshire in 1992 are still around in 1996 and is delighted to hear that they are. ("Toothbrush Man" dressed himself up as a giant toothbrush and ran on a platform of mandatory flossing.) He wonders whether I agree that Federal Reserve chairman Alan Greenspan's confirmation hearings, at which Nader was the lone dissenting voice, were "the closest thing we have to what it must have been like in the old Soviet Union." He asks if I ever noticed the way conservatives are more likely to be compassionate when they actually see what happens in the world. His favorite example of the phenomenon is George Will, who, immediately after seeing a woman die in a car crash outside his home, penned a column demanding mandatory air bags. "It was a rare event," says Nader. "A professional conservative forced to confront reality."

For my part I am preoccupied. As we whiz off the Beltway and into the countryside I notice that everyone but me is strapped down tightly; it's not often you see people so well trussed to a backseat. I confess my negligence. "I can see the headlines," I say. "'Nader Dies in Crash: Impaled on Pen of Rocketing Journalist.'" In a flash Ralph turns and locks my door. "I've just increased the likelihood of that," he says. Then he adds: "Don't worry. I'll be your air bag."

At Gettysburg, Nader takes the stage for what will be a two-hour lecture, followed by question time. He won't leave the stage until the last student has asked his last question. He begins at seven o'clock. He will not finish until nearly eleven. In those four hours the entire Nader worldview—and a partial Nader presidential campaign—emerge.

The worldview can be broken down roughly into two parts: Nader's critique of free markets and Nader's critique of American democracy. Nader is no socialist—he is too acutely aware of the power of market incentives. The difference between Naderism and socialism is that Nader picks his spots—he accepts the logic of the market but focuses his fierce energies on the places where it has failed or might fail to work efficiently: monopolies, public goods, and so on. Underpinning his views is his belief that markets are made up of consumer psychology and that psychology can be tinkered with for the commonweal. "For example," he says, "there is now a market for seat belts. People will pay for them. Why did that happen? People learned. You have to teach people what they want. Corporations understand this—they create wants all the time. But we need to create other wants."

Nader's view of democracy forms a kind of corollary to his view of markets: What he calls the "two-party duopoly" has so ossified that the difference between Clinton and Dole, for instance, is negligible. Both parties are equally beholden to corporate interests, which intersect with the well-being of society only by accident. Just as Nader's solution to market problems is an active, well-informed consumer, his solution to political problems is more active, better-informed voters.

In a nutshell, that is Nader's message—and, in a nutshell, it can sound naïvely technocratic. But as he speaks, something more than the message emerges. You can see the students edging out on their chairs. Forty minutes into his talk he has moved away from his detailed arguments against the toxic effects of hot dogs and fossil fuels and onto an entirely new plane. He is drawing his audience into his peculiar vision of life:

> There are very few people [he says] who are happier than active citizens, even though they take a lot of brickbats and ostracism and ridicule and are in uncomfortable positions. They are furthering their sense of values. They are trying to help other people. That's deeply ingrained in our religious/secular ethics psyche—some people think it's more deeply ingrained than that: it's biologically ingrained.

149

This theme, once established, expands and contracts until Nader reaches yet another plane. And you realize that he is offering up a way of life that can be embraced fully only by people who have not been broken by disillusion. He is speaking to youth:

> Time is the essence here. As young people, you have a different sense of time than people who are older. The longest year in your life was probably when you were fifteen waiting to get your license. And, as you grow older, a year is like six months, then three months, then one month. And then it's over. I mean you're seventy years old, and you've lived a fairly good life and raised your kids, and you have some money in the bank for the children and grandchildren. Your grandchild comes and sits on your knee and says, "Grandparent, what did you do with your life?" . . . And you're thinking, How am I going to answer this? You're thinking . . . what are you going to say? I developed an advertising campaign for Geritol? I built up a chain of manicure storefront shops? I represented mergers and acquisitions to make investment bankers and golden-parachute-laden executives richer than the dreams of avarice? And, then, in the merger and acquisitions, all kinds of workers were laid off? How am I going to answer that question?

How strange, I think. The thing to say about Nader is that he is spiritually deficient, a man who worries more about American hot dogs than about world hunger. Yet when he asks, "How much has this nation lost because there are men walking around today with invisible chains?" you can hear it echo over Walden Pond. It's no wonder the Green Party has set upon him with such enthusiasm.

In the college parking lot I tell Nader that he has provided a keynote for his biography, if ever another book about Ralph Nader needs to be written. In praising the people who joined Ross Perot's United We Stand he had said, "It's a good thing that they did that. Some of them are eccentric. But so what? The eccentric of today is the normal person of tomorrow. There are a lot of examples of that." "You are the normal person of tomorrow," I say. No answer.

"You do consider yourself an eccentric?"

Pause.

And then: "No one calls Michael Jordan an eccentric because all his life he's been trying to get a ball through a hoop," he says. "One hundred and thirty years ago if some guy spent all his life trying to get a ball through some hoop they'd have stuck him in some cave."

"Where did you first see that the good citizen was an anomaly?" I ask, to shift the subject.

"There was a man in our town named Mr. Franz," he says. "He was the one who spoke in the town meetings—asking detailed questions of the auditors and so on. And people would look at him as if he were some freak. The guy who took his citizen duties seriously was a freak. You got your town fool, your town drunk, and your town citizen."

"Why do you live the way you do?" I ask, as we pull out of town. "The secrecy of your private life only creates suspicion and gives your enemies ammunition."

"That's what keeps me from becoming a jet-set celebrity," he says, "a diversion, an attention person. My parents always told me that the most difficult thing once you've become successful is to stay successful. To be able to endure it. To do it you need to control your time. To do that you need solace, you need privacy."

The impulse to suppress appetites and sympathies in the name of principle is the mark of a radical; and without it Nader would be just another smart guy trying to get through life without embarrassing himself. But radicalism is out of fashion these days; it is the sort of thing young people used to get up to but don't any longer. Indeed, in Nader's attitude to the world you can detect some important part of David Ifshin as he broadcast anti-American propaganda into John McCain's prison cell. And you can't help but wonder where it went.

We are passing the site of Pickett's Charge, where at two o'clock one afternoon in July 1863, Lee sent his army racing into the mouth of the Union guns, ending the battle and, eventually, the war. The battlefield is a monument to defeat but also to the victory of the idea that great failure is more ennobling than small triumph. As William Faulkner wrote in *Intruders in the Dust:*

> For every Southern boy fourteen years old, not once but whenever he wants it, there is an instant when it's still not yet two o'clock on that July afternoon in 1863, the brigades are in position behind the rail fence, the guns are laid and ready in the woods and the furled flags are already loosened to break out and Pickett himself with his long oiled ringlets and his hat in one hand probably and his sword in the other looking up the hill waiting for Longstreet to give the

word and it's all in the balance, it hasn't happened yet, it hasn't even begun yet, it not only hasn't begun yet but there is still time for it not to begin against that position and those circumstances. . . . Yet it's going to begin, we all know that, we have come too far with too much at stake and that moment doesn't even need a fourteen year old boy to think This Time. Maybe This Time with all this much to lose and all this much to gain; Pennsylvania, Maryland, the world, the golden dome of Washington itself to crown with desperate and unbelievable victory, the gamble, the case made two years ago; or to anybody who ever sailed even a skiff under a quilt sail, the moment in 1492 when somebody thought This Is It; the absolute edge of no return, to turn back now and make home or sail irrevocably on and either find land or plunge over the world's roaring rim. . . .

Now Nader is asking the driver, who seems to be something of a Civil War buff: How many men died here? Why did they do it? Why wasn't Lee's reputation more badly tarnished? Then Nader sees something that bothers him: the car window. In the old days, he explains, cars had small windows that enabled the passenger to get fresh air without making conversation impossible. They did away with them, he explains, to reduce the cost and to sell air-conditioning. People still want that small window, he insists, but the market will not provide it since it is such a small factor in the overall consideration of which car to buy.

It is well past midnight when we arrive back in Washington.

MAY 4

Where *did* it go? Aside from the dozen twenty-year-olds who wreaked havoc on behalf of People for the American Way, and a few dozen Buchanan aides, the fire of youth you might expect to find even now in politics was missing from Iowa and New Hampshire, and just about everywhere else for that matter. The vast majority of young people who had anything to do with politics were dressed up in blue suits and trying to please their bosses. Their common ambition was to become paid political professionals. Rented strangers.

Normally it would seem next to futile to head out into the land in search of the passions of American youth. But I have time, since neither Dole nor Clinton is yet bothering to campaign. And today there is a lucky convergence, the equivalent in youth culture of a solar eclipse. The MTV bus—called the *Choose or Lose* bus—is heading toward Seattle. American cities can be usefully classified as either offensive or defensive. Offensive cities—Los Angeles, New York—project their personalities onto the rest of the country and therefore are loathed by adults everywhere, like a dinner-party guest who won't shut up. Defensive cities sit back and listen, like aged grandparents. Seattle is now firmly offensive. One reason for that is Bill Gates and Microsoft; another is Kurt Cobain and Nirvana. In the past ten years some of the more offensive and successful rock music ever performed has been composed in Seattle.

When Republican politicians in the late 1980s made an issue of pop-music lyrics, and small groups around the country started to agitate for warning stickers on records, and Wal-Mart stopped selling offensive records (while continuing to peddle automatic weapons), MTV decided that politics was a natural way to expand its business. That was the end of 1990. Within two years Bill Clinton was standing before Tabitha Soren and a crowd of teenagers answering questions about his underpants en route to a huge margin of victory with the youth vote. People between the ages of eighteen and twenty-nine turned out in greater numbers in 1992 than anytime since 1972, when eighteen-year-olds first got the vote. It's hard to say how much of this enthusiasm had to do with the music-video people. But it was a nice illustration of the law of unintended consequences. If the Republican Party had been warned in advance that, by attacking musicians, they'd be stirring up a dormant, potentially hostile segment of the population, would they ever have listened hard enough to figure out exactly what it was that Tupac Shakur was rapping about?

As it cruises onto the campus of the University of Washington the bus is a sight to behold: a forty-five-foot billboard for MTV topped by twenty-two glittering silver stars that stick up from the roof like fairy wands. The interior is a Todd Oldham concoction of maroon wallpaper, leopard-skin carpets, mosaic-tiled cabinets, and gilt-framed windows. But the inside is not nearly so interesting as the outside. The *Choose or Lose* bus is plastered all over with quotes from rock stars and other famous people selected to inspire young people:

> I'm sure once Guns & Roses got as big as they did, the government checked up on it and realized that they didn't have the brains to be a threat to anyone. —Kurt Cobain

Actually, that didn't make it on. But this did:

Don't just stand there, let's get to it. Speak your mind, there's
nothing to it. VOTE! —Madonna (shortly before it was revealed
that she herself was not registered to vote)

Wherever the bus is parked it creates its own ecosystem. Today, as
every other day, it is quickly surrounded by reporters seeking interviews
and politicians trying to get interviewed. A pair of televisions on tall
stands drown out everything; they replay at great volume a tape of music
videos, journalists explaining politics in simple language, and rock stars
urging youngsters to vote. "If Snoop Doggy-Dogg can take the time
out to go deal with the pressure, you can too . . . ," blares Snoop himself,
who has taken time out from the courtroom, where he is on trial for
attempted murder. The environmentally concerned candidate for the
U.S. Senate who wanders in can barely be heard. "This guy has planted
half a million trees personally," shouts his campaign manager over
the din.

The noise (the pollution of choice for Generation X) is not quite deaf-
ening, but it's close, and it's out of sync with the desultory business at
hand. Short lines of students slowly form—one to register, the other to
fill in political surveys—between the television sets. The plurality of students who register claim to be "independents." The students who already are registered are asked to sign a pledge that they will exercise
their franchise come November. The pledge reads: "I will rock the system by exercising my right to vote on Nov. 5, 1996 because . . ." Beneath
this is a blank space for the students to fill in. The goal is to get them to
participate without suggesting that there is any particular reason to participate, other than to defend the interests of youth, whatever those
might be. The semiotics of the enterprise are the semiotics of the
sixties—a bus!—but the spirit couldn't be further removed. It's content
free, a kind of idealism about idealism.

As I wait for something to happen (I'm not sure what) I thumb
through some of the students' responses to the voting pledge. "I will rock
the system by exercising my right to vote on Nov. 5, 1996 because . . ."

I'm cool.
the shit is fucked up.
I want to keep the U.S. "choice free."

Bob Dole is an ass.
I care!
I have cable.
I want student loans!
I am gay and I want my rights!
I'm the smartest man alive.

A pair of mallard ducks stagger across the campus walkway and into the thin crowd of students, followed by a middle-aged woman on her way someplace with her hands pressed hard over her ears. I'm still waiting for something to punctuate the noisy tranquillity, and finally, barely, it does.

"Choose or lose *what?*" a voice hollers.

I turn around.

"Choose or lose *what?*" the voice repeats. I spot him: a young man with blond, shrublike hair, dressed in shorts and sneakers and a baseball cap. He's suddenly gone quiet, but the other fifty or so students milling about the bus are still flashing him the uneasy looks reserved for lunatics and homeless people. He notices my interest and hands me a flyer:

Get it straight. MTV doesn't care about you making a political or cultural choice, instead you are a consumer to be sold to and made money from.

Once I finish that one he hands me another:

Let's face it, if you vote for the lesser of two evils either you are the lesser of two evils, or you are not being represented.

"Who *are* you?" I ask. He's all alone, a stray alien life-form who landed on earth by mistake. And he's put his finger on the problem. It's the corporate risk aversion that's so bothersome, the mirror image of the political risk aversion at the top of politics. Democratic politics depends on direct confrontation and commitment to ideas. It is admirable only when it requires nerve. How can the immediate presence of a corporation using the political system to promote its own interests, nonpartisan in the most market-savvy way, do anything but contribute to the prevailing fashion in political attitude—the detached, ironic, and "independent" mode? (The critic Dwight Macdonald had a phrase for this. "The herd of independent minds," he called it.)

"You want my real name or my radio name?" asks this lone voice of dissent.

"Radio name," I say, out of curiosity.

"Clutch," he says, "from Naked Radio."

Naked Radio, it turns out, is a pirate station that broadcasts alternative music intermixed with long programs about local political issues. Within minutes Clutch is explaining in highly technical language—using words like "binary" and "switches"—how his station moves by stealth into an area of town, sets up its equipment, and, by sheer force of watts, poaches the frequency of legitimate stations. "If there is an area of town where the station's frequency is weak we can come in and dominate their frequency," he says. "Like, yesterday the station we took over was playing this demo tape, and you could just see it." Clutch places his hands on an imaginary steering wheel. "This guy is driving down the highway listening to his corporate music and then *bam!* All of a sudden he's hearing the Mamas and the Papas and then me saying: *This is Naked Radio and we're coming for your children!*"

I ask Clutch when I can hear his show.

"I dunno," he says. "We have to, like, switch our frequency, or we're going to get busted. Maybe tomorrow night you might want to check 89.9 FM." Then he adds, thoughtfully, "I don't mind infringing on someone else's frequency. It's a felony I don't mind committing." And with that we are interrupted, for good as it turns out. Rock musicians with stringy unwashed hair and tattered clothes—from bands called Sky Cries Mary and Goodness—emerge from the *Choose or Lose* bus, take the stage, and in weak, camp-counselor voices implore the assembled students to get out and vote. The students drift in and out of the crowd, with the perfected indifference of people who stopped listening long ago.

A few hours later the bus rolls back to the hotel to find waiting a redheaded, freckled-faced nine-year-old boy. "Is this the *Choose or Lose* bus?" he asks excitedly. It is, I say. "Cool. Can I look?" He hops on board, takes a quick peek. Then he races out into the back of a waiting slate-green stretch Mercedes-Benz with a personalized license plate that reads: QUORUM.

THIRTEEN

The New Dole and the Wild Grizz

MAY 27

You never saw a more unhappy looking group than the journalists assigned to follow Bob Dole into New Jersey on Memorial Day. "I got the best seat in the house to the worst show in town," grumbles a cameraman as we board the Dole plane at National Airport. "I just came in case he got shot or something," says a reporter, who doesn't even bother to take notes. You would never guess from watching them that they have the best jobs in journalism, or what used to be the best jobs in journalism. I, too, have my misgivings. Usually my campaign notebooks are crammed with anecdotes, observations, and incidents. Whenever I'm with Dole, however, they simply refuse to fill up. The Dole campaign remains an arid, sterile place. Not much grows there except a festering doom.

Today is the first day of the general campaign, which will be relaunched in earnest tomorrow with a bold journey across the country. After a month and a half of watching their candidate flounder in the Senate, the rented strangers have figured out that they no longer can play the same game as they played in the primary. They can't sit back and watch other people take all the risks and float all the ideas. The reason they can't do this is that Clinton already has done it: since his State of the Union Address, when he declared himself the enemy of big government, Clinton has been robbing Republicans of every last little bit of distinction. The Dole campaign hasn't even the resources to defend themselves against the tens of millions of dollars in attack ads being run across the country by the Clinton campaign. Clinton has done to Dole what Dole has done to everyone else.

157

Since the Dole campaign can no longer simply react to the world as they find it, they must go out and make the world anew. Somehow they must turn Dole into a challenger—an outsider—without also turning him into a loser. The first clue of what they were up to came two weeks ago, May 15 to be exact. On that quiet afternoon Dole walked into the U.S. Capitol and resigned his Senate seat. "I will then stand before you without office or authority, a private citizen, a Kansan, an American, just a man," he said, in what must rank as the most moving words he has spoken since he set out to become president. For the first time you had the feeling that a man was speaking his own mind to you in his own voice, and that it was a voice you could not only live with but admire.

But no sooner did Dole sacrifice his career than the rented strangers in the Dole campaign stripped the gesture of its value. The first leak came in *The New York Times,* in the middle of a flattering article about Dole's campaign manager, Scott Reed. Toward the end of the piece, almost by the by, we read this astonishing revelation:

> The element of surprise [in Dole's Senate resignation] was essential, Mr. Dole and Reed decided, if the announcement were to appear bold and make an impression on voters. "If it had leaked," Mr. Reed said, "he probably wouldn't have done it."

Think of it. Just two weeks ago Dole stood before the nation and said with apparent sincerity that "you do not lay claim to the office you hold, it lays claim to you. Your obligation is to bring to it the gifts you can of labor and honesty, and then depart with grace." But now, according to the stranger who runs his campaign, Dole's bold decision to end his wonderful Senate career was conceived right from the start as a public relations stunt. *If it had leaked he probably wouldn't have done it.* Not only does the campaign manager not see the shame in this admission—that it wasn't the act but the appearance of the act that counted—he is proud to admit it, for it proves that he knows all the angles. Presidential campaigns often accuse journalists of being cynical, but the cynicism of journalists does not compare to that of presidential campaigns.

The second leak is that the speech was not conceived or written by Dole, or even by a Dole speechwriter, but by a novelist named Mark Helprin. You can see why a novelist would be drawn to the Dole campaign; but you can see even more why the Dole campaign would be drawn to the novelist. Dole has no ability whatsoever to breathe life into his own life story. As John McCain says, "His problem is that other people sell him better than he sells himself." One reason for this may be that Dole does not think of himself as a war hero but as a kid who would have preferred not to fight and wound up getting shot. That is, he has never really packaged his own terrible experience for public consumption, and so the experience remains, in a sense, useless. He needs someone else to package it for him. The campaign, in effect, hired an expert to *create* Bob Dole.

This afternoon the creation is unleashed on the world, for the first time. A Better Man for a Better America, Dole is calling himself, stressing his war experience and the solid midwestern values instilled in him growing up in Russell, Kansas. He marches for a dozen blocks through Clifton, New Jersey, in front of the Memorial Day parade's single float, bookended by his wife, Elizabeth, and Governor Christine Todd Whitman. The crowd is quiet and sparse, less than one deep. The parade climaxes in a park, where the born-again Dole is meant to deliver his remarks and lay a wreath on a symbolic grave site. I wait for him there at the grave site, watching members of the local veterans' organization subtly jockey for position. Six old men form the color guard, dressed in red jackets, VFW caps covered with patches and buttons, and the apprehensive air of people who fear they might be asked to improvise. But the really striking thing about them is how old they look compared to Dole—although they fought the same war they now appear to belong to a different generation. "Any veterans of the First World War here?" I ask. "We just buried our last one last fall," says one of the men, who sports a POW-MIA pin in his cap. "Don't come around ten years from now," says the man beside him, "or we won't be here either."

As Dole approaches, a dozen more veterans with flags plead with the police to let them into the sacred space occupied by the color guard. "Where we gonna stand, Billy?" a veteran on the outside shouts to a veteran on the inside. "I'll get ahold of Eddie," says Billy. Two minutes later Billy returns. "Eddie says no," he says, with an apologetic shrug. "I dunno. For me, I'd let another member in." The plaintiff returns with a man in a blue uniform, white gloves, and a white pith helmet. The others call him General—though of what I have no idea. He wears no medals or insignias. "The police say no, General," Billy explains to him. "You got to be kidding," says the general, huffily. "Send one over to me. A *female.*"

After the ensuing scuffle—in which the general comes out ahead—I notice three very old men shuffling their feet at the back of the swelling crowd. The closer I get the more evidence of valor I see: Purple Hearts, bronze stars, and enough other medals to fill a helmet. "During the war we was at the front," says the one with the largest medal around his neck. "During the parade we're at the back." He points up at Dole, now ascending the bandstand. "I think if he knew that there was a contingent of Purple Hearts here he'd be different."

It was a nice illustration of a rule of military glory: The more of it you actually have, the less you are inclined to debase it for calculated advantage by, say, bullying the police into letting you into the winner's circle. This man with the medal, Jim di Stefano, has a picture of Dole taken in Normandy two years ago during the D-Day celebrations. It emerges that one reason he is willing to speak to me is that he hopes I might have Dole sign it for him. "You see how his face stands out," he says, pointing at the platform. "Even in a picture of one hundred people, his face just stands out." And it does. It is the face of a man who refuses to age in the midst of mere mortals.

"You could almost call it majestic," says one of his companions, who lost an eye in Korea.

MAY 28 AND 29

Dole plans to fly all the way across the country to spend less than twenty-four hours in California before picking up and flying back—first to Chicago, where he'll spend tomorrow night, and then to Cleveland. On May 28. Five months before the election. The only reason it doesn't seem insane is that several hundred seemingly sober men in dark suits follow Dole wherever he goes, some of them carrying automatic weapons. But the trip has a familiar delusional quality about it.

There is a kind of ambitious young person who mistakes frenetic movement for advancement in the world. He'll call you from the road and say, "I'm in Bangladesh on business, heading for Iceland," and you know that he thinks this is sufficient explanation of his purpose in life. The Dole campaign has something of this feeling. As long as the candidate keeps moving, everyone traveling with him is exempt from serious self-examination, which is a shame, since they have no idea why they are doing what they are doing. It's frequent-flier politics. And within a couple of hours I'm having my first Admiral Stockdale moment: *Who am I? What am I doing here?**

The first day is a perfect blur. Sometimes I'm close to Dole; more commonly I stand outside in the street while he does his thing in the presence of a few selected cameras and journalists. But no matter how close I get, the man remains inaccessible. The problem isn't the Secret Service protection; to slip past the Secret Service all you need to do is cut your hair, put on a blue suit, and walk as if you have a pole stuck up your butt. The problem is Dole's adamantine shell. I sneak up on him backstage before a political rally in Ontario, California, where he is standing with Governor Pete Wilson, Attorney General Dan Lungren, and a pair of congressmen, waiting to talk to the crowd about the last good war and Russell, Kansas. One by one the "celebrities" (as the master of ceremonies calls them) run onto the stage, leaving Dole all alone. The emcee is introducing him; the crowd is getting worked up. "You nervous yet?" I whisper into his right ear.

He jumps slightly, and turns, then reflexively sticks out his left hand for me to shake. "Not yet!" he says cheerily. The man has no idea who I am or what I am doing backstage, whispering in his right ear. He never asks. The guard, the perfect flatness, never drop—except on those rare occasions when his native wit gets the better of him, which happens often. (Yesterday, for instance, at a family picnic, with perhaps three hundred people swarming to get Dole's autograph in the street outside the middle-class home: "All those people coming for dinner?" Dole asks his hostess, motioning to the mob. "No," she says with a laugh. "Good," he says. "You'd be wiped out.")

Early the second morning we descend, in our motorcade of thirteen cars and two buses, on a seemingly tranquil park in Redondo Beach. The point of the event—and the trip—is to illustrate that Dole is against crime. The trouble is that Clinton is against crime, too. So Dole needs to show that he's more energetically against crime than Clinton, who at this very moment is en route to New Orleans to deliver his own anticrime speech. Dole and Clinton are like *Time* and *Newsweek*. No matter how much they claim to differ, they still run the same covers week after week.

---

*Admiral James Stockdale, a former fellow resident of the Hanoi Hilton with John McCain, was, of course, Ross Perot's running mate in 1992. He uttered his unforgettable lines in the vice-presidential debate, immediately before washing his hands of the whole affair.

The effect is to eliminate any edge Dole might gain from distinguishing himself from the president.

The park in Redondo Beach is being celebrated as an example of a neighborhood reclaiming its public space from urban marauders. But onstage, as various dignitaries disapprove of drive-by shootings, a small group of dissenters forms on the fringe. All but one are the Hispanics who bear the brunt of the new anticrime esprit. (They're hauled off to jail for all sorts of odd crimes—carrying baseball bats into the park after seven o'clock in the evening, for instance.) The exception is a gentle old soul named Art Campell, who for decades has cleaned the park, coached the local kids, and groomed the playing fields. The ball field at the center of the park is named for him: Campell Field.

Campell is a Dole supporter—"I'm for the man; I don't go by the party"—but he's mildly perplexed by the anticrime rally. "It isn't as bad as all that," he says, as Pete Wilson takes the microphone to praise the parents who have formed the neighborhood watch organization and to denounce "gang-bangers," which to my ears sounds a bit off-color. A policeman on the scene confirms that crime statistics in Redondo Beach are in line with those of the nation as a whole: violent crime has declined steadily here as it has in other cities over the past twenty years. More to the point, he cannot recall a single violent crime in the park. A few years ago someone shot a gun in the air as he drove past the park, he says, but no one was hurt. Campell stops the park custodian, a Hispanic man who speaks poor English. "Do you think this Dole thing is a good idea?" he asks the man. The man takes one look at my notepad and says, "I no want to say." He's afraid of offending his employers. The greatest fear in the park is the fear of offending the people on the platform who are spearheading the anticrime initiative.

Having successfully fed (and been fed by) the fear of crime, we wearily board the bus. After only two days with the new Dole I am now certain that he will suffer from the same problem as the old Dole: nothing interesting will ever occur in the close-cropped frame of his staged events. Where do politics come from, anyway? Not from listening to Bob Dole deliver a speech written by someone else to a group of people he knows nothing about in a place to which he will never return; not from creating a sense of crisis where none truly exists. The disjuncture between the world as we know it and the world as constructed by a political campaign leaves me gasping for reality. But I am naïve; I have never done this before; I have never seen a serious presidential campaign up close. I can't say anything about Dole's use of push polls, or about the cynicism of his staged events, without having some seasoned reporter look at me as if I were a child and say, "So what? They all do that." As I stare out the window wondering if this is so, a flyer lands lightly on my lap. I look up and find a middle-aged Hispanic man with a Frito Bandito mustache smiling at me. I take up his flyer. It is a religious tract done up as a tabloid newspaper. The headline is an apparently fresh, direct quote from Jesus Christ. "RUSSIA PLANS TO INVADE THE UNITED STATES WITH MISSILES"—JESUS. It is as plausible as anything I've heard today. Better sourced, too.

On the plane heading back east I look up and take a mental photograph, so that when I am old and used up I will be able to remember what it looked like in the days when politicians still campaigned. A wise old man once told me how to do this: Look hard, close your eyes, try to recall what you have seen. Repeat this procedure three times and you'll always remember the picture. In my mental picture, a Dole aide is standing in the aisle in front of me reading a copy of some movie magazine. Seated to the left of the movie magazine, a reporter is reading *Primary Colors.* Behind me sits Joe Klein, looking innocent. (Joe, of course, later admitted that he wrote the novel, published anonymously.) Behind Joe sits somebody else reading *Primary Colors.* The plane is partitioned into classes. From front to back: Dole and rented strangers, Secret Service and less trusted rented strangers, journalists, and, finally, cameramen. Every so often the cameramen roll an orange up the aisle with a message scribbled to Dole on the side (BUCHANAN FOR VP), but otherwise the classes don't mingle. The partitions between them are decorated with photos of Dole: one of him in Russell, Kansas, announcing his most recent presidential run, another in silhouette with a soldier behind him, standing at attention.

Before the picture is fully developed—between the second and third blinks—Nelson Warfield, Dole's press secretary, barges into the frame. He leans over us with a mixture of real and contrived self-assurance, pretending to treat journalists as his equals, but unable to prevent himself from condescending a bit. Nelson's status problem is the status problem of everyone who ever ascended to a high position in a presidential campaign. If Dole wins, he will be a Washington big shot entitled to condescend even to important journalists. If Dole loses, he'll be reduced to sending out his résumé to first-term senators. An authentic concern underpins his egalitarian pose.

Soon Nelson is engaged in heartfelt discussion with the TV people. It is so much more animated than any other conversation between Dole staffers—or Dole and the press—that I can't help but wonder what they're talking about. It turns out that the television people are upset with the Dole campaign for not providing them with an "establishing shot"—the image that leads each TV piece. They need something that says to the viewers: Dole for President. As long as the old Dole remained in the Senate the camera would pan the Capitol. Now with the new Dole they have nothing to shoot.

In times of crisis one must respond in kind. One must adopt a radical strategy. And I do. "I bet it's boring as hell out there," says Morry Taylor cryptically when I call him from a Dole rally in Chicago to see what he's up to. "Oh, it's not all that bad," I say, gamely, but he sees through it. "I'm glad they are all fucking boring," he says, "because I'm fucking going wild these days."

"It's *miserable*," I say, dropping all pretense. "It's not the same. . . ."

"Of course it's miserable, you dipshit," he says. "Whaddya expect? How many people in this country grow up and say 'I wanna be a politician'? How many people say 'I wanna be a bureaucrat'? Hell, you got more people who say 'I wanna be a car salesman' than wanna be a politician." (A couple of months later a poll appeared in the Miami *Herald* showing American parents wish for their children to be anything other than president when they grow up. Even journalism is more highly regarded than politics.) Morry, too, has soured on the Dole campaign, ever since Dole's rented strangers declined his invitation to introduce Dole to every businessman in a three-state area worth more than $200 million. "He's got to throw these advisers away and step up to the plate," he says. He doesn't exactly regret his endorsement of Dole. He's merely convinced that Dole is doomed. But before I have a chance to probe his analysis he says, "Probably you don't give a shit, but tomorrow I'll be applying what I learned running for president." The possibility hangs there between us for a moment and then drops. "I'm supposed to stay with Dole," I say.

MAY 30

Somewhere between Chicago and Cincinnati I realize that I don't have to do this anymore. I am not required to stay on this plane and witness the same mixture of half lies and bad theater over and over again. Once I realize this it is but a short step to prying my bags out of the luggage hold of Dole's plane and walking across the cold, dark tarmac into the Cincinnati Airport. From there I fly to Chicago, where I hope to catch a plane to Quincy, Illinois, the headquarters of Titan Wheel. I miss the last flight out, however, and so I dial the half a dozen numbers I have for Morry. Finally, I locate the man himself, in flight over McLouth Steel in Detroit on his way to Quincy, Illinois. "We'll pick you up," he says, still declining to explain any further what he's up to. Everyone who runs for president and loses claims to have learned from the experience; hell, people write whole books about what they've learned. But I've never heard of anybody trying to "apply" what he has learned. Anyway, my impression is that Morry learned nothing running for president, except that the American people are not yet ready to do business.

An hour later I'm standing alone in a bone-chilling rain beside a remote airstrip outside of Chicago. It's an odd feeling, waiting on the ground for an aircraft you've never seen to drop out of the sky and pick you up. Every few minutes a tiny propeller plane chugs through the mist and bounces to a halt a few yards away. Each time I expect it is my lift, and take a few quick steps toward the door. Each time the hatch opens laboriously and a comical number of overweight men in suits squeeze through it, like circus clowns popping out of a Volkswagen. They clump down the stairs onto the asphalt and into the back of sedans, leaving me once again alone. This happens half a dozen times before a long, sleek white jet dives spectacularly out of the clouds, like a hawk making a kill. It lands and makes right for where I'm standing. The door flies open and for a few long seconds there appears to be no one inside. Mysteriously, the dark oval hole in the side of the plane widens. Then, suddenly, out bounds a golden retriever. The dog emits a yawp of freedom and races down the stairs and halfway across the airfield before it is yanked up short by a voice over a loudspeaker: "Grizz! Get the hell back here!"

It's Morry. He's named his dog after himself.

After a short flight and a brief stop at the factory in Quincy, we head off to a local television station, where Morry intends to apply everything

165

he learned running for president. He still won't explain exactly what he learned that he means to apply. Instead he says, "You look at all of the political people. They're all nice people. Even Lamar. But what they really are—they're greeters. That's what they are. They greet people when they come in the door." Soon we're inside a chilly studio overseen by a tightly wound female television producer. One technician runs wires down the front of Morry's well-pressed shirt while another positions him squarely on top of an X stenciled on a patch of red carpet. A short row of television cameras faces him. Off to one side stands another executive of Titan Wheel. "This isn't politics," Morry continues. "This is for my investors' conference. They won't know what hit them."

"*Section one, take one,*" barks the producer.

Morry turns sideways and grins out at an imaginary audience, just like they all did before the first Iowa debate. Maybe for the first time in his life he speaks smoothly, like a man who does this for a living. "Hi, Morry Taylor, president and chief executive officer of Titan Wheel. Titan International is one of the fastest-growing companies in the U.S. . . . Wait a second."

"What?" asks the female producer.

"I gotta move," says Morry, like the Sundance Kid at the start of the movie. "I ain't gonna be standing here like some statue."

"You can try it," she says, uncertainly.

Again Morry turns and flashes the camera his Iowa smile. But this time he's rocking back and forth as if he's waiting for the pitch. He has the air of a pro ballplayer who, after eight hitless months in the minors, is now back winning major-league batting titles.

"Hi, I'm Morry Taylor. President and chief executive officer of Titan Wheel. Titan International is one of the fastest-growing companies in the U.S. We at Titan International do not spend a lot of time on theory. If we did we wouldn't be the world's largest supplier of wheel and tire assemblies, stuff we aren't supposed to be able to make in America anymore. . . ." And for the next minute and a half he rolls right along like the prize pupil in an elocution class, every comma in place. I'm not the only one who can't believe my ears. "He's really good," hisses the man in the control room. "The guy's got charisma."

"I think that was a keeper," says the lady, once Morry finishes his spiel.

"I *know* it was," says Morry. "What else would it be? Now that I know how to do this shit."

"Section two, take two," says the lady, signaling Morry to rip through another few long paragraphs, flawlessly. "Fantastic," says the lady, "I could kiss you on the mouth." The Mouth grins.

"Has the company done this before?" I ask the other Titan guy.

"Well," he says, dubiously. "There *was* a corporate video. But it was all product, no Morry."

That was it. That was what Morry learned running for president. Before his campaign he knew how to sell his product maybe better than anyone on the planet. Then, suddenly, for eight solid months he was no longer selling tires; he was selling himself. *He* was the product.

For the next half hour Morry brings across the full force of his presidential skills until at length he grows weary and says, "Okay, let's see the Grizz." With that he turns to me to explain. "You see, you got two hundred fifty investors in this room watching this video. They just finished eating dinner. They're bored as hell. They're all fallin' asleep." He remembers something and says to the female producer, "I want the decibel level so high they all hop out of their chairs and go 'Whaaaaa! What the shit was that?'"

On the television monitor at the back of the room Morry's face seems to melt. Hair sprouts from every pore. And then he roars, deafeningly. He's metamorphosed into a grizzly bear.

"The whole campaign Morry wanted to morph into a bear," whispers the Titan guy. "Now he's finally doing it."

"I'm doing it 'cause I don't listen to nobody anymore!" shouts Morry, suggesting, for the first time I know of, that he ever listened to anyone.

"He's becoming the Dennis Rodman of the tire and wheel business," the man from Titan whispers, more cautiously.

FOURTEEN

The Religious Party

One afternoon while I was getting my hair cut, my cellular phone rang. As the hairdresser snipped her stainless steel scissors around the phone that was glued to my ear, Scott Reed told me that he had just accepted the job as Dole's campaign manager. I congratulated him and hung up. "Dole is halfway to the nomination. Anyone smart enough to hire Scott Reed could go all the way," I said to no one in particular.

— RALPH REED
Christian Coalition director, from his political manifesto,
Active Faith

JUNE 1

"How fast can you write a book?" Morry asks, as the Titan corporate jet nose-dives toward some godforsaken tarmac in the Midwest on which he intends to deposit me. His realization that Dole almost certainly will lose to Clinton has led him to find within himself the desire to pen a manifesto—a tract that explains what is wrong with America and how to fix it. More precisely, he wants someone else to write his manifesto for him. The polls proving that Morry's political ideas are extremely popular, coupled with the complete failure of his campaign to sell them, have got Morry thinking of other ways to bring himself across to the public. I point out that I am the last person he should be looking to, as I am the only writer in America who actually has *failed* to bring him across to the people (I'm the only one who tried), but he's having none of it. I try to change the subject to anything else: the giant tractor wheels Morry sent to America's leading political journalists, the new grizzly bear tie he's about to

168

mail to his fellow Republican presidential candidates. But for once in his life Morry has no interest in anything but books.

"Patrick still writing that book about trade policy?" he asks, in the darkness of the plane cabin. The end of his cigar glows orange. Smoke hangs in the air between us, like some horrible misunderstanding.

"So far as I know," I say, uneasily. A few weeks ago I mentioned in passing to Morry that after the California primary Buchanan had returned to his home in Virginia to grind out a history of American trade. He was going to prove that the Founding Fathers were protectionist.

"We'll put that in there too," says Morry, now. "A chapter on trade policy. For all those educated wonders who never been in the war. Like Patrick."

"Look," I say, finally. "There's no 'we' involved here. I've got to get back to the campaign."

He snorts. "Like who else is out there to write about?"

"Like the people still running for president." But he's too shrewd; he knows my heart is not in it. It rebels at the thought of watching another Dole stump speech, or listening to another rented stranger, or watching another Clinton television ad attacking Dole, or waiting for Ralph Nader to call back. The sad truth is that square in the middle of the presidential campaign in the early summer of 1996 there really isn't much worth seeing, and Morry knows it. "Christ, if you are gonna do that you might as well go find Alan Keyes," he says. "He's still out there campaigning somewhere."

"He *is*?" This is news.

"Dipshit never dropped out. Still trying to have a religious party."

He's right. The other seven challengers all conceded. But Keyes never did. The soul man of the religious right is still at large. For that matter, so is the religious right. "I believe there is a Supreme Being," Morry is saying with total certainty. "But it ain't like Alan thinks of it. He ain't involved in politics. And you only got one real religion—they all got the same Father. Abraham. Some guy goes off and starts a new religion, he does it so he can get the money."

JUNE 14

I sit waiting on a hard bench beside the pay phone at a Quality Inn in Chicago, where Alan Keyes is scheduled to speak to the First Annual

Black Pro-life Unity Conference—a nice example of the cartographical logic of American politics. Black pro-lifers are like right-wing militiamen for gun control, atheists for school prayer, and feminists for all-male clubs. They are the explorers who complete the map of our politics. Still, I am not quite sure what to expect. The last time I laid eyes on Keyes he was storming out of a television station in South Carolina after being denied the chance to debate. His flipper feet were moving a mile a minute down a lonely stretch of highway, and he didn't seem very happy to see me or anyone else for that matter. All in all he conveyed the impression of a man who had come entirely unhinged. It was only a few days later, of course, that he was whisked away in handcuffs from a television station in Atlanta.

Five minutes after I take my place among the black pro-lifers Keyes does, too. He shuffles swiftly past a poster board decorated with grisly photographs of fetuses aborted in the third trimester and into a banquet room filled with the faithful. Keyes has been campaigning steadily since our last encounter, says Jim Kennedy, an aide who travels with Keyes wherever he goes. Only in the past couple of weeks has he relaxed a bit. "A couple of more television appearances, and this thing would have taken off," says Jim, dropping the large square black briefcase he carries for Keyes that is stocked with food, medicine, and clothing. Jim was on hand when Keyes was arrested in Atlanta. He fasted right alongside Keyes for the three days it took to get him back into the televised debates. "Everywhere we go now," says Jim, "the police come up to Alan and joke that they're going to drag him away in handcuffs." Jim illustrates an important rule in politics: The less well paid the staff, the more devoted they are to the candidate. To follow a loser you have really to believe in him. No rented stranger, he.

Half an hour later Jim and I are seated at a table with eight pro-life blacks—four men and four women—in a banquet room filled with maybe three hundred others. It emerges that two of the people at our table are pastors; and it isn't five minutes before I am forced to admit that I am an atheist. I do this knowing full well that I have now cast myself as the villain. Atheists have a bad name in American public life. There is no positive culture of atheism: no awesome buildings in which committed atheists congregate, no poems to godlessness, no bumper stickers to proclaim ATHEISTS AGAINST HELL or ATHEISM IS FOR LOVERS, no Atheists' Coalition with a lobbying arm in Washington. The idea of the Good Atheist is just not very well established; the closest thing to it is the witty infidel who, in the end, no one much cares for. Atheism, in short, might benefit from a well-constructed public relations campaign.

The news is met as it always is, with uncomfortable smiles all around. Tell a politically charged Christian that you are an atheist, and he invariably responds as if a joke were being played on him. Either that or he'll argue with you until he has proved his case for the existence of God to himself, for the thousandth time. Sure enough, the one calm man at the table leans in.

"Let me ask you this," he says. "The atom is the basic building block of the universe, right?"

"Right," I say.

"And man just discovered the atom thirty years ago, right?" he asks.

"I guess," I say, in hopes that he will come quickly to his point.

"But here is my question," he continues. "Who created the atom?"

I'm stumped. "Evolution," I say, uncertainly. He and everyone else at the table smile, knowingly.

"But who created evolution?" he asks.

"God?"

"Right!" he says.

"But then who created God?" I ask.

It would have been his turn to be stumped, I think, but just then we're both saved by the loudspeaker: the ceremonies begin, and Keyes is introduced. ("The man with the message," says the emcee. "The man with the tenacity. The man with the audacity.") To a standing ovation he takes the podium, shoves his hands into his jacket pockets, and rocks back and forth on his flipper feet. A room full of black people is cheering at the top of its lungs for a Republican presidential candidate, and he hasn't spoken a word. Now he does:

I am reminded [he says] of that great phrase which moves me so from the New Testament. Because as Christ refers to himself so I have always felt he refers to black Americans. "The stone that the builder rejected." See, in a very real sense in American history this is who we are. You know this? We are. Because there in the beginning when they fashioned the Republic and put the Constitution together and so forth and so on, where were we? As slaves and rejected and deprived of rights and citizenship. Interpreted as three-fifths of persons in the South—you remember that?

This is the first time I have seen Keyes address a black audience, and, typically, he is speaking to them, without notes, words he has spoken to no one else. There is a real thrill in the listening, partly lost in the reading, but worth trying to preserve. The audience murmurs. "That's right," mumbles the Reverend Hiram Crawford, seated at the high table beside the podium. He has the timeless craggy face of an Old Testament prophet with deep-set raccoon eyes, and the authority of an arbiter. As Keyes speaks he remains perfectly still, except for a slow circling of his mouth, as it prepares to judge the speaker.

After a rousing description of the history of black America, Keyes arrives at his theme: the nobility of suffering. His voice rises and pulls the audience along as he ascends the mountaintop of their racial experience:

And even though the great ideas and ideals on which the nation was based required a respect for our whole humanity, yet we were denied that respect, and rejected out of the body of this human race which otherwise was being set upon the path to liberty. See? "The stone that the builder rejected."

"That's right!" murmurs the reverend. "Amen!" shouts a woman at my table. "And yet," says Keyes:

Throughout the history of America that stone that the builder rejected sat there in various ways—during the slave years and during the years of discrimination and segregation and injustice. And where did we sit? We sat as a great reproach and as a great reminder. Always representing to the conscience of America the true founding principles that are indeed the foundation stone of this nation's life.

The audience erupts. "He tells the truth! He tells the truth!" shouts Reverend Crawford.

Now, I *know* [Keyes continues] that there are people who look back on the history of black Americans, and they don't see much we've been given. They see freedom taken away and goods taken away and dignity defiled and so forth. They don't see much we've been given. But I look at it with a different eye.

172

"Tell it! Tell it again!" shouts the reverend. Tears now flow freely down the face of the woman at my table, and she's not alone. The audience is on its feet, while Keyes, now plunging down toward the end of his talk, makes a masterful twist—a kind of rhetorical full pike.

> All the trials and all the tribulations and all the tragedies and all of the sacrifices simply lift us up upon the cross along with Jesus Christ and give us a chance, if we will, to save the world. And I think there is no issue that puts that chance before us so much as the issue of abortion. . . . The womb is our auction block. And the dignity of life is being bought and sold in order to establish a selfish regime of irresponsibility. And who is going to call this nation back to itself if we do not? Who is going to call this nation back to the great principles of human justice and equality grounded in the will of God if we do not? [Now his voice softens; it is barely audible.] We are indeed the stone that the builder rejected. And today the foundations are crumbling.

It's maybe the twentieth time I've heard Keyes speak. Before each speech I promise myself that I won't let myself become swept up again in what he is saying; yet after he speaks I am always someplace different from where I started out. So rarely are we persuaded of something we didn't think it possible to be persuaded of that when we are, however temporarily, we think it a kind of miracle.

A few minutes later I hop into the back of the car taking Keyes to his hotel. From the front seat, he makes chitchat. His mind has clearly shifted from the crusade to the world; he's come back down into the universe. He tells me that he needs to figure out how to pay for his son's college tuition, that he's still burnt out from the campaign. He opines that Dole was foolish to offend the religious right with an offhand comment about Gary Bauer, the head of a Washington think tank called the Family Research Council. By offending Bauer, Dole offended Bauer's effective boss, James Dobson, director of the mammoth quasi-Christian media empire Focus on the Family. "It took *tremendous* effort to wake these people up to politics," Keyes says. "Bob Dole thinks that they'll vote for him over Clinton, but that's not the choice. If he keeps this up they'll just go back to church. That's what they were doing before. They'll go back to tending their garden, praying, and waiting for the Second Coming."

I tell him that I'm thinking of heading out into the world to examine this particular proposition: if people who are moved by passion can be persuaded to vote for a passionless candidate. Even during the primaries, while the Christian organizers favored Dole, the people they were attempting to organize favored Keyes or Buchanan. My problem is that I don't know where to go to find the slumbering giant. "Colorado Springs," says Keyes. "Colorado Springs is the capital of American Christian activism."

JUNE 15

This afternoon I discover in the Colorado Springs yellow pages a promising advertisement:

The New Life Church
Making It Hard for People to Go to Hell
from Colorado Springs

As the sun vanishes behind the mountaintops I set off from beneath Pike's Peak to find the New Life Church. As I exit the highway and wind my way up the single-lane road to the church I am able to see what Keyes meant. Just beyond the New Life Church is the International Bible Society; just before it is the sprawling headquarters of Focus on the Family. The horizon is all churches: churches planned, churches under construction, churches built. What all of these churches have in common, I soon learn, is a dream that they might one day be half as big as the New Life Church.

Drive across America and every so often—usually in a suburb, usually in the Sun Belt—you will be pulled up short by a building that claims to be a church but looks nothing like any church you have ever seen. The model for these strange places stands forty minutes outside Chicago, in a suburb called South Barrington. It is called the Willow Creek Church, and it was created in 1975 on the foundations of a shrewd marketing survey. Having first identified a plausible neighborhood, Pastor Bill Hybels went door to door asking people what they wanted from him. What they wanted was nothing like what you think of when you think of the word "church." They didn't want crosses, for instance, or other traditional religious imagery and design. The structure Hybels created in the end was

174

aesthetically unpleasing—barely distinguishable from one of Morry Taylor's tire factories. But within a few years Willow Creek had become the largest church in America. Each week seventeen thousand people pass through its doors. Hybels became, and remains, the informal spiritual adviser to President Bill Clinton.

Colorado Springs's New Life falls squarely in this new tradition, though its pastor, Ted Haggard, is unlikely to be called into this White House. After a quick tour of the framed press clippings and photos of his world travels ("There I am on top of the Dome of the Rock asking God to pour out his spirit on the mosque"), we sit thigh to thigh on the visitors' side of his desk. Between us lies the very Bible—the New International Version of the New Testament—created by New Life's next-door neighbors. The NIV has become the best-selling English translation of the Bible, Pastor Ted explains, and a quick glance through the index tells you why. It has been updated for contemporary life. Under "Entertainment Media," for instance, it cites Luke 23:35. Turn to the page and you find not only the passage ("The people stood watching . . .") but a footnote that tells you how to interpret it. "One of the surest proofs of depravity of the human heart," it reads, "is the fact that people take pleasure in violence, blood and death."

If anyone ever set out to prove that a person's occupation derived from his physiognomy, they would start with Pastor Ted. Even when he's relaxed his face assumes an expression of concentrated beatitude, smiling broadly with his eyes squinted tightly into pillbox slits. As he becomes agitated he squinches his eyes more tightly as if blinded by the light of his feelings, and his mouth breaks out into silent laughter. Other than that, and his native wit, he is the spitting image of Dan Quayle.

It is with a broad smile that he tells me about the spiritual rejuvenation of Colorado Springs. It began with his vision in 1985 on the back side of Pike's Peak, where he and his wife, Gayle, had gone camping. Pastor Ted believes in the power of cumulative prayer: the more prayers you focus at once on a particular problem, the more likely the problem will be solved. When Pastor Ted came down from the mountaintop, he prayed constantly for Colorado Springs. He prayed over buildings, he prayed over streets, he prayed over empty suburban fields. When he'd finished praying over the real estate he tore the phone book to pieces, and prayed for each name in it. "You can't explain the Colorado Springs phenomenon in natural terms," he says. "These ministries didn't come here for political reasons, or simply because of the low cost of living.

They came because they heard about the renewal that was occurring in the churches." Last year Pastor Ted coordinated the prayers of 44 million Christians worldwide.

Almost by chance I have stumbled upon the cultural turmoil that is reshaping the Republican Party. The social conservatives—Buchanan and Keyes—create some demand for their services. But the market for new political ideas is opened up mainly by forces beyond conventional political control, by people who don't even think of themselves as political. Pastor Ted has attracted the attention of the country by taking the lead in the war against homosexual rights. Together with a few others he is behind a proposition on the state ballot designed to strip gays of legal redress for discrimination. Reporters trundle constantly through the office of Pastor Ted, whom they present as Colorado Springs's leading evangelist. "ABC News came here a while ago," he says, "and they really needed to have me be the guy who wanted to take control of the school system. They were hoping to find a guy dressed in black with one of those stringy black ties. When they saw me and I gave them my answers I could see they were disappointed."

In one important respect Pastor Ted defies the stereotype of the evangelist: he seems undisturbed by modernity. He wears running shoes to work. He saw that the church needed to adapt, and so he has adapted it. It was too uncomfortable—a hard wooden bench in a Barcalounger culture—and so he loosened it up. The rewards it offered were too slow in coming, and so he promised anyone who attended an immediate "power encounter" with God. It is all rather enterprising of him, I think, much like a heathen might approach it, if it paid well enough; and after an hour or so with him I am beginning to think of him as a kindred spirit. But then I ask Pastor Ted what he saw when he first arrived in 1985 in Colorado Springs.

"I saw discouraged Christians and Satanists," he says.

"Satanists?"

"People who believe Lucifer is Lord and needs to be worshiped. I'm glad you asked me that because the media doesn't understand it."

"But . . . how did you know?" Our conversation is suddenly tilting wildly, like a Ouija board. Pastor Ted's eyes squint shut. His mouth bursts with silent laughter.

"People would tell us about it," he says, with the clarity of simplicity. "People would try to escape from covens and tell us about the struggle to get out. I have an interest in Satanic meetings. If people are going to covens, I have more of an interest."

From there the tone of the conversation is no different than the tone of, say, a lecture on physics. Pastor Ted explains to me how cows and babies were being eviscerated in the dead of night when he arrived in Colorado Springs; I nod and write and try hard to think of a follow-up question. Each time I feel like maybe we're about to wander back onto common ground, the ground washes out from under me in a flood of superstition. I am a bit uncertain where to go from here. I know that he is going to tell me things that will make him appear perfectly ridiculous in print. I know also that I will put them in print. But it is not the usual duplicitous journalistic encounter. For Pastor Ted knows exactly what he is doing. He *likes* the idea of me reporting these crackpot beliefs.

"Is there still Satanism in Colorado Springs?" I ask after a while.

"Not that we can detect," he says, smiling—or, rather, laughing.

"How do you know?"

"Genuine Satanists are very in-your-face kinds of people," he says. "They're really rough. But it's true, you can't always tell. Some Satanists, like Generation X Satanists, they look like Satanists. They dress in black. Other times they are totally cloaked. They look like the guy who manages McDonald's. But if Christians pray it makes it so Satanists cannot get a spiritual response. . . ." Pause. "Does that sound weird?"

It is getting close to 9:00 p.m., and the view of Pike's Peak through the pastor's window has vanished in the dark. I think Pastor Ted would let me interview him until midnight if I were so inclined. As I beat a retreat to the door I recall the purpose of my visit, to establish the nature of the link between religious leaders like Pastor Ted and their political organizer, Ralph Reed. As head of the Christian Coalition Reed claims to speak for 1.7 million right-wing Christians. "If Ralph Reed wanted to come to speak in this church would you let him in?" I ask him.

"Who is Ralph Reed?"

JUNE 16

My Episcopalian grandmother used to say that Father's Day was a contrivance of Jewish merchants to get the goyim to buy more stuff than they needed. If she were alive to see Pastor Ted in action, she might argue instead that it was created by evangelical preachers to pluck the heart-strings of their followers. At the start of his Father's Day sermon Pastor Ted calls fathers to the front and tears to the ducts. "The more you hang around here," he tells the 3,500 people who have turned up, once they are well oiled with sentiment, "the more strange you are going to become." But actually that is not true; it would be more true to say that the more you hang around New Life the more you will resemble most everyone else in Colorado Springs. The entire upper crust of the city is represented here—from the police chief to the richest real estate developer. The congregation is white and prosperous. The glass case in the lobby is jammed with the business cards of salesmen from the better companies. It's a sign when ambitious salesmen start turning up in evangelical churches—like the return of the Jews to Jerusalem.

Pastor Ted delivers a sermon on the meaning of God the Father, sprinkled with tiny editorials. In the course of forty minutes he bashes liberals twice and likens the recent brouhaha about Clinton and the FBI files to the Watergate cover-up. It works. A young woman comes forward to report that she has been healed of back pains; a man says that his pew has been cleansed of racism—the Lord is generally agreed to be present and accounted for. "We emphasize that all the gifts of the spirit are available today," Pastor Ted tells me, when he returns to his seat during one of the many intermissions. "You mean that evangelicals offer immediate returns?" I ask. He jolts slightly and says, "Immediate responses." Undoubtedly he is right. The appeal of his brand of God is that he doesn't require much up-front investment before he starts paying dividends. In this way and many others evangelism is simply mirroring the culture in which it flourishes.

As I stand in the front row of the morning service I can see Pastor Ted —between trips to the pulpit—glancing at me out of the corner of his eye. I know what he is thinking. He's thinking he has a convert. I haven't even time to spare for the afternoon service, however. It is Gay Pride Week in Colorado Springs. ("I don't understand it," says Pastor Ted, when I explain why I am leaving. "It would be like having Murderer's Pride Day.") The parade begins an hour after the morning service ends, and though it is a bit of a hike from the New Life Church it seems worth the trouble. There I am met by Frank Whitworth, the head of the local gay activist organization Ground Zero and this year's parade marshal. He is nearly twenty years older than Pastor Ted and about twenty degrees rounder. If the two men were placed side by side, nine out of ten objective observers would say Pastor Ted was the gay activist and Whitworth the evangelical pastor. That is unlikely to happen, however. In a town of three hundred thousand in the middle of nowhere, the protagonists of a struggle that has attracted the attention of the world have never met. Pastor Ted has made no more effort to meet Whitworth than Whitworth has to meet him.

As we leap into a car at the head of the parade, Whitworth offers me a quick overview of Pastor Ted's political life. To Whitworth, the link between a new social phenomenon and a radical political initiative was never so clear: the boom in evangelical Christianity in Colorado Springs led directly to the antigay Amendment Two, the attacks on the public library, and the marches outside of Planned Parenthood that now occur frequently in Colorado Springs. The proposal to restrict the civil liberties of homosexuals passed with 65 percent of the area's vote largely because of the influence of local churches. "I really believe that homosexuals are just a horse to ride," Whitworth says. "If the horse dies, they'll just find another horse."

Maybe a thousand people march in the gay pride parade, and for a glorious few moments there is on display the varieties of the homosexual experience: dykes on bikes, gays for God, homosexual cowboys, men dressed as women, women dressed as men, even a pagan lesbian dressed in black robes. But no one turns out to watch them. Indeed, it's astonishing how empty the streets of Colorado Springs remain, given that it is the only parade in town. Whitworth is reduced to shouting from the lead vehicle at people who just happen to be out on the sidewalks. We finish the half-mile course in eighteen minutes.

JUNE 18

Pastor Ted had scheduled a prayer session for six o'clock in the morning, but when the alarm rang at five-thirty I must have slapped it to death in my sleep. At nine I work up the nerve to call him. "You slept in, didn't you?" he asks, in the manner of an indulgent uncle addressing a small child. "I almost came over there and brought you breakfast." We agree that I'll be at the prayer session tomorrow.

Although the hours are grueling, the most difficult part of this chasing after evangelicals is packing the literature. I've been wandering around evangelical America for more than a week, and it shows. On one bed sit three Bibles and a stack of photocopied scripture. Beside the scripture lie half a dozen hysterical religious tracts. *The Coming Historical Crisis,* that sort of thing. On the floor between the beds lies a collection of videotapes and a biblical defense of homosexuality. Still more papers and pamphlets clutter the second bed—Alan Keyes's latest manifesto, Pastor Ted's slim volume explaining exactly how he drove the Satanists out of Colorado Springs. God knows what the maids must think.

I spend the afternoon on the hill beside Pastor Ted, at Focus on the Family—yet another tax-exempt Christian organization that more closely resembles in spirit and appearance a global corporation. Each day *Focus* is heard by 3 million North Americans and some fantastic number of Latin Americans. Each year 250,000 followers of Focus founder James Dobson trundle through the visitors' center. They are shown a video about the founding of Focus on the Family in the 1970s—in response to the "excessive permissiveness" of American society. They are permitted to touch a screen that provides Dr. Dobson's views on homosexuality, divorce, pornography, and a lot of other topics. "Focus is a nonpolitical institution," the tour guide explains, standing before a sign that reads: ELIMINATE DEPRAVITY! At the end of the tour they often head for the "chapelteria," where perhaps they may notice the inscription on the wall above: THE GOVERNMENT EXISTS TO MAINTAIN CULTURAL EQUILIBRIUM AND TO PROVIDE A FRAMEWORK OF SOCIAL ORDER.

The most striking aspect of the Focus campus is its perfect spiritual homogeneity. Everyone walks around wearing the same beatific smile as they do at the New Life Church; everyone assumes that everyone else operates in a spirit of kindness and generosity. It's as if a whole world has been created in the image of Lamar Alexander. I'm not sure at first why I find this so creepy; after all, it's nice to be kind and generous even if you have to fake it. But it's harder to remember to be kind and generous when you are only allowed to be kind and generous to people who feel just as you do.

JUNE 19

After the prayer session Pastor Ted takes me up the street to the International Bible Society, creator of the world's best-selling Bible. Maybe the best measure of the strength of the evangelical movement is the market share of its Bible. The New International Version, conjured into existence with the help of evangelical pastors in the late 1970s, has sold more than 100 million copies. The International Bible Society has figured out among other things that this new market can be segmented. It has created NIV Bibles for women, for couples, for recovering addicts, and for teenagers. It has created a comic-book Bible for incarcerated youth and a third-grade-reading-level Bible for adult convicts. It hasn't, however, created a Bible for homosexuals. "You couldn't have one," Pastor Ted explains, with his usual shrewd business sense. "You might have one for people *dealing* with homosexual issues, but if you had one that said 'homosexual' on the cover people couldn't carry it when they went to church—unless they went to MCC." MCC is the gay church.

That evening I return with Pastor Ted's personal copy of the NIV and dig out from the hotel desk drawer the King James Version. I turn to a verse Pastor Ted has shown me in Romans 1:26–27:

> For this cause God gave them up unto vile affections: for even their women did change the natural use into that which is against nature: And likewise also the men, leaving the natural use of the woman, burned into their lust one toward another; men with men working that which is unseemly, and receiving in themselves that recompense of their error which was meet.

Not so bad, I think. At any rate, in its obscure phrasing it leaves the well-meaning homosexual with a bit of wiggle room. Then I flip into the NIV study bible—the very book Pastor Ted had held in his hands when he wed. Here is the equivalent passage:

> Because of [their bad behavior] God gave them over to shameful lusts. Even their women exchanged natural relations for unnatural ones. In the same way the men also abandoned natural relations with women and were inflamed with lust for one another. Men committed indecent acts with other men, and received in themselves the due penalty for their perversion.

The last line guides the reader to this footnote:

> The apostle likely regarded the homosexual/lesbian abomination as the greatest evidence of human degeneracy resulting from immorality and God's abandonment. Any nation that justifies homo-

sexuality or lesbianism as an acceptable lifestyle is in the final stages of moral corruption.

That footnote has probably had more influence on public attitudes toward homosexuality than Ralph Reed and all the gay-baiting Republicans in Congress. Yet the NIV has attracted hardly a peep of protest from homosexuals, who are relegated in a book read by millions of credulous readers as the literal word of God to a moral rung below serial killers. You read it and you say: Here is where politics comes from. And the politicians don't even know it. Will politics and culture ever meet?

FIFTEEN

Ghosts

The entertainment industry is an easy target for politicians who want to identify a villain so they can be the hero. Ironically, Washington is where the real breakdown of values has occurred.

—MORRY TAYLOR,
"Kill All the Lawyers and Other Ways
to Fix Washington" (unpublished manuscript)

JULY 27

Before rejoining the Dole campaign I fly with my friend Barbara Feinman to Detroit. I have made a deal with myself, as an incentive to get out of bed in the morning. From now until Election Day, for every three days I spend with Bob Dole, I will allow myself a day with someone who is not Bob Dole. Normally, I would have waited until I had earned the reward to collect it. But circumstances—namely Barbara—intervened.

Until a few months ago Barbara was happily making a living helping famous Washingtonians—Ben Bradlee, Bob Woodward, a pride of senators—write their books. Her reputation as the best ghost in town led Hillary Clinton to hire her to help with *It Takes a Village*. For eight months Barbara toiled, to the apparent approval of the first lady. But then suddenly and without warning everything changed. One morning Barbara was First Ghost; the next she was First Enemy. She still isn't quite sure how or why she fell out of favor. But she later learned that her desk in the White House had been just a few feet from the files that proved Hillary had taken more than a casual interest in the Whitewater land deal. Not long after she learned this she was invited in for questioning by New York senator Al D'Amato's Banking Committee and special prosecutor Ken Starr's office. Since then journalists friendly to the White House have accused Barbara, without evidence, of all manner of ill deeds, from dishing the dirt on Whitewater to helping Woodward with his book *The Choice,* which painted an unflattering portrait of Hillary.

Barbara may be the least likely person ever to get caught up in a Washington scandal. She has no lust for publicity, and she would require training before she could successfully scheme or lie. When I phoned her a few weeks ago she sounded fairly certain she didn't want to have anything to do ever again with Washington or journalists or politicians. Morry Taylor's political manifesto was another matter, however.

After a few days Barbara agreed to become Morry's ghost and to fly with me to Detroit to meet the subject. The chief appeal of Barbara to Morry was that the first lady had mistreated her; she was the human equivalent of a badly managed factory. The chief appeal of Morry to Barbara was Morry's reluctance to spend a lot of time on his book. (The bane of every ghostwriter is the author.) As long as Morry stays occupied with other projects, she claims, she needs only a few sessions with him and a couple of months at the typewriter. For an entire book. "I've written whole books that the authors have hardly seen before they are finished," she explains. Already she is brimming with ideas about how to deliver Morry to the American public. She insists that the book must be written in the first-person singular, so that the reader experiences the full force of Morry's personality. "It's easier for me to remember what Morry is trying to say if I'm channeling him through me," she says. "That's a frightening thought, channeling Morry," I say. "I've channeled worse," she says.

By midafternoon Barbara is sitting in front of a big-screen TV clutching a Grizz T-shirt, drinking a Grizz beer (brewed by Morry in New Hampshire during the primary), and watching Morry—in a pink shirt with a cigar dangling from his mouth—fast-forwarding through a videotape of his various performances. He speeds right past his triumphant speech to the People, his various debates in Iowa and New Hampshire, his concession speech. At length he arrives at his new commercial for Titan Wheel—the one I watched him create merely a month ago. "Here," he says. "This is the best part." On the screen Morry morphs into a grizzly bear, and as he does he emits a roar even more menacing than the one I recall. "That's my roar," he shouts with glee. "My real-life roar. They just slowed it down."

Soon enough Barbara is taping her questions and Morry's answers.

Q: Did anyone encourage you to run?

A: No.

Q: What did your friends say?

A: You're nuts. You're crazy. You can't win.

Q: Did you ever think you could win?

A: I ain't no dummy. I knew what was going to happen. On the other hand, it relieves some guilt for me. I said what I had to say.

Q: It wasn't just a publicity stunt?

A: If you want publicity there are easier ways to get it. If it was the publicity I wanted I woulda piled up a million dollars in the street out there and set it on fire. You woulda never seen so much press in your life.

All the while, Morry watches the Olympics on television. The whole book, it would appear, will be generated by an author who has one eye on the tube.

Slowly Morry reveals how difficult it is for any multimillionaire who enters politics to exit. The Republican Party is refusing to let him or his money go in peace. Not long ago a representative of Michigan governor John Engler called him and demanded a one-hundred-thousand-dollar campaign contribution. "There isn't a governor in the world who is worth one hundred thousand dollars to me," Morry told him. No sooner had Morry put down the phone then it rang again, and Phil Gramm was imploring him to build a new factory in Texas. After telling Gramm that he'd think about the proposition, a Dole man called Morry and asked him to join Dole for lunch in Washington. This time Morry agreed.

The lunch was a primary reunion. Every one of the Republican presidential candidates attended, except for Pat Buchanan; and every one remained true to form, including Buchanan, when you come to think of it. Gramm, for instance, displayed more of the political acumen that led him to run in the first place. When asked by Dole whether he thought Ross Perot would join the race, Gramm said no. "Gramm said he had just been with Perot and that he didn't have the look in his eye," says Morry with glee. "Lamar was Lamar!" he continues, making his imitation Lamar smiley face, "and no one could make Keyes shut up.

"And Forbes!" Morry grabs the inside of his cheek with his index finger and yanks hard to illustrate the point he's about to make. "Forbes is completely hooked. He'd run over a kid to get to a camera."

By the end of the lunch Morry's role was firmly established as the fat-cat businessman who bankrolled the Dole campaign. He agreed to fork over one hundred thousand dollars for a party at the Republican convention next month in San Diego. He retained artistic control of the event or, rather, reseized it from the rented strangers. At first, like a fool, he simply handed over his hundred grand to the Dole people. But then he saw what they did with it. Fifteen grand on some second-rate country singer! These people had no idea about money! In a rage Morry called them up, demanded his money back, and told them that he'd plan the party, intelligently. Whatever is left of the hundred g's, he said, he'll donate to the Republican National Committee.

Once Morry took control the party ceased to be an ordinary political gathering of people standing around with drinks in their hands listening to a second-rate country-music singer in the background and trying to think up things to say to each other. It became a "motorcycle rally." A friend of Morry's in San Diego who goes by the name of New York Mike has arranged for five thousand bikers to roar into San Diego on Harley-Davidsons the day before the convention begins. Bruce Willis, Arnold Schwarzenegger, and Ben Nighthorse Campbell (whom Morry keeps calling "Senator Lighthorse") will ride along with them. Morry himself is unsure whether he'll ride a hog, but either way he'll lead the parade, together with Dole and a truck carrying a giant Titan Wheel billboard: a grinning grizzly bear wearing a tractor tire and holding a triumphant thumb in the air.

The party is merely the beginning of Morry's new master plan to infiltrate the political world. In the same way he once lay awake at night thinking of the 70 percent of Americans who claimed they hated politics, he now turns over in his mind the polls that have shown that voters clearly preferred his political ideas to those of the other candidates. Running for president clearly didn't further the Taylor agenda. The manifesto, he believes, will. He figures if Barbara can help him to simplify politics for ordinary people, the book might encourage more businessmen to get into it. The main purpose of Morry's manifesto, in other words, is to inspire more people like him to run for president.

And so within minutes of our arrival Morry is explaining to Barbara the brutal facts of presidential politics. "There are a whole group of people who want people to think that things are too complicated for them to understand," he begins. "They are called *consultants.*" He reaches deeply into a bag of potato chips while Barbara looks on, flashing nervous glances in my direction. She thinks I can help her, but I can't; if she's going to extract the manifesto from its author she'll need to learn to understand Morry for herself. I drift slowly out the door, like a parent leaving his child on his first day of school. Morry simply waves me away, as he does with everyone. He shakes your hand when you arrive but never when you leave—another little quirk that no doubt contributed to the brevity of his career as a presidential candidate. It's as if he can't believe you have anywhere better to go.

Outside, for one last moment, I linger to listen. Almost immediately Morry takes the conversation away from the politics of his manifesto to its potential sales. "Who buys books in this country?" he asks Barbara, rhetorically. From the tone of his voice I know that he's got his hand extended and his fingers spread out like the beads on an abacus. "You got three groups. You got the Jewish princesses first. Then you got the uppities—the more wealthy. Then you got the universities. Professors. If you get these people to buy, then *maybe* it gets enough attention so that the business guys hear about it. Otherwise you might as well flush it down the john."

The tape recorder records; Barbara remains silent.

"But if the business guy hears about it the Jewish business guy buys first," he continues. "Why do you think that is?"

More silence. Barbara already must understand that when Morry asks a question it is not because he is looking for an answer.

"Because it turns off the queen who is yellin' at him," says Morry. "When the poor guy is watching TV the wife thinks she can yell, it's like he's doin' nuthin'. But when he's reading a *book,* she shuts up. She respects that."

"How do you know so much about Jewish women?" asks Barbara, who happens to be one.

"I observe," says Morry, simply.

JULY 28

After landing at Washington's National Airport, the plane taxis right up beside the Dole campaign plane, which, since Dole's resignation from the Senate, has changed its name from *Leader's Ship* to *Citizen's Ship.*

The passengers who see it gawk and whisper, even though most of them probably couldn't care less about the Dole campaign. The danger for a presidential candidate, particularly one like Dole who simply cannot connect with his audience, is that he might mistake this sort of curiosity for sincere interest.

I walk out of one gate and find milling around the next the same group I left six weeks ago in Cincinnati: forty journalists, a dozen Secret Service men, and ten rented strangers in blue suits waiting to board the Dole plane. For the next ten minutes I try hard to think of something better to do, secure in the knowledge that as soon as I am aboard the Dole plane I'll want to be off it. No sane person could possibly be interested in this trip, I think. But then I remember: more has happened in the campaign than meets the eye. For a start the Dole people have decided that they can afford not to speak to the Buchanan people. There has not been a single line of communication between the Buchanan campaign and the Dole campaign. Not a letter, not a phone call, certainly not a lunch. Blood was bad to start with; to go this long without speaking is bound to make it worse.

The other thing that has happened is national campaign strategy.

With the help of outside consultants employed by the campaigns, and of Charles Cook of the newsletter *The Cook Political Report,* I have taken to drawing a campaign strategist's map of the United States. On the map, I try to pinpoint which states each party will legitimately contest in the presidential election. The map attempts to describe not what is true but what the campaigns *believe* to be true. In the minds of the strategists states fall into one of three categories: those such as Minnesota, which neither campaign believes to be in dispute; those such as Michigan, which both campaigns believe to be up for grabs; and those such as Arizona, which probably aren't up for grabs but you never know. This third category holds the most delicious possibilities for the campaign strategists, because it is just possible they might dupe each other into ill-advised expenditures. For example, there are a number of states in which the Clinton campaign is running ahead in the polls but nonetheless expects to lose. Clinton is now spending money in Nevada, for instance, but only because he is hoping that his ads, alongside his lead in the polls, will spook Dole into wasting his precious time there. Dole's people are hinting that he may try to do the same thing to Clinton in California.

Sure enough, that's where the Dole plane is headed.

One of the stranger aspects of flying around with the finalists of a presidential campaign is that only about a fifth of the journalists at any one time are allowed into all the events. This rotating cast of cameras and scribes is called the pool. The pool's job is to observe and question, and then to report back to the other journalists what it has seen. There is no economic incentive for a reporter to see anything different, as anyone who does is immediately required to share it with the rest.

This afternoon in Los Angeles there is a spare seat in the pool van waiting on the tarmac, and so I take it. I am breaking the rules—and risking the wrath of the rented strangers—because the event is not to be missed. It turns out that Dole has flown to Los Angeles to see a movie. He will attend *Independence Day* today and praise it tomorrow. The speech has already been scheduled. "He's going to cite *Independence Day* as an example of a major motion picture that makes money but preserves the notion of patriotism, mankind coming together, and the fight between good and evil," says Nelson Warfield, his press person, just before we depart for the theater.

The high point in Dole's career as a presidential candidate came last summer, when he denounced Hollywood for its sorry values. Since the primaries he implicitly has been comparing these values to "Russell values," or the way of life in the small town in Kansas where he learned how to behave. The only glitch in his performance the last time was that he had neglected to see the movies he denounced. When you read Bob Woodward's account in *The Choice* you realize how weird our political life has become. After Dole's first Hollywood speech, writes Woodward:

> Scott Reed realized that the campaign had made two mistakes. First, Dole was receiving some legitimate criticism because he had to acknowledge that he had not seen the movies. Reed should have made Dole watch the movies so he could speak with authority. But Reed figured they had barely convinced him to give the speech, and long sessions watching movies would have likely increased his resistance. . . . Second, the mention of (ardent Republican) Arnold Schwarzenegger's movie *True Lies* in a list of the top-grossing movies that "were most friendly to the family" made it appear that Dole was . . . pandering.

This time the rented strangers have wised up. They will make certain that Dole sees a movie, and that America will see Dole seeing a movie, before Dole passes official judgment on Hollywood.

No one seems to care at all that there is still a small problem: the speech is written *before* Dole has seen the movie. Think of it. The response of Dole and his advisers to the perfectly reasonable criticism—if you are going to express moral outrage about Hollywood movies, you should at least have seen the movies—isn't to hide their heads in shame and resist the temptation to feign moral outrage for votes. It isn't even to have Dole go out and see a few movies and come back and tell us what he thought about them—the honest approach to moral philosophy. It is to orchestrate a tableau for the American public in which Dole *seems* to see the movie before he offers up his moral judgment. To remain sane, I have to believe that the end result of this crap is the continued indifference of the American public.

On the way into the movie theater from the airport you can see the power of Clinton's $100 million ad campaign. Seven old codgers are strung out along the freeway twenty yards apart, holding signs for Dole to read:

BOB

THE

GRINCH

31

YEARS

AGAINST

MEDICARE

Several times each day Californians (and Floridians) are told that Bob Dole wants to strip them of their Medicare benefits, when, in fact, the difference between the two parties on Medicare spending is tiny. The ad's brutal effectiveness is yet another example of how well dishonesty pays in this business. In the geriatric mind "Dole" is starting to rhyme with "death."

An hour after we pass the signs we crowd around the ticket booth, watching the Doles walk up and buy their tickets to *Independence Day*. They proceed inside, surrounded by cameras, where they buy popcorn and a box of Goobers. Interestingly, none of the journalists or campaign staffers has to go through any of the rigmarole that's supposed to create the illusion this is a regular trip to the movies. Everyone in the motorcade but the Doles—journalists, staffers, Secret Service agents—simply marches into the theater and takes a seat he hasn't paid for. The Doles, on the other hand, buy their tickets for themselves not because they are having an ordinary experience but in an effort to pretend that they are having an ordinary experience. They have come full circle to a kind of alter-reality. The serious candidates don't have the will to acknowledge that their lives are unlike other people's.

The theater is already pitch black. For the next two hours the Doles remain invisible, save for the moments when an American city is blown to bits by the alien spacecraft and the theater lights up. From my seat down in front I can see the Doles staring impassively into the abyss. One hour and forty-five minutes later the earth is saved, and Dole emerges blinking in the sunlight. Immediately he is asked what he thought of the movie. Fifty-odd journalists swarm around him, and I can't make out what he says. It doesn't matter. In the van on the way home the reporters replay their tape recorders and try to decipher Dole's comments.

TAPE RECORDER: Mumble, mumble.
REPORTER ONE: What was that? "We won in the end"?
REPORTER TWO: No. Just "We won. The end."
TAPE RECORDER: Mumble, mumble.
REPORTER ONE: What was that? "It's a good movie. You can bring your family, too"?
REPORTER TWO (impatiently): No. It's Dolespeak. Just "Bring your family, too."

And so it goes until Dole's full moral appraisal of *Independence Day* is assembled:

"We won. The end. Leadership. America. Good over evil. It's a good movie. Bring your family, too."*

*The Wall Street Journal later reported that *Independence Day* figured into the Clinton campaign strategy. On June 22 Clinton watched the movie in the White House screening room with a businessman named Roger Tamraz, who had forked over $177,000 to the Democratic Party. A few weeks before the screening, Mr. Tamraz, with an introduction from the State Department, met with a senior official at the National Security Council to discuss his desire to build an oil pipeline from the Caspian Sea to Turkey. His former business partners included Saddam Hussein and the governments of China and Libya.

JULY 30

Bob Dole wakes up, climbs into his motorcade, and is driven to 20th Century Fox Studios, where he delivers his speech on Hollywood values. The podium has been planted in the same studio where Nikita Khrushchev, on a visit to America, became outraged at the sight of ladies dancing in cancan costumes. "Khrushchev thought it was not proper and got very upset," says a Fox employee who oversees the vast, empty warehouse.

As Dole explains why Hollywood should make more good movies like *Independence Day* and fewer bad ones like *Striptease* I am struck by the shabbiness of his own product. His argument is confused. He starts out by saying that Hollywood should make more good movies and fewer bad ones because goodness *pays:*

> If our ticket windows are a kind of cultural ballot box, then the results are in and we can call a winner. By a landslide, Americans are choosing the good over the grotesque. Excellence over exploitation. Quiet virtue over gratuitous violence, and character over pointless cruelty.

But if it pays to be good, of course, the market would take care of the problem and there would be no need for Dole to stand up and make a speech about it. Filmmakers would make only good movies because only good movies would pay. And if some stupid filmmaker happened to produce a bad movie it wouldn't matter, since no one would pay to see it. Toward the end of the speech Dole—or his speechwriter—seems to realize the contradiction. He tacks back and argues nearly the opposite, that bad movies pay just as well as good movies:

> Anyone with influence over our culture has to choose one or the other. And maybe no one expressed that choice better than Clark Gable's character, Rhett Butler, in *Gone With the Wind.* He says: "What most people don't seem to realize is that there is just as much money to be made out of the wreckage of a civilization as from the upbuilding of one. I'm making my fortune out of the wreckage."

It makes no sense. But from the point of view of the rented strangers the sense of Dole's argument does not matter. What matters is that their strategy works. The newspapers publish their straightforward accounts, without mentioning Dole's attendance record at the movies. This time no one dares to suggest that Dole hasn't seen the movies of which he speaks. "The nice thing about this place," says the Fox employee who tells me about Khrushchev's visit, "is that you can create anything in it." But the effect of Dole's speech on an attentive listener, I think, is precisely the opposite of what Dole intended. Instead of enraging him about Hollywood's values it causes him to wonder about Dole himself, and the Russell values he claims to champion. How can you even try to sell a moral vision when you don't honestly share the view? How can you speak to men's hearts when you house your soul in the aluminum siding of modern politics?

From California Dole is heading to Russell with a few days in between back east. In Russell he plans to announce his running mate, and to underline, as always, the small-town midwestern values that distinguish him from other politicians. In Russell, Dole's rented strangers promise, the seventeen-point lead in the opinion polls that Clinton has held over Dole since January will shrink. One of them takes me aside to tell me that Russell is not to be missed. I should travel with Dole, he says. Or I could quit the Dole plane and watch Dole's trip to Russell on C-Span, which would be more comfortable and just as informative.

There's a third option, however.

AUGUST 7

I don't really expect anyone to answer the door of Bob Dole's house in Russell, but I stop by anyway, just to see what might happen. When you travel with Dole, you see the world as it is constructed by the Dole campaign, until you almost forget there is a world outside where people do the unexpected. Indeed, as I reach for the screen door I half wonder if some SWAT team will leap out of the bushes and haul me back to *Citizen's Ship* for questioning.

But in my attempt to discover what on earth Dole means when he invokes "Russell values" I'm well ahead of the posse. The Dole campaign plane is a few days behind me, and the neighborhood remains undisturbed by politics. The only sign that I'm in the right place is the faded pink mat beneath my feet: WELCOME TO THE HOME OF THE DOLES. After a single ring, the front door swings opens and an elderly woman steps outside. "Just cleaning up before Bob gets here," Dole's sister, Gloria, says matter-of-factly. She then disappears inside, leaving the door open for me to follow. I do.

Bob Dole's boyhood home—his official residence, in fact—is instantly recognizable to anyone who had grandparents in the 1960s: 1960s old persons' furniture (low-backed lounge chairs), 1960s old persons' colors (unnatural shades of green), and 1960s old persons' smells (1940s perfume). Over the roar of the 1960s vacuum cleaner, Gloria opens various drawers and tosses onto various counters items for me to inspect. The drawers contain hundreds of loose photographs of Dole in his youth that neither Gloria nor anyone else has looked at in years. One shot depicts Dole modeling clothes in a fashion show staged by a local department store; another shows him shirtless with his muscles slightly flexed. As a collection, they capture both Dole's natural obedience—he always poses—and his intense physical vanity. (How many eighteen-year-olds in 1940 lifted weights?) "He looks like a movie star," I say to Gloria. "He was a movie star," she says, quickly. "He *is* a movie star." Next Gloria digs out an old shot of Dole with Barry Goldwater. "First he's for Bob one day," she says, referring to Goldwater, "the next day he's not. Senile, I think."

The whole thing happens so fast it seems only natural that I'm ransacking the home of the Republican presidential nominee. After a thorough search of the premises we move to the garage, passing, beside Dole's bed, a strange pair of Little Black Sambo rag dolls of the sort they don't even allow in the South anymore. The inside of the garage is a welter of ancient possessions that have long since ceased to serve any useful purpose: five-pound cameras, medicine balls, that sort of thing. The outside is equally unremarkable save for the jury-rigged system of sausage-shaped weights that Dole used to rebuild his arm after the war. According to Gloria, the contraption has simply hung there for the past fifty years, untouched by time or fate. Dole just likes having it around.

As I watch the white rope spool through the eye of the silver pulley, I realize I am also watching Bob Dole's campaign in microcosm: somewhere Dole is either giving a speech or preparing to give a speech in which he invokes the place where I now stand and the things he once did here. "Now, let's just take Bob Dole," he'll say, typically. "Nothing special about me. I grew up in a small town. My dad wore his overalls to work every day for forty-two years and was proud of it. We grew up living in a basement apartment. Six of us. To make ends meet. In Russell, Kansas.

We didn't have any money, but we had a lot of values." Then he will allude artfully to his war wound and his heroic recovery from it.

The insistence on the importance of events that occurred fifty years ago in a place where he hasn't lived for thirty-five years is more than a little strange. It's as if Dole has made a bargain with himself and with those who would judge him that enables him to cease all serious self-examination after the age of twenty-five. The deal is something like this: Dole agrees to believe that it was worth it to have his arm and his vanities shattered for the sake of his country; in return the country agrees not to question what lurks inside him. Thanks to a single decision he made fifty years ago, he is forever the war hero. It's a strangely stunted view of seventy-three years on the planet.

Time and again a person is reminded that the hardest thing in life is not meeting some challenge but knowing what the challenge is that needs to be met. Challenges have a way of slipping by unnoticed; most lives are the story of a series of unseen struggles. Defining the challenge is precisely Dole's problem. He has a superhuman ability to struggle; there's no question about that. But he needs to be told what the struggle is: staying alive, rehabilitating his body, getting elected, passing a bill. The gift of imagining the world for other people, as he now is trying to do, is beyond him; he cannot even imagine the world for himself.

AUGUST 8–10

After three long days in Russell I realize (a) that I can never quote anyone here saying anything truthful without bringing the wrath of the town down upon that person and (b) that any scene or person I depict will be instantly recognizable to the entire population. I will try instead to summarize what I have learned, briefly.

Those who are attracted to Dole's vision of life in Russell, Kansas, need to spend a little time here. It turns out there's a reason ambitious people like Dole have been fleeing the place in droves: while its mythical counterpart grows in stature, the actual Russell has been slowly withering. A bleak local economic history could be written from inside any store on Main Street. For example, the biggest and oldest store—a department store called Bankers, for which Dole modeled clothes—opened in 1881, ten years after Russell was founded, beside the new tracks laid by the Union Pacific Railroad. It prospered through the oil boom of the 1920s and the farming boom of the 1940s, reaching its apogee in the 1950s, when it stocked three full floors of dry goods. Since then the store's business has gradually waned so that it now occupies barely one floor, some of which is given over to the sale of Bob Dole paraphernalia. Where once there were gardening tools there are now rows of Dole buttons, stickers, T-shirts, and caps. The oldest family-owned business in Kansas will probably soon close for lack of business and of a family member willing to live in Russell. "I'd manage the place," says one of the heirs, who lives in Kansas City, "but only if you put it on a truck and moved it to another town."

The economic history of Russell consists of a series of faraway events turning the place upside down: oil and wheat price fluctuations; railroad and highway construction; and, most recently, Bob Dole's national political career. The Dole campaign is Russell's last best hope for prosperity. If Dole wins, the town booms. Local estimates see the current population going from 4,700 to as high as 80,000. If Dole loses, Russell may join the thousands of other hamlets compiled in a five-volume local classic, *Ghost Towns of Kansas.*

So it is not surprising that the town kicks into full gear each time Dole arrives. In just a few days I watch Russell become "Russell." The newspaper generates thick special editions about Dole, with "news" stories written by some of Dole's old pals. The chamber of commerce donates office space to the Dole advance people. The high-school band practices Dole's favorite song, and the adult choir works on its repertoire. People who ordinarily offer tours of town beg off. "The Dole campaign asked me to refer journalists to the chamber of commerce," one tells me. I know I'll never get a straight answer on the record when I stop a lady on the street and ask her if Russell strikes her as a good site for a presidential library. She pulls herself up and recites like a pro: "Russell is a small town that does things in a big way."

But it is true—as Dole repeatedly suggests—that Russell's value system is different from that of a big city, or of Hollywood. The difference springs less from the intrinsic qualities of Russell's citizens than from a single extrinsic circumstance: everyone who lives in Russell knows everyone else in Russell. This in turn leads people to be a bit more considerate. Initially, probably, their consideration arose out of the small-town fear that if they weren't, everyone would find out and they'd be ostracized. But now it is a pleasant habit. It does not even cross the mind of the owner of a local motel, for example, to raise his prices when the national media come to town and take every room in a fifty-mile radius. "That would be wrong," he says.

But the power of the community obsesses and controls those within it. Residents of a big city are constantly reminded that the most important events of the day take place far away; residents in Russell are not. As a result, in a big city, events that occur far away—foreign policy, vacations in Borneo—acquire a ridiculous prestige. In a small town, the reverse is true: events that occur around the corner become ridiculously important. The world slowly shrinks until it is smaller than the town. When recently a small local businessman moved away, for instance, a rumor raced around town that he had gone to Detroit and acquired 51 percent of the Ford Motor Company. People believed it.

SIXTEEN

San Diego

The drug war could become very simple. The first thing I would do as President is build gazebos in every town, glass encased, where you could put drug offenders—primarily minors who needed to be taught a lesson—on the weekends. They'd have a little area that they can sit there and lie down on a cot and a little toilet and sink in each one. That's it. Open the door, stick them in there and shut it. I'd give them box lunches but they would have to stay behind that glass wall. . . .

— MORRY TAYLOR,
*"Kill All the Lawyers and Other Ways
to Fix Washington" (unpublished manuscript)*

AUGUST 11

Morry asks me to meet him in the parking lot by the San Diego Convention Center, but the convention center is closed, and the police who surround it have no idea where to find the parking lot. After a half-hour search, I ask a cop if he has seen five thousand people on Harley-Davidson motorcycles, the number Morry promised to deliver to the Dole campaign.

The cop looks at me as if I am mad. "How many?" he asks, incredulously. "Five thousand," I say. "There is no way you get five thousand motorcycles anywhere near here," he says. For the first time since I met him seven months ago, I doubt Morry's ability to throw a party. How do you find five thousand bikers, anyway?

Soon enough I find the parking lot. It lies directly behind a small cluster of protesters a half mile or so from the convention center. It consists

The bubble forms moments after Pat Buchanan
enters the Republican convention.

of maybe four acres of concrete with a full concert stage at the back. Over the stage is an American flag and in front of the flag a huge banner. It reads, TITAN: AMERICA'S NEWEST TIRE COMPANY. On the stage are five large black men loudly playing instruments. Each of them wears a bandanna that says, THE GRIZZ. At the front of the stage, with a cigar jutting straight out from his mouth, is Morry, gyrating slightly to the funk, oblivious to the first of several insults he's received from serious Republican politicians: just a few moments ago Massachusetts governor Bill Weld said he preferred to be dropped from the Republican convention entirely rather than play the role he'd been assigned inside the hall, to introduce a brief video of Morry's endorsement of Dole.

The roar of approaching motorcycles soon drowns out everything. Not 5,000 but almost 7,000 motorcycles are streaming across a distant bridge. On top of them are close to 7,000 Republican loyalists, led by half the United States Congress: Newt Gingrich, Trent Lott, Ben Nighthorse Campbell, Dick Armey. An aerial photograph will later show a thick line of more than two miles of Harley-Davidsons stretching along the California coastline. If ever there was a chance for Dole to shatter every conceivable stereotype, here it is. From the moment the bikers arrive at the gates, however, the Dole campaign ensures that pretty much everything goes wrong. Dole's promise to attend is the most immediate problem. It causes the police to detain 6,800 bikers on the highway rather than let them anywhere near the Republican nominee. The thick line dutifully comes to a halt and the bikers wait, restlessly. The Dole campaign goes back and forth on whether Dole will in fact turn up until everyone is thoroughly unhappy.

To pass the time the politicians speak, in order of their importance, to the small group of bikers who have been admitted, starting with Trent Lott and ending with New York Mike, a local Harley dealer. ("We're bikers, right? And we're tired of being discriminated against. We're tired of helmet laws. . . .") After an hour or so of this the Dole campaign finally radios its admission that Dole won't be coming after all. The effect is immediate: the senators and congressmen vanish. Poof. They exit out the back gate, just as the first three thousand bikers on the highway enter through the front. Morry claims most of the bikers are actually doctors and lawyers, and if this is true, then doctors and lawyers are not what they used to be. These are doctors and lawyers with wild, distended bellies and facial hair that falls to their knees and terrifying messages tattooed all over their bodies and clothing. Their most popular cause by far is the Vietnam War. Every one of them seems to be either a Vietnam veteran or a friend of a veteran. HANOI JANE: TRAITOR BY CHOICE, COMMIE BY INJECTION, reads a typical armband. The glee on Morry's face as 6,800 huge men on motorcycles—he was already calling them "my bikers"—roar into the lot calls to mind a small child on Christmas morning. "It's the only event at the convention that is open to everybody and you don't have to pay," he shouts, by way of explanation of the huge turnout. The bikers for their part seem thrilled, especially when Morry moonwalks across the stage and hurls Grizz T-shirts into the raucous crowd. As he does the band strikes up a new song:

> It's your thing.
> Do what you gotta do.
> I can't tell you.
> What not to do.

Within minutes the motorcycle rally is the single biggest party of this year's Republican National Convention. Yet the only candidate in sight is Morry Taylor. A thousand bikers swarm at Morry's feet clamoring for his attention, like vassals cheering their lord. "I don't want to be here when they run out of food," Morry shouts back over his shoulder, as he hurls a Grizz cap into the crowd. "If they run out of food it's gonna get ugly." They run out of food. Luckily, at the rear exit a white stretch limo awaits the Grizz. In a final flourish Morry tells me to meet him tomorrow at the convention, hurls his final T-shirt, splays his arms and legs into a Greek cross, and exposes his empty palms like Saint Francis displaying the stigmata. Then he's gone.

AUGUST 12

In the lobby of John McCain's hotel I am nearly plowed over by Steve Forbes, who has the unnerving habit of walking straight ahead without blinking, like a blind man. On my way into the restaurant I brush against the leg of a table occupied by Norman Mailer. By the time I reach McCain, who sits chatting with a senator from Alaska, I am almost too jaded to notice. Such is life at the Republican convention, where you can hardly strike up a conversation without being charged a lecture fee.

Ever since I met him late one night in a private air terminal in South Carolina, McCain has caused me problems. I know well enough how to talk to an important person who shades the truth; they all do that. But I don't know how to interview an honest man who occupies high political office. A strange reversal occurs whenever I speak with McCain. I know I should be plumbing him for information, trying to get him to say things he shouldn't, the usual journalist thing. But the minute he opens his mouth he says something impolitic on the record, and some inner voice cries out in me: "For God's sake, don't say that! There might be a journalist around!"

Somehow, despite his alarming preference for the truth, McCain's name ended up on the shortlist of possible running mates for Dole. Along with four others he was invited to submit the nineteen-page questionnaire prepared by Dole's rented strangers. A lot of the questions clearly were designed to expose and eliminate anyone who in their lives courted risk or adventure. For example:

> Have you or your spouse ever been publicly identified, in person or as a member of an organization that was identified with a particularly controversial* national or local issue? If so, please describe. [A footnote explains the asterisk: "Reference to 'particu-

larly controversial' is intended to focus on issues that could be used, even unfairly, against you." Fully one third of the questions come with this warning.]

When I ask McCain why Jack Kemp, whom Dole has ridiculed for years, and not he was chosen, he laughs and says, "I've lived a rich and full life, my friend. A better life than you even. And when you do that you end up with a few skeletons in your closet." This is true. He went through a messy divorce. He was charged with (then exonerated from) aiding and abetting savings and loan crook Charles Keating in exchange for campaign contributions. But mainly what he has against him, I think, is his willingness to say pretty much what's on his mind. I'd like to think that Dole secretly enjoys this quality in McCain. ("Any man who has spent five years in a box," Dole has said, "is entitled to speak his mind.") But honesty is kryptonite to the rented strangers.

That's the other reason McCain may have been passed over: Dole's most senior staffers—Scott Reed and John Buckley—once worked for Kemp. Kemp's selection is the best evidence yet that Dole has given himself over entirely to them.

Nevertheless, a couple of weeks ago the Dole campaign asked McCain to speak tonight at the convention about honor and duty. God knows what this means to the rented strangers, though McCain believes it means a lot to Dole. McCain sent in a draft of a six-minute talk that the Dole campaign revised heavily. "No words more than two syllables" is how McCain describes the revision. Every freelance magazine writer knows the feeling, I say, then immediately realize McCain's position is different. At the time of this exchange he was a leading candidate to be Dole's running mate. That he told the rented strangers to stuff it could not have helped his cause, though the minute McCain pulled his speech the strangers caved and told McCain he could say whatever he wanted.

After breakfast McCain drops me at the convention center in time to see the chairman of the Republican National Committee, Haley Barbour, open the proceedings. Barbour played an important role in Dole's coronation. During the primaries, when the rented strangers were busy hiring pollsters to spread lies about Forbes and Buchanan, Barbour covered Dole's flank by telling the others he'd put a stop to it. Now he's addressing the two thousand delegates, all of whom, interestingly, paid their own plane fare to get here. Against this is set the fifteen thousand journalists covering the event, all on corporate expense accounts. Probably the best investigative journalism to be written about the 1996 Republican convention is the search for the journalist who has the least compelling reason to be here. Compared to the meandering editors of glossy New York magazines, the TV crew from the Netherlands has the keening urgency of firefighters during a roaring blaze. ("I think I secured the Dutch vote," says McCain, after a brief interview with them.)

With twenty thousand or so white men to sift through I don't find Morry until late this afternoon. He's leaning against a wall at the back of the hall looking distinctly out of sorts, like a man trying to spend lire in Spain. On the rare occasion someone recognizes him he seems shocked. I try to restore his spirits. I tell him that just a few hours earlier a man named Ed Harrison took the podium and started his speech with the immortal words, "Now I'm not a politician. And I'm not a lawyer. I'm a businessman." He had stolen Morry's precise words. This, too, Morry can't quite believe. He hasn't entirely grasped the power of the modern media. Finally, a Fox TV crew without anything to do stops by to interview him.

"Mr. Taylor," begins the reporter.

"What do you mean with this 'Mr. Taylor' shit?" asks Morry.

"Morry?" says the reporter, uncertainly.

"The Grizz!" booms Morry, effectively bursting the media bubble.

More silence. We've stood together for maybe twenty minutes without anyone in the audience of freshly scrubbed, white, prosperous, shiny happy faces spotting him. Then suddenly a voice calls out.

"Mr. Taylor?"

A handsome young man in a wheelchair presents himself. "Are you Mr. Taylor?" he asks.

The achingly earnest look on the man's face is one I've seen ten thousand times. Every time it dents my ability to suspect anyone of anything but sincerity. I become, momentarily, a midwesterner. Sure enough, the young man in the wheelchair is from Ohio. He's gazing up at Morry, with adulation. He wants a picture with him. Morry is touched, but he hides it well.

"You're a great American, sir," says the young man.

"Give me your address," says Morry, as I snap their photo together. "I'll send you a box of Grizz stuff."

That's it, I think. That's all for Morry here today, where people are only interested in the real politicians. But I have forgotten the general rule of American politics: if you hang with Morry Taylor, action will follow. It continues to obtain. We're sitting in the section reserved for the primary candidates when Pat Buchanan appears in the convention hall, for the first time.

When Buchanan enters he's already got maybe fifty journalists with him; he quickly accumulates another hundred, plus several hundred delegates keen to shake his hand. The result is a human tsunami that breaks across about a third of the convention hall and lays waste to anything in its path. "People are being trampled!" an enormous security guard shouts into his wrist mike. "Send me fifty people!" But the crowd has its own logic: people attract more people. For every added security man, three curiosity seekers join in.

The tension rises as Buchanan circles the hall. He's like a ball bearing in a roulette wheel before it stops on a number. Every appearance by a significant politician attracts a mob. The bigger fish know better than to stop anyplace; when they need to cross the hall, they racewalk before the mob can congeal. And Buchanan is the biggest fish of all. At length he comes to rest in the seat directly behind Morry. Fully one-third of the convention is watching him and ignoring Texas governor George W. Bush, who is speaking piously from the podium (". . . open up a child day-care center at your church or synagogue . . ."). "I need more help here!" the fat security guard is blaring into his wrist mike. "Send help! Send help!"

All the while Buchanan is acting as if nothing out of the ordinary has occurred, that every day he goes out and ruins someone's convention. Then he fixes on Morry, standing eight feet in front of him.

"Morry Taylor is the problem here!" he shouts. "He's ruined the convention."

"Did they do this to you when you got here, Morry?" shrieks Bay Buchanan, joining her brother in ganging up on Morry.

It seems needlessly cruel. Morry stands watching and minding his own business. "It's you, Pat," he replies. "Leave Shelley with me, and take these people out in the street." The two former rivals vie to condescend to one another. Buchanan is winning on points until he pushes it one inch too far. "Where's the keg, Morry?" he shouts. "Go get the keg."

Morry looks up and licks his lip like a grizzly bear who has just spotted his next meal. "Hey, Pat," he says. "You're unemployed now." The combination of truth and daring pulls the entire circus up short. Then Morry turns to the cameras, which have swiveled to face him. "He needs a job," Morry explains to the world's news media. "Or else he'll have to take unemployment."

Buchanan shakes his head like a boxer who didn't expect the under-cut. But before he can swing back Steve Forbes rolls up alongside him with his family in tow. The sight of Forbes clearly means nothing to Buchanan, but it arouses some feelings of solidarity in Morry. Here they are: the losers. Relegated to seats far away from the podium, in rows fifty-eight and fifty-nine out of sixty. "They chased poor Lamar out of here," says Morry, forlornly. Forbes looks at him as if he's mad.

Former presidents Gerald Ford and George Bush speak, but no one around Buchanan listens. All eyes now refocus on the Peasant King, who has fled Morry for serial interviews with the networks. He parcels out his choler for twenty minutes at least, until Nancy Reagan appears to eulogize Ronnie and causes everyone to go silent. (Republicans behave as if Reagan has already died, whereas Nixon, who has actually died, is treated as if he were still alive.) Then comes what I am sure will be the defining moment of the convention. Not today, not next year even, but four years from now when Republicans reassemble in New Hampshire they will remember this moment more than any other: Colin Powell, who follows Nancy Reagan, raises his voice above the crowd and pro-claims his belief in abortion rights:

> You all know that I believe in a woman's right to choose and I strongly support affirmative action. And I was invited here by my party to share my views with you because we are a big enough party—and big enough people—to disagree on individual issues and still work together for our common goal: restoring the American dream.

As the journalists applaud, the delegates bicker, and to make himself heard over the din Powell has to repeat himself. I turn around and meet Buchanan's gaze. In that gaze I see the future of the Republican Party; I see Buchanan four years from now staring at Powell, or someone who thinks like Powell, across a stage in Iowa and thinking: If he wins the nomination, I'm leaving the party. In these circumstances it is as a rule impossible to think of a decent question. "Any reaction?" I ask, idiotically. "What?" Buchanan says. "Any reaction?" I shout. But the noise from the crowd trying to decide whether to cheer or to boo is too loud.

When it's over Morry tells me that Dole has invited him to join him onstage on the final night, but Morry has for the second time in as many days declined Dole's invitation. He figures it will merely be another meaningless free-for-all, with everyone who ever thought of running for office crammed onto the stage. Although Morry's aides—he has two—plead with me to try to change his mind, I can't tell him he's wrong. It's nothing personal, though he is still irritated that Dole lacked the sense to address seven thousand raving loyalists on motorcycles. Convention life is less than it's cracked up to be, he's decided. In the morning his plane will take him and his friends to Las Vegas.

AUGUST 15

Last night, the next-to-last night of the convention, before McCain nominated Dole, the party bosses played a video featuring Alan Keyes. It showed Keyes and Ralph Reed expressing solidarity with Dole and with the Republican Party. Keyes was loudly cheered and Reed was ignored, a reaction that pretty well reflects their respective influence in the hearts of evangelicals.

When I finally track down Keyes upstairs near the fast food, however, I discover he's blind with rage. It turns out he made the video to express his views on abortion; the Republican National Committee edited out any mention of the issue. The Dole campaign and the RNC actually lied to him, says Keyes, by saying they'd either include his pro-life message or not air the video at all. "They showed it without my approval," he shouts at me, as we sit on a remote bench to avoid the autograph hounds who chase Keyes wherever he goes. "They showed it against my wishes." This is in keeping with the party's strategy of grafting a pro-choice TV show onto a pro-life platform.

"They want the life issue to be off the table," Keyes says, "but it is not off the table. If this party will not carry the pro-life message we'll start another party." Another party? "Howard Phillips has got the Taxpayers Party on forty ballots," he says. "It will soon be a very nice, very viable party." Nearby, a lone adoring fan gasps and claps. At Buchanan rallies, the mere mention of the Taxpayers Party brings the crowd to its feet. The

206

Taxpayers Party gives hope and solace to pro-lifers. It's what they think of first when they think of what they can do to destroy the Republican Party.

AUGUST 17

Great men are people who are willing to make asses of themselves in public.

— HOWARD PHILLIPS,
founder, U.S. Taxpayers Party

Four days ago, in a town called Escondido, Buchanan came clean with his intentions. He told a furious California audience of a thousand followers that he intends to remain inside the Republican Party—for now. "Did you see Ollie up there?" he asks, laughing loudly. (Ollie North preceded Buchanan on the microphone.) "Ollie expected them to *cheer* when he told them we had to stick together. Instead, they nearly got up and lynched him." In his speech Buchanan refrained from endorsing Dole, however, and even claimed a kind of victory over Dole, by saying that his people had written the abortion plank in the Republican platform. And, indeed, when you turn to page 34 of the 1996 platform, which hardly anyone has read, you find this:

> The unborn child has a fundamental individual right to life which cannot be infringed. We support a human life amendment to the Constitution and we endorse legislation to make clear that the Fourteenth Amendment's protections apply to unborn children.

On the other hand, a bit lower down, the same platform reads, "we oppose abortion, but our pro-life agenda does not include punitive action against women who have an abortion," which is a big point of dispute between Buchanan and Dole. At any rate, Dole claims he hasn't read—and won't read—the platform. The platform lends itself to this treatment. It is long, wordy, litigious, and a neat illustration of the political uses of bad writing. Pick up a copy of the 1964 Republican platform and you find a slim, elegant, terse statement of beliefs, mostly shared by the candidate. The whole document ran nineteen pages. From its very first lines you see the clarity of expression, and of belief, that so frightened people about Barry Goldwater:

Humanity is tormented once again by an age-old issue—is man to live in dignity and freedom under God or be enslaved—are men in government to serve, or are they to master, their fellow men? It befalls us now to resolve this issue anew—perhaps this time for centuries to come.

The 1996 platform is one hundred pages of blather that Bob Dole wouldn't be caught dead reading, and neither would you. Or so Dole hopes. Buchanan for his part had much less to do with it than Dole thinks. Once he saw that his followers had taken over the platform committee Buchanan sent his sister Bay out to San Diego to claim credit for the result.

In any case, anyone who thinks that the war between Dole and Buchanan ends with abortion hasn't been paying attention. The Buchanan brigades won't be satisfied until they are rid of their association with old-fashioned conservatives such as Dole. One moment at the start of the Escondido ceremony spoke volumes about what Buchanan's followers are up to, as opposed to what Buchanan claims he's up to. At the end of the Pledge of Allegiance, a claque at the back of the room tacked on a pro-life appendix. After "with liberty and justice for all," they hollered "born and unborn." When I expressed astonishment that they have dared to amend the Pledge of Allegiance, a friend gave me a where-have-you-been look and explained that the Buchanan people have also rewritten "The Star-Spangled Banner" to incorporate some pro-life language.

Nothing illustrates so well how anticonservative Buchanan's movement truly is. Its goal is not to conserve the past but to advance a radical agenda. Given this, it will be difficult to yoke these people to the Dole campaign. It's like trying to transform a lightning bolt into useful current.

Today, in the short drive across the thin and steeply arched bridge between San Diego and Coronado, I trace the path that a few days ago many had hoped Buchanan would follow on his way out of the Republican Party. From the top of the bridge you can see both the white tent-like San Diego Convention Center and the antique turrets of the Hotel del Coronado, where on the Sunday before the Republican convention Howard Phillips sat holding his breath. Phillips created the Taxpayers Party four years ago, more or less as a vehicle for Buchanan. Had Buchanan crossed the bridge, several thousand journalists would have crossed with him; the event would have overshadowed everything at the

Republican convention. The unhappy coalition of economic and social conservatives would have splintered. Dole would have been finished.

It never happened, of course. Instead, the road to Coronado became the road to Escondido. "My friends, this party is not just their party," Buchanan said to the people who came mainly in hopes he would stick a plastic explosive on the side of the Dole campaign. "It's our party, too." What that means for the Taxpayers Party I am not quite sure; and I'm curious to know what happens to such a highly charged political movement when it loses its leader. If Buchanan had chosen not to run, Phillips told me just a month ago, the fall-back plan was for Phillips himself to be the candidate; to hold Buchanan's place for four more years, as it were.

Upon entering the Taxpayers convention's Hotel del Coronado I am immediately assaulted by a middle-aged man streaked with grime. His long black toenails curl over the ends of his sandals. His chest is plastered over with soiled buttons: CHARLES E. COLLINS FOR PRESIDENT. He is not alone. The courtyard of the distinguished old hotel teems with passionately devoted followers of Charles E. Collins, all of whom emit terrific noises and even more terrific odors. Something has gone badly wrong. Collins is a Florida businessman who finished seventeenth in the New Hampshire primary. Ever since, his stinky brigades have been roaming the country in search of a party. Many of them believe the decline of America began with the U.N. conspiracy to fluoridate the water supply. Fluoride destroys brain cells and makes America weak, they argue. Maybe the most important practical consequence of their belief is a refusal to bathe. Massing together, waving signs, and cheering loudly at the center of San Diego's oldest hotel, they are as disruptive as Klingons.

As I marvel at the difference between what is and what might have been, I spot K. B. Forbes. Not long after the California primary K. B. left a prominent job in the Buchanan campaign to work for Phillips. A lot of people—me included—took the move as a sign that Buchanan was about to jump. Just a month ago I shared a hamburger with K. B. and Phillips and listened to them explain how Buchanan might win the White House in 1996 as the Taxpayers candidate. Phillips had devoted massive energy to getting the party on as many as forty state ballots. When he sat down with an electoral map he could, making plausible assumptions about Ralph Nader and Ross Perot, tell a story that ended with Pat Buchanan in power.

Then, K. B. was the embodiment of hope and optimism. Now, he looks as if he has just spent a night at the Munsters'. He doesn't even bother trying to spin me. "I'm getting out of here," he says, as a few followers of Collins leap from the bushes. "My political reputation is on the line." He slaps his palms together and points his index fingers toward the exit.

I follow K. B. Forbes to a chair in the hotel's elegant courtyard, through which disheveled supporters of Collins stream. Wearily, he sets about persuading me he has nothing whatsoever to do with the people around us. There comes a point in the career of every public relations man when he must cease to worry about his client's public relations and start to worry about his own. The Taxpayers convention is such a moment for K. B. Forbes. Even B-1 Bob Dornan, projected on the program as a possible convention speaker, decided to give it a miss.

The speakers inside the hall provide a mad sound track of political rhetoric. Apparently news of the political party in need of a candidate has inspired anyone who ever dreamed of being president to travel to the Del. "Eighteen years ago," wafts a female voice over our bewildered heads, "I was asked what I would like to do with my life, and without much hesitation I said I should like to be president of the United States." As K. B. tries to make himself heard over this, a group of maybe a dozen supporters of Collins pass through the courtyard, followed by the man himself, who sports a giant mane of red hair and a boutonniere. They walk strangely, though at first I can't quite figure out why. Then the soiled man at the front of the procession shrieks back over his shoulder, "Don't step on the lines!"

Some meaningful contingent of the Collins campaign is trying to avoid stepping on the cracks in the sidewalk.

"Put it this way," says another journalist, who stops to explain both to me and to K. B. just how loopy the Taxpayers Party has suddenly become. "In this crowd, the role of the Birch Society is as a *debunker* of myths." K. B. eyes me, hopefully. "All I know," he says, his eyes darting wildly in many directions, "is that I am outta here."

A few yards away, the convention proceeds at speed. Inside is a grand twelve-sided chamber lit by six magnificent chandeliers. For the moment the Taxpayers convention consists of maybe three hundred people (six hundred attend, by the end) and no mass media, only a pair of camcorders making home movies at the back of the room. Soon the presidential candidates are nominated, argued over, and voted on. There are five nominees, including Collins, Phillips, and Buchanan, who is of course not present to accept his nomination. A woman named Diane

Templin, clad in American flag panty hose, rises and says she realized she was destined to be president while attending a spiritual retreat. She lists among her credentials for high office her sixty-seven foster children. She is followed by a former CIA agent named Ted Gundersen, who explains to the several hundred assembled listeners that the CIA has been abducting small boys in the Midwest and carting them to Washington, D.C., to participate in homosexual orgies. Only when Collins rises to speak on his own behalf does the crowd explode with true enthusiasm. Collins lays out his platform, the centerpiece of which is returning to the American people the secret trillions hidden inside the Federal Reserve.

At length I spot Howard Phillips, pacing at the back of the room. He pauses in front of one of the tiny booths that sells T-shirts and bumper stickers (the Taxpayers Party's favorite: I LOVE ANIMALS—THEY'RE DELICIOUS!). He is looking distinctly unfazed. Howard is a man of ideas; and for the sake of his ideas he's willing to subject himself to much ridicule. This tells you all you need to know about the role of ideas in contemporary politics. Ideas are what serious politics is believed to be all about and what serious politicians love to claim politics is about. But if the two biggest political parties have anything in common it is their indifference to ideas; their willingness to trample on their ideas is what makes them electable. Only fringe parties—Taxpayers, Greens, Libertarians—exhibit any fidelity to their ideas, and it is precisely this intellectual fanaticism that consigns them to oblivion.

I set out to interview Howard, but an extraordinarily scented woman intervenes. She hands me a flyer. The Taxpayers convention is rigged, she shouts, in so many words. Supporters of Collins are being prevented from voting, she claims, and Howard Phillips has even taken to spreading "dirty lies" about Collins. And it appears someone has gone to the trouble of printing flyers that attack Collins. I can't find the document but the Collins flyer in response to it is worthy of the occasion.

CHARLES E. COLLINS FOR PRESIDENT OF THE UNITED STATES, it says in bold print. It continues: "Chaos reigns at the U.S. Taxpayers Party Convention as the registration of delegates turned into a circus. . . . 'This is politics as usual in spades,' said George Gruner, campaign manager for Charles Collins. 'Howard Phillips should be ashamed of himself and this farce he calls a convention.'"

For the next six hours I watch Howard bravely weave his way through a human stink bomb looking distinctly unashamed. To judge from his countenance you would never guess that anything at all has gone wrong.

He holds his head high, delivers a long, proud speech, and in the end rescues his party. Collins finishes second, ahead of a dormant Pat Buchanan, who finishes third. All in all, a stirring performance in the face of overwhelming odds. As I leave, I can still hear Howard's voice receding in the distance. "The victory of our cause is certain," he is saying, "though we know not the day, the year, or the hour."

Later, I return to my hotel and find a fax from K. B. Forbes. "Dear Howard," it begins.

This is my letter of resignation as Communications Director of the U.S. Taxpayers Party effective today, Sunday, August 18. Howard, you truly are a great man dedicated to conservative principles and preserving America's Constitutional Heritage. However, this convention has attracted—what I believe to be—the rudest and most mentally unstable wannabe political activists and "media" in America. I will not sacrifice my honor nor my reputation to assist these elements. . . .

SEVENTEEN

Chicago

The road from San Diego to Chicago, where the Democrats are scheduled to meet in a week, passes through Los Angeles, where the Green Party convenes this afternoon. The Greens are the left-wing response to the Taxpayers, and their convention site on the UCLA campus is a mirror image of Howard Phillips's fiasco on Coronado Island. Tables groan with the same hysterical T-shirts and bumper stickers and literature as the tables at the Taxpayers convention. Once again even the most casual observer can see that people drawn to the far left and the far right have more in common with each other than either do with the politically apathetic masses at the center. The man who wears a T-shirt that says FIGHT CRIME—SHOOT BACK! has more in common with the man who wears a T-shirt that says THINK PEACE! than the man who wears no T-shirt at all.

By the time I arrive Nader is seated beside a large bowl of sunflowers in a dark auditorium facing 150 journalists, including the networks, CNN, and MTV. Polls have shown Nader stealing as much as 11 percent of the vote from Clinton in California, but that's not the only reason for the coverage. The coverage arises from the fact that Nader is more entertaining than either of the two major parties. His celebrity is all the excuse the TV people need to follow him around in their futile search for interest in American politics. A day with Nader and you can see that one slight force in American politics working against the general tendency to phoniness is the ever-more-pressing requirement that everything be good TV. At the moment the two major parties are generating some of the most dreary entertainment ever broadcast, in part because they operate under the assumption that intraparty disputes are disreputable.

213

But their desire to present a unified front leads ultimately to a death of interest and causes the networks to cut back on their coverage. (The ratings of the Republican convention were the lowest ever.) The minor parties with their taste for conflict make for much better television.

Nader uses his forum to explain that though he is the Green Party candidate for president he is not running on the Green Party platform. He likes the Green platform but feels its breadth detracts from his real message: that both major parties are so deeply in hock to corporate America that neither can credibly claim to address issues of social justice and public welfare. As the cameras roll Nader says what no candidate of either major party will say, although many think it:

> Politics has been corrupted not just by money but by being trivialized out of addressing the great enduring issues of who controls, who decides, who owns, who pays, who has a voice and access, and why solutions available on the shelf are not applied to the existing and looming crises of our society, both local and global.

This message, Nader claims, strikes fear in the heart of Bill Clinton. Three weeks ago, Nader says, someone from the White House approached one of Clinton's major donors and said, "You know Nader, why can't you get him to withdraw?"

AUGUST 21

One moment I'm sleeping soundly in my hotel room, the next the phone is ringing and a voice on the other end of the line is asking, "This is the vice president's office, can you take the call?" Al Gore himself is on the line. In a moment of weakness, thinking that maybe I should interview someone important, I had made a call to Gore's office saying I wanted to speak with him. I hardly expected him to take it seriously. "It's nerve-racking getting a call from the vice president," I say. Gore chuckles unhappily; I've made him uncomfortable. "No, seriously," I say. "This is the highest I've climbed in the world." This merely makes things worse. "I don't believe that at all," he says, nervously, attempting to maneuver me back into some acceptable mode of political discourse.

I have only five minutes of interview time, and two of them are now gone. I'm (sort of) curious to know if Gore's environmentalism has, as it appears, vanished down the sinkhole of practical politics. There was a time before he became vice president when Gore's strong stand on the environment distinguished him from other insiders; whatever you thought about the issues it showed that he was willing to risk ridicule for his beliefs. But now the vice president's conversation is littered with "frankly's" and "to-be-honest-with-you's" and "it-is-my-understanding's," all of which translate into civilian English as "I'm never going to tell you the truth about anything, so why on earth are you asking?" So I ask him elliptically if he's spoken to anyone in the Green Party since he's taken office. He has not, which probably goes some way to explaining why the Green Party likens him to Judas. ("The vice presidency has long been a sinecure of sycophancy," Nader said yesterday, for instance. "But when you are a sycophant to Bill Clinton you are a new breed of sycophant.") I'm not going to get much more out of him, however. Before he hangs up Gore tells me that (a) Americans truly are committed to nature; (b) he's not more intimidated having to debate Jack Kemp than having to debate, say, Florida senator Connie Mack; and (c) the collection of speeches written by White House speechwriters and now published as a book by Bill Clinton, *Between Hope and History*, was penned entirely by Clinton himself. It is his understanding, Gore says.

AUGUST 26 AND 27

Your first day at a convention is like your first day at school: your first instinct is that something important is happening, that everyone must know something you don't. For the first few hours in Chicago I am engaged in a wild, undignified scramble to find out what that something is. During this uncomfortable period all sorts of information lands on my lap—a stack of old articles from *Chicago* magazine, drafts of speeches by retired Democratic congressmen, lists of delegates—stuff no one in his right mind would read. But nothing can be ignored; I even interview a delegate. But then there is this tremendous noise on one side of the convention hall, a spontaneous outbreak of whistles and cheers that draws all attention to the entrance beneath the Nevada delegation. The sound is exactly what you would expect if a billionaire were handing out sacks of cash, or if a woman were performing a striptease. I plow through the crowd.

It is Al Gore.

A normal person might well wonder what fifteen thousand journalists are doing covering an event of dubious importance for the second time in three weeks. It's not an easy question. The journalists who write about other journalists, like Howie Kurtz of the Washington *Post,* write about the futility of being a journalist at the Democratic convention. (The *Post* has as many people here as in all their foreign bureaus combined.) The famous journalists invert their occupation and give interviews to other journalists, like Kurtz. The rest of us are resigned to finding some nugget slightly different from the nuggets of others. Joel Achenbach of the *Post,* for instance, scored the scoop of the day by persuading Tipper Gore to take him jogging with her along Lake Michigan. Since both Joel and Tipper live in Washington, it's a little strange for them to have flown to Chicago to construct a newspaper article about jogging together. Context is everything, I suppose.

It turns out few of the journalists actually attend the convention, except during prime time. The journalists remain in tents outside the United Center. During the first two days, between three-thirty in the afternoon and seven o'clock at night, only a few dozen people pass through the section of the hall reserved for the "periodical press." This is a shame, because the best time to be in the hall is when no one is paying much attention. Hillary Clinton pops in in midafternoon to check the mike levels and the height of the podium. She steps up in her pink suit and, when she sees that it's the wrong height, kicks off her pink heels. She stands there girlishly in her stocking feet, asking too many questions of the men around her, and you can see that, like everyone else who plays her adamantine role, she is far more vulnerable than she lets on.

Even after the convention begins, no one pays it much heed. (People appear briefly like mayflies during prime time.) So when Dick Gephardt speaks I am able to crawl right up behind him on the platform and see what life looks like from the speaker's point of view. Essentially, life looks predetermined. The speaker stares into four TelePrompTers: one at his left shoulder, another at his right shoulder, a third mounted straight ahead of him across the hall just beneath the cameras (so that he can appear to be looking at you when you are watching him on TV). The fourth is embedded in the podium just above his navel. His speech—in letters four inches high, like the text of a book for the elderly—scrolls gently across. Gephardt only has to swivel back and forth between the prompters to pretend not to be reading word for word, which he is. "We meet here to offer a vision, not just a show for television," he is saying.

No wonder no one listens. Part of the thrill of watching a public speaker lies in the risk the speaker takes in putting himself before you. The magic microseconds between a speaker's thoughts and his exact words keep his audience on some subtle edge about what might be coming next. Jesse Jackson, for one, understands this: in the first two days he alone shuts down the prompters and speaks from loose notes, and he alone fully engages the crowd. It is the very moment that Jackson abandons his notes and struggles to mold words around his ideas that he first brings the crowd to its feet. His speech is gloriously messy—he gets New York Harbor confused with Pearl Harbor and mixes more metaphors than James Fenimore Cooper—and for this he earns the scorn of his enemies. But he speaks from the heart, and to an issue, economic justice, explicitly unaddressed by either major party since Pat Buchanan retired from the field. And for this he might well win the attention of all sorts of people who otherwise might not care about politics:

> What is our challenge tonight? Just look around this place. This publicly financed United Center is a new Chicago mountaintop. To the south, Comiskey Park, another mountaintop. To the west, Cook County Jail. Two ballparks and a jail [paid for with public funds]. In that jail mostly youthful inmates, eighty percent drug positive, ninety percent high-school dropouts, ninety-two percent functionally illiterate, seventy-five percent recidivism rate. They go back sicker and sicker. Between these mountains of the ballpark and the jail was once Campbell's soup and Sears and Zenith and Sunbeam and stockyards. There were jobs and there was industry. Now there's a canyon of welfare and despair. This canyon exists in virtually every city in America.

But Jackson is the exception. The ordinary Democratic convention speech makes no attempt to connect Democratic politics to the world around it. It arises not out of the need of the speaker to say something important but out of the speaker's desire to have delivered a speech at the convention, to establish his position in the official structure of the Democratic Party. The only exceptions to this rule are the speeches designed to make people cry. Grief once again fills a gap that should be occupied by more relevant and potentially objectionable sentiment. The constant parade of personal tragedy signals to the delegates, the cameras, and most of the journalists that they should respond with synchronized nods and similar expressions of pain. Ron Brown's widow, Jim Brady's wife, and Christopher Reeve are of course well-known victims. The speeches delivered by relative unknowns in the wee hours of the afternoon contain wagonloads more of the same. Here is a representative sample of opening lines, snatched in a single pass of the press table:

"As the father of a child brutally murdered by a habitual, violent criminal . . ."

"As many of you know, my husband . . . was a former tobacco lobbyist who died this past March. . . ."

"December 7, 1993. That was the day a man with a semiautomatic weapon boarded the train . . . my husband was one of those killed."

Say what you will about this technique for eliciting public sympathy. (Should we be more inclined to vote for Bill Clinton because an actor who fell off a horse speaks at his convention?) But once you start dealing indiscriminately in tragic sentiments it's hard to keep feelings running high. By early in the second day, people's capacity to absorb bad news has dwindled to nothing. A pleasant middle-aged woman describes the recent death of her husband from lung cancer, for instance, and no one in the United Center pays her any mind. It is an incongruous sight: a woman in bright yellow on the verge of tears as she relates her tragic loss over the loud hum from the audience below, most of which is engrossed in small talk and hot dogs.

Raising my binoculars from the floor to the ceiling, I can't help noticing something: the higher you get, the whiter the people get. Almost all the black people are on the floor. The faces in the skyboxes are lily white.

At the end of the first evening I make my way up to the skyboxes. The skyboxes at the convention, it turns out, are much like the skyboxes at the Bulls games. They have been reserved by the Democratic National Committee for the rich people and their companies, who can afford to pay for them. These include some of the seventy-two CEOs, many of them Republicans, who coughed up one hundred thousand dollars each to be an honorary vice chairman of the Democratic convention. Here, near the money and the cameras, is where *Weekly Standard* editor Bill Kristol kibitzes with Senator Joe Lieberman. Here is where you see curtained-off rooms decorated with signs that say: THE DCC WOULD LIKE TO THANK ESPECIALLY THE CHICAGO BOARD OPTIONS EXCHANGE AND PATTON, BOGGS, LLB. The people here sit sipping red wine and nibbling on goodies, looking down upon the politicians who will have no choice tomorrow but to take their calls.

By now pretty much everyone has left. But inside one of the many suites toils a middle-aged woman in a black-and-white penguin suit. For maybe half an hour the woman works alone, tossing out opened but untouched bottles of wine, dumping large silver trays of food into giant green trash bags. The food tumbles into the bag in mouth-watering heaps: chicken and beef satay, fried potato puff balls, shrimp rémoulade, thinly sliced meats rolled up like Oriental carpets. "This was one of the rooms reserved for the White House staff," the woman says, idly. "They never came. But they never called to cancel." That's when you know you've arrived in the Democratic Party, I think, when you don't even care to use your reserved suite. When I watched George Stephanopoulos in a Chicago health club earlier today, reading the newspaper as the convention unfolded on the TV above his head, I didn't appreciate what I was seeing. The coolest thing to be at the Democratic convention is a no-show.

I'm curious what the woman is being paid to chuck out thousands of dollars of untouched food. Instead, I ask more generally about salaries at the United Center. "You mean, what do I make?" she asks, cheerfully, as she empties a cow's worth of beef satay into the garbage. "Four bucks an hour."

AUGUST 29

I had been investigating what turned out to be a false rumor that the city of Chicago had renovated only the sides of the Henry Horner housing project visible from the United Center. On my way back from the ghetto, in the desolate no-man's-land created by a phalanx of police officers between the Democratic convention and the poor, I bump into John McCain. The shock of finding a Republican outside the Democratic convention is followed by a disturbingly pleasant sensation. I'm beginning to understand the war that must occur inside a fourteen-year-old boy who discovers he is more sexually attracted to boys than to girls. The longer I hang around McCain the harder it is to fight the feeling that just maybe I'm . . . Republican.

McCain has become so involved with the Dole campaign that he might as well be the candidate. His assignment for the next few days is to travel south from Chicago through Missouri and Kentucky, keeping one day ahead of the buses Clinton will ride out of town in the morning.

The idea, as I understand him, is to poison the local media against the president, which sounds like fun. Tonight he's been stirring up trouble at the TV stations covering the convention; now he is headed out to a rich Chicago suburb for a big fund-raiser. Suddenly I face a choice: to go with McCain, or to stay behind and watch Al Gore's acceptance speech. No sane person would stay behind.

On the way out of town McCain shows me a small album of photographs from the Republican convention. After Morry Taylor, Pat Buchanan, and perhaps Colin Powell, I think McCain had the most interesting experience in San Diego. After he gave his speech in prime time on Monday night he assumed he was finished; but then on Tuesday night he got the call. "It's the *night* before the nominating speech," says McCain, "and my portable phone rings. A voice says, 'McCain, will you nominate me?' It's Dole. You know, what are you going to say? 'It'd be an honor,' I say. Dole says, 'Okay, we'll be in touch.' Then he hangs up."

There are any number of things that are remarkable about this anecdote. First, that in a campaign as thickly greased with hired strangers as any in American history no one thought to drum up a nominating speech. The Dole campaign plans its trips to the bathroom four days before it goes. Yet Dole waited until the day before the event to select his nominator. Second, that the speech came off better than anything the hired strangers have done when they've been given time to plan and scheme. (Is it possible that it came off so well *because* it was spontaneous? And that Dole procrastinated precisely so that the pros wouldn't get their grubby paws on it?) And finally, that Dole chose McCain, who in the early primaries backed Phil Gramm. Some would say that this is merely another illustration of Dole's willingness to do anything to increase his chances of winning, like his selection of Kemp as his running mate. I'd prefer to think not. Dole is forever being painted as vindictive, on the basis of a handful of sound bites ("Stop lying about my record"). In fact, he has shown himself in his actions over and again to be admirably free of the quality. Last year, when McCain came out for Gramm, Dole took him aside and said not to worry: "When this thing is all over, we'll be together."

After forty-five minutes on the road McCain and I find ourselves in an enormous house in a rich neighborhood. About one hundred prosperous people mingle with drinks in their hands beneath Impressionist paintings, discussing just about everything except what has brought them together. The only people who look slightly out of place are the Illinois

Republican candidate for Senate, Al Salvi, in his middle-class polyester suit, and his wife. The slight tension is dispelled, however, when Salvi's wife accidentally knocks over a crystal lamp. "Hope you have liability insurance," someone shouts, and the crowd breaks out in knowing laughter: everyone understands liability insurance. Everyone has property to lose.

The exact words spoken are not nearly as interesting as the tone of the event, which is that of a private club gathered to discuss its affairs. At length, Salvi introduces McCain, who performs what is essentially a stand-up comedy routine written for an audience of people who make more than half a million dollars a year. "I want to thank Rich for hosting this event in his modest middle-income tract home," he begins. "The difference between us and President Clinton is that President Clinton believes that everyone should own a home. Rich and I believe that everyone should own a home like this." It turns out that McCain has done a lot of these events, and in his experience the folks are interested not in what Al Salvi has to offer America but in being humored. The host knows this, too. He goads McCain to give the crowd what it's after: "Tell them how Dole asked you to nominate him," he says. Politics—as opposed to McCain's celebrity—becomes immediately superfluous. "The good news is that Al Salvi has enough money to win this race," McCain concludes, gamely. "The bad news is that some of that money is still in your pockets."

And then he stops, without making the case why giving money to Salvi will matter to anyone. The reason is that it won't. In the lives of even big benefactors, politics occupies a ridiculously small place; campaign contributions are akin to paying the electric bills. A year or so ago I sat across a desk from hedge fund manager Michael Steinhart and watched him squeeze some major decision about Democratic Leadership Council funding between a huge trade in the stock market and a problem with one of the animals in his private zoo. The DLC—what Jesse Jackson calls "Democrats for the Leisure Class"—would hardly exist if it weren't for Steinhart. But to Steinhart it was just another of his many hobbies. It interested him, of course, but not nearly as much as his zoo. Thus people who take their power for granted share something with people who have no power: in neither is there any strong impulse to activism. The rich, like the poor, lead lives filled with foregone conclusions.

Returning to the convention hall we find the first piece of news in weeks: Clinton's confidante and chief campaign strategist, Dick Morris, permitted a prostitute to listen in on his calls to the president. Among other things, he leaked to her news of the discovery of life on Mars, six days before it was on the front page of *The New York Times*. Clinton's response to the new fact comes in the form of a short press release:

> Dick Morris is my friend, and he is a superb political strategist. I am and always will be grateful for the great contributions he has made to my campaigns, and for the invaluable work he has done for me over the last two years. (August 29, 1996)

For the first time all week I am, inexplicably, happy. And I am not alone. Real pleasure fills the faces in the convention hall as people discuss the story. This reaction is in part sadistic, no doubt, but it is also a legitimate reaction to being constantly told by people like Dick Morris that gray is white and two and two make five. No disinterested person who spends a few days in the middle of this process could view it as anything but a fraud. That much is so obvious it isn't worth saying. Lying— or "spinning" in the preferred jargon—is actually highly thought of in political circles. One of the consequences is that when some shockingly authentic event occurs people pay it more attention than they pay the last year of press releases or the $40 million infomercial in the United Center. When people are fed only what the insiders want them to know, it comes as a huge relief to find out something the insiders do not want them to know. "It's a one-day story," I hear one of them explain to a group of salivating journalists. Of course it is! When the hooker turns up on *The Tonight Show* no one is going to be the slightest bit interested. When *The Star* publishes her diary no one will read it. When it finally came out it proved not only more revealing but also, in places, more accurate than Morris's own account of his political life. Compare two extracts, describing Clinton's strategist's reaction to the Iowa primary. First Sherry Rowlands, writing in *The Star:*

> He called someone [at the White House] and said, "Yeah, I see Buchanan is at 28 [percent] and Dole is at 25. Yeah, well, we want Dole to win because he's easy to blow away. So get it in the press about his age [about how he'll be 80 by the time he's in office four years]. And point out about the problems which come with age— like physical and mental conditions. . . .

Now Morris, in his memoir, *Behind the Oval Office:* "Forbes might have come closer had he kept his wits about him. . . . After he finished a close second in Iowa, he was euphoric. But that set him up for disappointment. . . ." Buchanan finished second in Iowa. Forbes finished a distant fourth, and was hardly euphoric about it. We've come to the point where the insiders are less reliable than their prostitutes.

Later that night I receive a message from Barbara Feinman, who is still trying to ghost Morry Taylor's political manifesto. I hadn't heard from Morry since he left San Diego after two days out of sheer boredom. (*Nightline* anchor Ted Koppel made the same move, for the same reasons.) Barbara, who has just returned from three days with Morry, sounds shaken up. I'm hardly surprised.

It turns out that Morry rented a pair of trained grizzly bears—a six-hundred-pound female and a one-thousand-pound male—to deploy in yet another round of commercials for Titan Wheel. For no apparent reason he dragged Barbara to the filming. During the event, as Morry went to kick a field goal over the outstretched paws of the female grizzly, the bear was stung by a horsefly. In a flash the grizzly forgot she was tame: she rose up eight feet in the air and roared so loudly that Barbara, fifty yards away, sprinted off the field. Morry, to his credit, didn't flinch.

To add insult to insult, Morry seems to be growing tired of his manifesto, and of politics. The Grizz is returning to the wild. "You couldn't have any more questions about politics," he growled at Barbara's tape recorder at the end of three days. "I answered all the questions that exist." Barbara racked her brain for some issue of public policy that she had failed to consider and that Morry would need to address if he ever were to become president. "What about flag burning?" she asked. "Where are you on flag burning?" "If a guy wants to burn the flag," said Morry, "he can burn the flag." He pulled on his cigar, thoughtfully. "But here's the thing: If you burn the flag, then anyone who wants to do whatever they want to you can do it—there's no punishment for that."

EIGHTEEN

The Leftovers

Democratic nations awaken and foster a passion for equality which they can never entirely satisfy.

—ALEXIS DE TOCQUEVILLE

AUGUST 30

The first stop of Clinton's official 1996 campaign is Cape Girardeau, Missouri, known mainly as the place Rush Limbaugh came from. Everything is tailored for the cameras, of course, and the campaign decides with great precision what the cameras do and don't record. For example, before Clinton's first official campaign interview on the MTV bus, all other TV channels are barred from filming the president boarding or leaving the bus. The intention presumably is to make MTV's young viewers feel that Clinton is keenly interested in their problems without insulting the viewers of other channels or rousing the ire of those who loathe MTV.

Before the MTV interview Clinton stumps a rally of perhaps twenty-five thousand putative supporters. On this first day the crowd is uniformly pro-Clinton, or at least that is how it seems to the cameras' eyes. But when you wade into the middle of the rally you find a small family of Perot voters. They wave their mad signs (STOP THE U.N., GIVE US BACK OUR POWS) and shout, but no one pays them much attention—that is, until a middle-aged man grabs the U.N. sign from the woman and runs for it. "Get your hands off my wife!" shouts the man with the POW sign beside her as he takes off after the culprit. The culprit is a Clinton campaign volunteer, who keeps one step ahead of the Perot supporter until he reaches the edge of the crowd, maybe one hundred yards from

Clinton on the stump.

the podium. There they stop and argue. The Perot supporter isn't violent, but he does go on a bit noisily about his constitutional rights. "That man will grab a woman's sign, but he won't grab a man's sign," he says to me, the lone witness. As the culprit smokes a cigarette with shaking hands, the Perot man explains to me that he intends to press charges. "But that's my job," complains the culprit, a sixty-year-old construction worker who up close is more pathetic than dangerous. "I was told to take signs away—to make sure no signs came in here." Behind him the crowd is waving maybe five thousand Clinton-Gore signs.

From there a strange scene unfolds. First the police descend and separate the two men. They humor the sign stealer and interrogate the Perot supporter as if *he* were the criminal. They are followed by a young, fresh-faced Clinton campaign staffer, who whispers to the police to avoid making any kind of scene that would create media interest in the Perot man. Then the *Perot* man is dragged away from the media (me), leaving the culprit to stump for Clinton. "I'm a yellow-dog Democrat," he says, happily. "That means I'd rather vote for a yellow dog than a damn Republican." Who can blame the Perot man for thinking that everyone is out to get him? The modern need to script every last televised detail right down to a few signs in the middle of the crowd merely feeds the paranoia of those who already feel enough of it.

By the time the struggle is over, so is Clinton's speech, which was up-lifting as usual. No matter what you think of Clinton's campaign there is an undeniable joy in watching someone do something he is so good at. Traveling with Dole you are always forgetting where exactly you are; a Dole speech in Ohio is indistinguishable from a Dole speech in Califor-nia. Traveling with Clinton you are reminded of not just the state but the town and sometimes the part of the town; everywhere he goes Clinton finds some way to evoke a sense of place, almost by the by, even as he de-livers pretty much the same stump speech. ("I look out at the bean fields and the river bottom," he says in Cairo, Illinois, for example, "and I feel like I've come home.")

But the most important difference between Clinton and Dole is that Clinton is able simultaneously to address both the crowd and the televi-sion audience and make both feel as if he were speaking to them and them alone. All of the TV producers on the bus trip say the same thing: While Dole is forever mangling what are meant to be sound bites, Clin-ton generates so many crisp ten-second passages that, by the end of the day, they have little choice but to make Clinton look great and Dole look like a dope. This is maybe the most important difference between the two candidates, since most Americans will experience the campaign as no more than sixty days of juxtaposed sound bites.

The rest of the trip is more of the same, with a twist because finally something unexpected has occurred in this campaign—the Dick Morris business. In every small town two hundred journalists pour off their buses and into the crowd to quiz anyone they can get their hands on about the rapidly developing scandal. Since most people have never heard of Dick Morris or his scandal, this often involves first informing in-nocent people and their children about Morris in order to get a reaction. You really haven't seen modern campaign journalism until you've watched a twenty-eight-year-old TV producer from New York City ex-plain foot fetishism to a slightly deaf seventy-nine-year-old female voter in rural Kentucky.

In the end there is about as much sense in a journalist's traveling with Clinton as in a journalist's traveling with Dole. A serious presidential campaign is no place for anyone who cares about anything. The whole point of Clinton's campaign is to avoid making any kind of mistake, and to steal any opinion of Dole's that looks like it might be popular. "Protective imitation" is how Ralph Nader describes it, accurately. As long as the winner is going about this ruthless business of winning, the passion is elsewhere, and so am I.

SEPTEMBER 7

I've always thought of Las Vegas as the place where celebrities fly to die. In the Las Vegas airport you are coaxed down the moving walkway by Connie Stevens and Frankie Valli; on the strip downtown you are drawn to the casinos by billboards featuring Rich Little and Wayne Newton. Better than any other place in America, Las Vegas knows how to squeeze the last few drops of credibility from people, like one of those machines that combs tailings of abandoned Colorado silver mines for tiny fragments left behind by the original miners. And so, at first glance, it would seem appropriate that Las Vegas is where I have come to find Jesse Jackson.

I seek out Jackson for the same reason I seek out John McCain or Morry Taylor. There is a sense about him that there isn't about any of the principals currently running around trying to get themselves elected. He's fighting the intense pressure to be something other than who he is or say something other than what he thinks. Political passion seems always to arise out of the inchoate need to resist some force larger than oneself. That is why it is so conspicuously absent inside the two major parties. At the Democratic convention Jackson was the only speaker who gave the impression of a man engaged in a struggle with his society. He was the only speaker who shut down the TelePrompTers and just *talked.*

Jackson is in Vegas to see the Tyson-Seldon fight and, incidentally, to win back a House seat for the Democrats. Over the next couple of months he'll travel to every district that has a close race and exhort the black and poor to the polls. In some cases, he'll make the difference. Today, for instance, he's speaking to churches in West Las Vegas, where the Republican incumbent, John Ensign, won in 1994 by 1,470 votes. In a three-block strip are nine black churches inside of which are enough votes that went uncast two years ago to throw the House seat to the

Democrats. And today is Sunday. Several hundred people have crammed into the Greater New Jerusalem Church, but none of them seem to know where Jackson is—not the pastor, not the TV crews, not the Democratic candidate for Congress who was stood up an hour ago at Jackson's hotel. Half an hour after he was meant to speak, Jackson pulls up in a Cadillac. It turns out he's been visiting with Mike Tyson, whom he baptized eight years ago and now considers a good friend. It's just the first sign of the harmonic convergence of dangerous black people that is occurring today in Las Vegas.

Jackson's church performance is pretty much always the same, but, like a Buchanan stump speech, it has the force of being delivered for the first time. The reverend doesn't so much stand at the pulpit as dance back and forth on the balls of his feet, like a prizefighter. The most curious aspect of his delivery is how much *less* formal it is than his private speaking voice, which goes some way to explaining why he doesn't always translate to white audiences. I can understand him perfectly when he talks to me; when he addresses a crowd I find him incomprehensible. Even his accent plunges down the social register: "joy" becomes "jie," "hungry" becomes "ongry." Maybe he senses that at some level he's more likely to reach his poor black audience if he reaches *only* his poor black audience. The first part of the speech is a nostalgic call to arms in which he asserts that black Americans face the same struggle they always have. ("Las Vegas, Mississippi. Ain't nuthin' changed but the heat.") But even here this sounds like a stretch, and it fails to arouse the crowd as much as the second part of his speech. The second part is a plea for economic justice, and the room heats up as he delivers it:

> They say poor folk are lazy [murmurs of recognition]. Who works the hardest and the longest? Every day? ["Tell it, preacher!"] Who raises other people's children? Who changes the beds? Who vacuums the floor? Who wipes the toilets? Who cleans the slopjohns? ["It's the truth, Jessie!"] Furthermore. Furthermore. Most poor folk are not on welfare. Most poor folk work every day. They work every day. Still can't send their children to college. Most poor folk are not black [loud cheers]. They are white. And they are female. And two-thirds are children. And whether white, black, or brown, *of* the earth. And it is our moral obligation to feed all of them whether black or white or brown [crazed applause]. Misery is not black or white, it's wrong or right [standing ovation].

Watching the roof explode off the top of the church at the end of each performance, you can see that something important has happened since the primaries. An awful lot of things that less fortunate people want to hear are no longer being said by any candidate in a major party. Commencement of the full-scale war between the two parties has shut down a lot of messy little debates. The Jacksons and the Buchanans have been folded into their respective tents. You can see that Jackson is struggling against the circular logic that excludes his group from a democracy: because their concerns are not explicitly addressed, the poor don't vote; because they don't vote, their concerns are even less likely to be explicitly addressed. How this resolves itself, God only knows.

From the third and final sermon we head off to the local trauma center, where the rap artist Tupac Shakur lies in critical condition with three bullets in his chest. Rap music, oddly enough, has become the nearest thing to a political voice of the poor. Tupac says he discovered his music and its themes "when I was out there with nowhere to stay, no money," and that theme runs right through his lyrics, along with an impressive indifference to mainstream politics. When not long ago Shakur was asked in an MTV interview if "anything Bob Dole says about rap music means anything to you," his reply was far more acute than Dole's attack on him. "I don't have no disrespect towards Bob Dole," he said. "I know he don't know what he's talking about. He's just talking. Some card that somebody gave him and he's just reading off that card. But he's cute. He's my grandfather." Tupac was actually trying to say something nice about Dole, which makes what he did say all the more withering. ("They speak the language of the other half," says Jackson about the gangsta rappers from the front seat of our car. "They speak the language of the hopeless. They are in the valley of dried bones—of recycled pain.")

It is the second time in two years that someone has tried to kill Tupac, and the second time that no one saw a thing, even though Tupac travels with bodyguards. We arrive at the trauma center to find it more or less empty: a handful of indigent kids, a couple of policemen, a young white woman who introduces herself as Tupac's personal assistant, and a businesslike representative of Death Row Records, the company that posted $1.4 million in bail to spring Shakur from jail last October. The phone in the hospital waiting room rings: it's one of the three men who plausibly can claim to be Tupac's father. He's calling from jail.

Not long after Jackson is promised entry to the hospital room, four men from the Nation of Islam arrive. They look sinister, though it takes me a moment to figure out why: it's this business of making uniforms out of clothing that isn't designed to be worn uniformly. They wear well-pressed dark suits, shiny black shoes, and clip-on bow ties. They all have the same haircut—close cropped with a part cut into the side. They all wear the same cologne. They walk and stand in loose formation, with the most senior in the lead. From there it's all a game of whispers: Jackson whispers to Death Row Records; Death Row Records whispers to Farrakhan's people; Farrakhan's people whisper to Jackson. There is some question about who gets to see Tupac first, which is strange since Tupac is in a coma, blissfully unaware of the struggle for his political value.

There's no point in even trying to pretend I understand what is going on. But one thing is clear: everyone with ambition to speak for the black community wants a piece of Tupac Shakur. As poor young black men drift away from mainstream political activity and toward sheer alienation, a kind of displacement occurs that leaves official spokesmen like Jackson and even Farrakhan high and dry.

From the hospital we visit the boxing promoter Don King at his home, completing in a single day a kind of hat trick of black culture. Once again, more whispers: while Jackson goes inside King's phony stone mansion I am left to wait for an hour in the car gazing up at the dozens of ersatz-gold light fixtures and then down at the limousine running lights at the base of the steps. I seek consolation in the thought that the world would not be quite right if Don King had good taste. When the reverend finally emerges, King is with him in baggy brown shorts and a sloppy joe shirt. His hair is flattened down on his head, belying his oft-repeated story that it has stood straight up ever since he met God. Like Tupac Shakur, he wears not one but two gold watches, one on each wrist. An absurd display of wealth, on the one hand; on the other a funny parody of mainstream success culture: If you are going to turn your wristwatch into a status symbol, why have only one?

It isn't until we arrive at the airport that I have a moment alone with Jesse Jackson. I want to ask him how it feels to strike the sort of compromise he has had to strike this year. (Clinton's genius has been his ability to push the left to within one inch of its breaking point without pushing it over.) After Clinton sandbagged him in 1992 with a speech to the Rainbow Coalition about rap lyrics, Jackson told his biographer, Marshall Frady: "I can maybe work with him, but I know now who he is, what he is. There's *nuthin'* he won't do. He's immune to shame. Move past all the nice posturing and get really down there in him, you find absolutely nothing . . . nothing but an appetite."

I want to show Jackson the passage, and ask him about it and one other, concerning Al Gore and their respective 1988 presidential bids. Last year, speaking to a group of black ministers in Los Angeles, Jackson aired out his views:

> Y'all know who my *real* hero is? 'Course there's King out there, he has his place. And Gandhi, him too. But my real hero is Albert Gore. That's right, Al Gore. Father a senator—mine a janitor. He went to Harvard—I went to a little black college in North Carolina, A&T. Albert was elected to the U.S. Senate—I was just in the Movement, worked with Breadbasket and PUSH in Chicago. Then, in 1988, I beat him in Iowa, a state ninety-eight percent white. He said it was 'cause of liberals and farmers. So I beat him in New Hampshire; he said it was because he was off campaigning in the South. So I beat him in the South on Super Tuesday. He said Dukakis had split his support. I beat him then in Illinois, in Michigan; he said he wasn't really tryin'. I beat him then in New York; said he ran out of money. But now, here I am this afternoon, talkin' to y'all in this church in South-Central L.A.—and he's vice president of the United States. How'd he manage to do that? *Amazin'*. Al Gore's my real hero, bein' able to do something like that. They attackin' affirmative action now 'cause of what they call racial preferences. Preferences? Racial preference? Don't be comin' to me talkin' about racial preference.

He's looking at me with superhuman indifference as I produce the book from my bag and flip to the first passage. We've spent much of the past hour racing through the airport a step ahead of the hounds. His plane is just about finished boarding, and I have time for this one question. But just then a pair of airline employees interrupt with a demand for more autographs. Jackson takes way too long to supply them, and I can tell what's going to happen next. He's going to hand back their pens, turn to me, and say, "Gotta go." Then he'll vanish down the jetway. Which he does.

The poor people in my Manhattan neighborhood long ago discovered workfare: those who remain on welfare supplement their stipends by collecting aluminum cans and glass bottles and returning them to the receptacle at the Key Food on the corner, which pays them a nickel a throw. The freelance recycling business has become the leading street industry in New York, and for all I know the rest of the country: all over the city you now find people—most of whom are homeless—pushing shopping carts overflowing with cans and bottles. Around the hub of maybe sixty receptacles on the sides of Manhattan supermarkets swirl thousands of poor people who have discovered the free market.

At any given moment on my little corner you can find several dozen men and women of all ages and all races lined up to deposit their hauls a can at a time. But the line is clearly subordinate to the secondary market in cans and bottles that forms twenty yards down the block. The center of all action here is a slim young black man who for the past few months I've studiously avoided. He's always standing amid ridiculously tall piles of giant clear garbage bags filled with cans and bottles; by midnight the sidewalk is completely blocked; occasionally the police show up and move him. It never occurred to me that he might find me more dangerous than I find him. But when I walk across the street to introduce myself, he, together with two of his customers, jumps up in terror. The two others sprint down the street and vanish around the corner. The black man packs up his things as fast as he can.

"You with the IRS, man?" he asks, frantically.

I explain I'm not and hand over my business card, which he holds at a distance as if it might bite him on the nose. At first he's pretty sure that I am either an undercover cop or a tax collector; then he caves and believes my story. "This is NYC," he says, when I ask what on earth he's doing with what looks to be about five thousand cans and bottles. "You gotta survive by any means. *This* is by any means."

The Key Food grocery store does not really seek the recycling business, it turns out. Its machines dispense only about two hundred dollars a day, or enough to compensate the street people for only four thousand cans and bottles. The gap between supply and demand is filled by Rob— the black man's name—who sits at the center of a small economy of poor people premised on recycling. He buys the precious discarded cans and bottles for half what Key Food pays, sorts them into piles—Coke with Coke, Pepsi with Pepsi, Bud with Bud, and so on—and sells them to a Russian in a pickup truck for a nickel each.

The dizzying string of middlemen in the recycling business calls to mind the brokerage industry; each can seems to pass through four different hands on its way to reuse. Indeed, a few hours with Rob and you can see how finely attuned to market logic homeless people have to be. Rob commutes forty-five minutes from a small apartment in Harlem and works the streets twelve to fourteen hours. On a good day he can earn two hundred dollars, which implies, at a spread of two and a half cents a can, that he trades eight thousand cans a day. He supplements his recycling income with a side business in the amazing assortment of goods that homeless people find on the street: today his cart holds a Walkman, two pillows, a desk chair, and some empty cigar boxes. He also conducts a brisk trade in Pepsi points, the stickers on the side of Pepsi bottles that can be redeemed for various products. An elderly Vietnamese woman offers Rob a couple of stickers for which he is willing to pay two cents a point (she refuses), since Pepsi points are useful only in bulk. The price goes up the larger the quantity for sale. "My brother got two thousand points," he says. "He's holding on for someone who'll pay five cents a point."

Rob buys sacks of cans and bottles off homeless people as he explains the ins and outs of the trade. He treats his customers—most of whom, he says, have drug problems—politely and honestly. "I'm looking out for the poor people," he says, "because I represent the poor and unknown." His customers reward him by refusing to deal with anyone who tries to steal his turf. If another middleman seeks to move into the Key Food collection area on, say, a day that Rob is sick, the homeless people who collect the cans on the street will simply live with their cans until Rob returns. "But then you got guys trying to steal each other's cans when they sleeping," says Rob. "Man, you know things is bad when you got people trying to steal *cans* from each other."

Rob's view of the government is curiously similar to Steve Forbes's: most of what the government does, he feels, just gets in people's way. The IRS is forever disrupting the can-recycling trade, for instance. He was on welfare for a bit but got off because the time it took to collect his check wasn't worth it. He now views the welfare office chiefly as a good place to collect discarded cans and bottles. Rob finds the minimum wage laughably low—how could he ever feed his four-year-old son on five bucks an hour? "People coming by and saying, man, 'He's a bum, he homeless,'" he says. "Man, I'm not homeless. I *was* homeless. But if they come into my little place they be shocked at what I got. Fifteen boxes of records. 'Damn! He got all that shit.' My mixer alone cost four hundred dollars."

Even worse than the IRS is the government's continuous threat to interfere with his true love, music. "Truthfully," says Rob, "I don't want to work for no man. I am deeply into hip-hop. I want to have my own production company. Rap is my heart and soul and where I come from. They tryin' to stop it but it's real." He waves his hand over the heads of three elderly Korean ladies busy counting out cans on the sidewalk. "It's *here*." Rap music is Rob's main political issue. Right now he favors Clinton only because "he ain't so much like Bob Dole and them trying to stop my rap music." If his support is not deep it is because he feels Clinton is no longer for the poor. "Ain't no one for the poor anymore," he says. "I just signed up independent. I'm going to vote for the person who's gonna be for *my* people."

NINETEEN

The Fall

Dole's poll numbers are like a fever that won't break. Very briefly, during the Republican convention, he closed the seventeen-point gap with Clinton. But then it widened back out again and stayed there. Even to his friends it is pretty clear that Dole will lose; it may even be clear to Dole. But if he loses he will lose in a spirit different than Buchanan, or Morry, or Ralph Nader, or Alan Keyes. His loss won't resemble the loss McCain suffered in the running-mate sweepstakes. He's going to lose having made all the decisions one must make to win. He'll lose ugly.

Late last night as the Dole plane flew back once again to California, Dole left his seat at the front, walked back half a dozen rows, and stopped. For several strange minutes Dole just stood there in the gloaming, gazing toward the back of the plane, saying nothing. Since everyone else was asleep, or seemed to be, Dole probably thought he was unobserved. The one staffer who looked up and saw Dole standing there was at first alarmed at the sight of his candidate so seemingly null and void. But then Dole cocked one dyed black eyebrow in the darkness, and the staffer thought: He looks exactly like Dan Ackroyd imitating Bob Dole.

Probably there is a moment in every not-very-closely-fought presidential campaign where the loser thinks: Here is what they'll talk about when they look back on this race. Here is what they'll point to when they say that my losing was inevitable. Here is my inexorable fate, in a nutshell. Today after his midnight stroll Dole gave them the moment. First he went out and gave a speech in which he referred to the Los Angeles Dodgers as "the Brooklyn Dodgers." Then he walked up onto a stage in Chico, California, reached over a railing to touch the hand of a small boy, and fell over. He dropped four feet onto a photographer and landed flat on his back, where a Reuters photographer named Rick Wilking promptly snapped off half a dozen rounds of one of the most painful sights you've ever seen. To all the world, it appeared as if Dole had been shot.

Of course, Dole got up immediately, and for the next few hours made a lot of good jokes about his fall. And, of course, the rented strangers did their best to explain why Dole's fall was actually the best thing that had ever happened to the campaign. "This should put to rest the age question once and for all," Nelson Warfield said. "If Bob Dole can take a tumble like that and hop right back up on his feet and deliver a great speech, he's strong enough to be president and go a couple of rounds with Mike Tyson, too." And I almost bought it. But then I remembered something from the primary. At first I thought I was just imagining it, and it took the better part of a night of digging through old notes. But at length I found what I was looking for. On March 11, 1996, Dole was asked why he thought Lamar Alexander was so slow in quitting the race. "I think Lamar believes I'm going to fall off the podium somewhere and he'll be there for the last rites," he said. "Not going to happen."

The reason this particular metaphor occupied Dole's mind was that he had just spent two and a half months worrying about just this event. Over and again on the New Hampshire snow the rented strangers had told him: *Whatever you do, don't fall.* If he fell, they said, he would look old. And if he looked old, he would lose. And if he lost, well . . .

SEPTEMBER 27

I'm too old to cry.

— GEORGE McGOVERN,
in his concession speech, November 7, 1972

Once, during a brief stint working for a dealer of Old Master paintings, I was assigned to show pictures to Thomas Hoving, the former director of the Metropolitan Museum of Art. Hoving made a religion of first impressions. He'd stand with his back to me at one end of the showroom, staring into the wall, as I set the picture on the easel. When it was ready he'd swivel like a gunfighter and virtually shout the first three words that popped into his head: *"Sublime! . . . Tactile! . . . Fake!"*

When I met George McGovern today I thought of Hoving for the first time in years. Maybe because McGovern himself is sort of a living work of art. Or maybe it was just the noise of the adjectives—*Wise!* . . . *Decent!* . . . *Real!*—going off in my head. The man who drove Dr. Hunter S. Thompson mad with his inability to get himself across on the stump makes an overwhelming first impression, especially when you catch him on location. His office here in Washington is a kind of stage set crammed with mementos: a portrait bust of Kennedy, McGovern presidential campaign posters, pictures of McGovern with (I almost wrote "other") presidents, photographs of McGovern's daughter, whose death after years of alcoholism McGovern recently chronicled in his sad book, *Terry.* The effect is talismanic, as if keeping these objects around allows him to control and redefine the original experience. It is the same impulse that leads a man to write a memoir or to speak to young people who have no memory of distant events, McGovern's two principal occupations these days.

Once we are seated across a coffee table from each other, McGovern offers me what amounts to a loser's tour of presidential campaigns. "I have to live with the knowledge that, not only did I lose the election, but I lost it to the most discredited man ever to occupy the White House," he once wrote, and you can see how much work has gone into managing this knowledge. "You feel sort of personally repudiated," he says now. "It's not really true. People love you. But you have to grapple with that. In some respects it is like a death in the family." Maybe for this reason McGovern has formed what sounds suspiciously like a support group with other losing presidential candidates. "I ran into Walter Mondale," he says, ". . . what was it . . . sometime around 1989. He said to me, 'George, you are the only person alive who can answer this question: How long does it take before it quits hurting after you've lost forty-nine of fifty states?' I said, 'Well, Walter, I'll let you know when I get there.'" Both Gerald Ford and Barry Goldwater are now McGovern's friends. ("After I lost," says McGovern, "Barry wrote me a letter that said, 'Dear George, If you must lose, lose *big.*' That letter gave me the first big lift I had after the election.")

I decide to come clean, as delicately as possible. As Clinton races around seducing everyone he meets, Dole seems bent mainly on keeping his tan. The rented strangers say that he was not injured in the fall, but clearly something has broken inside him. The long weekends lounging outside his sterile condominium in Florida are punctuated only briefly during the week by light day trips on the East Coast. His staffers tell me that Dole plans to fly to San Diego *three* days before the second debate, on October 19, "to adjust to the time zone." In reading about the McGovern campaign, I was struck by the similarity of his reaction to incipient political disaster. "At a street corner rally in Philadelphia that [last] morning, George McGovern had hoarsely spoken his favorite words from Isaiah," wrote Timothy Crouse:

> "They that wait upon the Lord shall renew their strength. They shall mount up with wings as eagles, they shall run and not be weary; they shall walk and not faint." A number of reporters had bitten their lips to keep from crying. For George McGovern grew stronger and calmer as his staffers grew more desolate. The reporters could not help being awed by his incredible serenity.

"Do presidential candidates quit?" I ask.

"I didn't," McGovern says, then quick as a flash vanishes into the past. "It is discouraging, but I never got demoralized. The news story would be that George McGovern took his failing campaign to California in a desperate attempt to revive his political career, but that's not what you see. I can still see those hands by the thousands and those faces and those tears and those cheers. And that pulls you up." And then, interestingly, he segues into his view of Dole and his campaign. "He's better than people know," he says. "He'd make a fine president. But his campaign appears to be frozen—it's almost as if he were frozen in time."

On June 11 Dole spoke his final words on the floor of the Senate. The speech was a rambling but moving collection of memories, one of which concerned McGovern. It is worth quoting as much for what it says about the way Dole processes his experience as it does about McGovern:

> I have also been proud to be involved in nutrition programs. Somebody mentioned that earlier today. I remember working with Senator McGovern on that, and there was a conservative article saying I cannot be a conservative because I know George McGovern. I think George McGovern is a gentleman and has always been a gentleman. But we worked together on Food Stamps. I will confess, when I made my first tour with George McGovern, I said, "This guy is running for president?" I was not convinced. There were a lot of skeptics in this Chamber; probably some on each side. You cannot have truer motives. It is always something

political. But, after being on that trip about two or three days, I changed my mind.

Although it reads like the rantings of a lunatic, it is just Dole thinking aloud to himself, as usual, one sentence at a time. Still, you can't help feeling that the whole purpose of the passage was to give Dole a chance to say that George McGovern is a gentleman; that is how McGovern interpreted the remarks, and he is clearly still touched by them. "It came to me completely as a surprise," he says. "Dole never called me and told me he was going to do it."

Then McGovern remembers something else that, he thinks, might explain Dole's tribute. "I saw him fall once," he says. "On the tracks of the shuttle under the Senate. He lit on that withered arm of his. He was obviously in pain; his body was twitching. I helped him get up. You know when you lose the use of an arm it throws off your balance. *You can't break the fall.* And while I was helping him I said, 'Oh, Bob, this really is *too* bad.' And he looked at me in a way I hadn't seen. There was genuine friendship in his eyes."

Everyone who has run for president seems to have some special connection to the others. As McGovern walks me to the door I tell him I saw him on television at the Democratic convention, sitting in the rafters eating out of a bucket of popcorn with Michael Dukakis. "What'd you talk about?" I asked. "Oh," he says, "how Clinton is so much smarter than we are. How well he's masked some of his liberal views. . . ."

SEPTEMBER 30

DUKAKIS: *I hope many of you will go into politics and public service.*
  It is a noble profession, a noble profession.
AUDIENCE: *'92! '92! '92! '92! '92! '92!*

—MICHAEL DUKAKIS,
in his concession speech, November 8, 1988

The outside of the dun-brick building at Northeastern University is lined with dustbins while the inside is lined with professors of political science, one of whom is Michael Dukakis. The man himself occupies the corner office on the third floor, and as I walk to it I am faintly embarrassed for him, thinking, No, this couldn't be where he has ended up. But it is.

239

"Where is his main office?" I ask his (part-time) assistant as the strains of Dukakis's voice emanate from the open door a few feet away.

"This *is* his main office," she says.

I let that settle in. There is no indication that I am in the right place except for a plaque, tucked at the back of a cluttered bookcase:

JAW JOINTS AND ALLIED MUSCULU-SKELETAL DISORDER
FOUNDATION WISHES TO HONOR MICHAEL DUKAKIS

"Do a lot of journalists come to interview him?" I ask.

"No . . . not very often," she says. Then she adds, "Sometimes they call."

That fact lingers in the air, begging for elaboration.

"Because, you know, this time of year they want him on some of the shows."

"*Hi, howahya?*" It's him. In the flesh. With his hand out. Not for the first time since I started doing this job I take pleasure in finding a man who almost went all the way who is shorter than I am. A *lot* shorter. I wonder if maybe America wouldn't be well served by a short president, a man we could all look down upon. It might lower expectations.

I follow Dukakis into his office, where he asks me what I take in my coffee. "Just milk," I say, prompting him to grab for a pair of mugs and a carton of nondairy creamer. "My life is nothing but a bunch of powders these days," he says, then takes off down the hall to make the coffee, leaving me alone in his corner office with a few long rows of books about health care.

A number of thoughts pass through my brain, but the one that sticks is: He hasn't cashed in. Up and down K Street former politicians are growing fat selling off pieces of their prestige. Dukakis, if he wished, could have installed himself in a fancy office with a fancy salary. And yet he chooses to be here. The effect could not have been more powerful if he were wearing a hair shirt.

"Okay," he says, handing over the powdered coffee. "Tell me about yourself." I do, sort of, concluding with some vague reason for being in his office.

"*If* I knew anything about presidential campaigns I wouldn't be here," he says, cheerfully. "I'd be finishing eight successful years in the White House."

I tell him that the first thing I don't understand is how when people look back on a campaign's defining moments they are always pointing to ridiculously trivial events. Just yesterday, for instance, *The New York Times* ran a piece saying that Dukakis lost the debates when he shook hands with Bush and showed the audience just how much shorter he was. "Absolutely ridiculous," he says. "That had nothing to do with anything, in my judgment." But then I mention Willie Horton and the picture of him in the tank. "Bush was in a tank three times," he says, defensively, neglecting to consider that Bush never was compared to Rocky the Flying Squirrel.

It's hard to think of a man whose life was turned upside down by a campaign as Dukakis's was in 1988. He didn't just lose; he was destroyed. When he came home the next day he found that his state hated him as governor and his wife was swallowing diet pills. And yet the day after his loss—which Dukakis thought was entirely due to Bush's nasty campaign—Dukakis was asked if he could forgive James Baker, Bush's campaign manager. "Mr. Dukakis replied with a rare touch of humor," ran the account in *The New York Times*. "'I believe in the redemption of souls,' he said." Back in 1988 I was still an ordinary, well-adjusted person with only a passing interest in presidential campaigns. But even then that phrase got my attention, both for its felicity and for its sangfroid. Is it possible to lose so terribly, I wondered, and not feel a thing?

I keep trying to take the conversation in the direction of Phil Donahue—Let me feel your pain!—while Dukakis keeps dragging it back to the Issues. "My preference was to come up with a national version of the Hawaii health system," he says, typically. "Did you know that Hawaii is the only state with universal care?" I didn't. The man is full of passion. It's just that he lacks passion for ordinary things, the sort of things that inspire passion in ordinary people.

The phone rings; Dukakis quickly picks it up. "What? We need a disk for you guys?" Dukakis is saying. "Okay, okay. We're going to try to get it for you." I feel almost embarrassed watching this. I am staring at a man who believes that the only thing between him and the White House was a decent strategy for defusing attack ads, and he is answering his own phone. It occurs to me that former political big shots scramble for the golden phones of K Street not only for the money but also to disguise the fall they have taken—so that they don't have to be pitied by assholes like me who come to place flowers on their grave.

"Have you read that little book over there?" he asks, pointing to his well-thumbed copy of *Putting People First*, Clinton's manifesto from the last campaign. "You should read it. I reread it from time to time." I ponder the implications of anyone not reading but *re*reading *Putting People First* as I pull the copy down and page through it. The chapter headings are checked in pencil, though there is only one passage marked, under the section about energy efficiency on page 98: "Increase U.S. reliance on natural gas—which is inexpensive, clean-burning and abundant, and can reduce carbon dioxide emissions—by issuing an executive order to purchase natural gas–powered vehicles for the federal automotive fleet, following Texas's lead."

The phone rings again. This time when he hangs up I am ready with a question. He had learned all about the importance of responding to attack ads in 1978, when he lost the governorship of Massachusetts, so why wasn't he ready for them when he ran for president? "That's a good question," he says. "I can't answer that question." Not only does he think he could have been president, he doesn't know why he didn't do what it would have taken to be president. That's the sort of interpretation of events that could kill a man. But it seems barely to have registered in Dukakis.

"Poor Dole," he says, suddenly. "Once you win the nomination there's a walling off that takes place. I found it frustrating. Anytime I wanted to talk to constituents, buy a suit, buy groceries, I was walled off by the Secret Service. Clinton was asked what he thought about living in the White House and he described it as the 'crown jewel of the federal corrections system.' It drove me *up a wall.* I look at Dole and I think it's *killing* him. Then all of a sudden you fall off a platform *and it becomes a three-day story. And it becomes a metaphor for your entire campaign.*"

The phone rings *again;* again Dukakis picks it up. "Hello, who is this? No. They *canceled* the lunch."

Although I know I am wasting my time and his, I ask Dukakis if he ever loses sleep over his loss. Of course he says he doesn't. "Look, I had my shot and I blew it." The amazing thing is: I believe him. The preternatural rationality that kept Michael Dukakis from being president enables him not to dwell on his loss. If there is a less useful role model for Dole—or for that matter for Clinton—I can't think of who he is.

TWENTY

Experiments in Higher Living

Then Jackie Kemp came on and we seemed to collapse, offensively and defensively. The final score was 50–20. It was the most humiliating moment of my life. I had never lost a game by that kind of score, even in high school.

—O. J. SIMPSON,
The Education of a Rich Rookie, 1970

SEPTEMBER 23 AND 24

I can't say how or why, but word arrives that if I travel with Jack Kemp he will see me. All I can say is that, the first time since the end of the primaries, a real live candidate has promised to give me an interview in the flesh. Neither Dole nor Clinton is granting interviews to anyone other than the editorial boards of the big newspapers and a few important television people. (Word spread later that Dole was hiding out of fear that he would be asked about a mistress he kept in Washington during the early 1970s. This story was never confirmed.) And so this is the closest I am likely to get to what they call Power. Power is not what it used to be, however. Mainly it means holding a job that is widely regarded as important or prestigious. The likelihood of this happening to Kemp is rapidly dwindling to zero, which is one of the reasons he's happy to see me.

Immediately I land in Kemp's press pool, chiefly because no one else wants to be; no one else wants to be because tagging along with the running mate of a presidential candidate who trails by sixteen points with forty-three days to go is not journalism but a death watch. When I ask one of the five other print journalists on the Kemp plane what my pool

243

responsibilities are, he says, "Normally you'd have to come back and tell everyone else what happened, but since no one gives a fuck what happened you don't have to do anything." So it is more for spiritual reasons than professional ones that I stand watch in the lobby of an old hotel in Grand Rapids, Michigan, waiting for Kemp to emerge from his fundraiser. It's closed to the press, as the fund-raisers usually are, to help the donors believe that they are being told secrets.

Despite the general indifference to Kemp, he is actually the major candidate most worth listening to, mainly because he takes lots of little risks and occasionally says something he isn't supposed to, as when he reminds crowds that just a few months ago he endorsed Steve Forbes. His endorsement of Forbes was another risk. And though it was widely decried as kooky by the insider political culture it was actually a brave, principled stand. (Precisely because it was decried as kooky.) Kemp likes to wing it. Although he is cast as a man of ideas, he is essentially a creature of high emotion. The enthusiasm that leads Kemp's tongue to run away with his brain is so infectious that it seems churlish to stop and ask what he means when he talks about the need for prosperity in "Second, Third, and Fourth World countries," or when he says that "we are living in the most exciting country, *the most exciting millennium,* in the history of mankind," or when he promises "we're going to cut your taxes *and* balance the budget."

At length Kemp leaves the fund-raiser and joins his motorcade. We're meant to head straight to some factory, but instead at Kemp's insistence we stop at the Gerald Ford Museum, which doubles as a repository of White House memorabilia. It is so chockablock with curios that it could be used to illustrate any point about presidential politics a candidate might care to make. Soon enough Kemp is standing without interest between Dolley Madison's ice-cream dispenser and William Henry Harrison's cradle. "Where's Lincoln?" he asks the curator. The curator points to a portrait on the wall. Kemp quotes from memory: "'If I had another face do you think I'd wear this one?' That's what Lincoln said. He had a great, great, great sense of humor."

Then Kemp's eyes pick out a display devoted to the Grant administration. "U. S. Grant," he says. "He did a lot of good things. He also lowered taxes." The curator nods, uncertainly. "Where's Kennedy?" asks Kemp. "Did he raise taxes or lower taxes?" Then he laughs and answers his own question. "He cut the capital gains rate from forty-nine to twenty-eight percent." "And what happened to the revenues?" asks

Joanne Kemp, by his side. "Revenues went up!" bellows Kemp. And then we're headed for the exit, with a brief stop at a display case celebrating Gerald Ford's high-school football career.

"Football," says Kemp, "is the training ground for . . ." He can't find the word he's looking for.

"Life?" suggests the curator.

"Life," says Kemp. "Absolutely. Well said."

It turns out that football and taxes are the only two certainties of life on the Kemp plane. In two days Kemp speaks at a hospital in Ohio, a lumberyard in Kentucky, a chair manufacturer in Michigan, and a police officers' association in New York. At each appearance, someone in the crowd presents him with a football to sign; invariably Kemp takes it and motions for the person to go deep. He then completes the pass as the crowd cheers. Often his first action upon taking the stage is to motion twice with his throwing arm as if he is hurling a bomb. He waves to the crowd by holding both hands out flat and wiggling his fingers in a fashion that is recognizably masculine only because quarterbacks do it in the middle of the game to get the coach's attention. He works the rope line not by shaking hands but by grabbing at them, the way players clasp onto each other in a huddle.

The speeches themselves rely even more heavily on the football metaphor—to the point where it is hard to see where the football stops and the politics start. He introduces his wife as "the only woman in history to be wife and mother to three pro quarterbacks," except when he introduces her as "the real quarterback of the Kemp family." (Only male politicians who clearly have control of their wives can get away with the pretense that their wives are actually in charge.) To a standing-room-only crowd at the chair-manufacturing company Kemp gives his most ambitious speech. Twenty minutes of hot rhetoric builds up to this:

> I close with this thought. Let's see, how many years ago? Nineteen fifty-seven. Wow. Almost forty years ago. I started my professional career with the Detroit Lions as their third-string quarterback. And they said I would never make it. I came from the wrong schools. I was too short. I threw too hard. I was too optimistic. I didn't have it. I tell you what. I never gave up. I got traded, sold, hurt, cut, booed, knocked out, but I never gave up. Bob Dole in his career never gave up. . . . Bob Dole and Jack Kemp are fighters. We believe in the American Dream.

Kemp claims a special affinity with blacks from his experience of playing ball with them. He implies a special understanding of business from his experience of being a team leader. His ability to pull this off has nothing to do with his actual experience of blacks and business (he was the whitest guy on the Bills, for instance, and he blew his football money on bad investments). It depends on the desire of blacks to believe in the myth of the white guy who plays sports, and is therefore "in touch," and of businessmen to believe that Kemp's football experience counts as business experience. I'm not sure about the black experience, but never in history have businesspeople been so prone to making this little leap of faith in football, as you can see wherever Kemp goes. At its moment of supremacy, commerce seems to be more in need than ever before of exciting metaphors to keep everyone interested in it. Could a similar phenomenon be at work in the Kemp campaign—his politics are so inert that people would much rather hear him talk football?

The starting point for almost all of Kemp's political beliefs is a single fixed idea, that lower tax rates will unleash so much economic growth that the government will end up with more tax revenues. Like most of the supply-siders Kemp is deeply sincere; his fierce loyalty to the supply-side doctrine in the face of all the evidence from the Reagan years is a mystery better solved by psychiatry than by economics. In Steve Forbes the impulse toward the supply-side religion seems to be repression—a desire to avoid grappling with objective reality. In Kemp the impulse seems to be expression—a need to get all fired up about an inherently rational subject. Whatever else it is, supply-side economics is relentlessly upbeat: all of our problems have a simple solution, and in solving them everyone gets more, forever. It is as if Kemp chose his economic theory not by its plausibility but by his ability to sell it in a language he speaks. ("Did you ever see anybody so enthusiastic about capitalism?" he shouts to the crowds.) In Kemp's hands economics ceases to be the dismal science concerned with allocating scarce means to alternative ends and becomes . . . football!

In New York I am led with other journalists to the thirty-eighth floor of the downtown Marriott. There we stand rigidly outside the door, like patients waiting for their booster shots, until Kemp's press aide comes to fetch us one by one. Interviews with national candidates are not usually designed to convey information or understanding but to strip the journalist of his complaint that the candidate is hiding, which he always is. I have been offered five minutes with Kemp—as I was offered five minutes with Gore. I am pondering the absurdity of trying to glean anything from anyone in five minutes when the journalist before me tells me that he only has two and a half—150 seconds.

Once my five minutes begin, I introduce myself. "You're the famous one from *The New Republic,*" Kemp says. But before I have a chance to fully absorb that notion, he adds, "The one who wrote that Kemp never had a new idea in his life. Well, you're right, I never had a new idea in my life."

"That's Michael Kinsley," I say. "I've never written about you."

"Oh," he says, "a tabula rasa." Just then Joanne Kemp comes in. "Joanne," he says, "this is Michael Kelly of *The New Republic.*"

"Michael Lewis."

"Right, Michael Lewis," he says, just as enthusiastically as if I had been Michael Kelly or even Michael Kinsley.

In his eyes I can see the lights of the stadium clock. Four and a half minutes. "What exactly," I ask, "is a Fourth World country?"

"A *Third* World country," says Kemp, "is a country that is trying to develop. A *Fourth* World country is a country that is so poor that it doesn't even have a *chance* to develop thanks to stupid IMF policies and . . ."

The clock is winding down; I have to cut him off before he eats up more of it with a disquisition on the international financial order. I ask how he became interested in economic ideas. He majored in physical education at Occidental College; it's a long way from there to econometrics. Kemp explains that he had "an epiphany" after he heard JFK speak on behalf of lower taxes.

Time for one more play: a Hail Mary. "If the Reagan years didn't do it, what evidence would dissuade you from your belief that lower tax rates will lead to more tax revenues?" I ask. Kemp explains that the Reagan years *proved* his theory and that he and Dole are now engaged in finding the precise point where the Laffer curve bends backward. (He is anxious that I not say he wants bigger tax cuts than Bob Dole, which until now hasn't occurred to me.) He uses not only the same logic but the same words he used in 1980. Nothing new has gotten inside his head. Kemp is the classic B student, but with a twist: he's also the star quarterback. After the grades are passed out he can visit the headmaster to argue his case. If he is charming enough, and a good enough quarterback, he'll probably persuade the headmaster to fire the teacher.

Afterward I went back and dug out O. J. Simpson's memoir of his first year with the Buffalo Bills, which was also Kemp's last. The beef about Kemp as a quarterback was his inability to adapt to new situations; the problem came to a head with the Bills. As O. J. wrote:

> When you have veterans on the line and a rookie in the backfield all saying that we should run and the quarterback still keeps throwing passes, it doesn't exactly qualify him as a strong leader. Jack was a heck of a nice guy and a pleasure to talk to—but I was beginning to wonder whether he really heard what you said to him. Telling him I had been open on pass patterns had been like talking to a door. . . . Even Dan Durragh, the rookie quarterback who had been in street clothes on the sidelines, had commented on how Jack often had his mind made up before he went back to pass.

OCTOBER 1

The Dole campaign treats me so oddly when I arrive this morning, fresh from my visit with Jack Kemp, for yet another trip to Cleveland that I find myself looking back over my shoulder to see if there's some other Michael they're talking to. That I have a name is in itself unusual—normally I'm just checked off the cargo list as *The New Republic,* that is, another magazine writer who together with his readership can safely be ignored. But this morning I am carrying my new Sony Digital Super SteadyShot Handycam DCR-VX1000, a palmable gray box that crack technicians from ABC spent nearly an hour teaching me to use. Like the Dole campaign's facing disaster after the Iowa primary, I've decided that the only chance I have of winning (of breaking through the artifice) is to play dirty.

Yesterday, I mentioned in passing to a Dole staffer that "I might do some shooting for *Nightline* tomorrow," as if I were the sort of person who did shooting for *Nightline* all the time. Now a Dole campaign worker named Charlie is standing over me like an old friend. "Hi, Michael," he says. "Good to see you again . . . you know you're not allowed to film on the plane." When I step onto the plane a second Dole staffer tells me the same thing. As I take my seat across the coffee table from a radio lady, a third Dole worker stops by and stresses the point. Apparently, the place where the campaign television journalist spends the vast majority of his time is considered outside the bounds of television journalism.

Before all these warnings, it had never occurred to me to film on the Dole plane. Now it does. Just before takeoff I stand up and take my first shot. A fat cameraman on his way to the toilet squeezes past a skinny stewardess, and I have him in my crosshairs. "You're not supposed to do that!" a voice shrieks out at me. It's the radio lady, playing narc. Charlie appears beside my seat to remind me of the Rule. He does a nice job of not being upset.

The day unfolds uneventfully (Dole gives a speech in a gym) except for my peculiar new relationship with the Dole campaign staff. Normally I have to set off a flare to get their attention; today, Charlie takes the seat behind me on the bus and for the rest of the day never seems to be very far away. Whatever they think I might do, I don't. By the time the rally starts I have busted the sound mechanism, lost the earplugs, and run out of batteries. I put the camera to one side. Charlie vanishes. But then we head back to the plane and a fresh battery. Which brings us to the shrimp episode.

Once we settle into our seats I set about trying to fix all the parts of the camera I'd busted. In order not to offend the Dole people, I decide to test the thing on what I figure is a declassified object—a large plate of cold mottled shrimp that has been laid on the table between me and a pair of radio reporters. I hunker right over the little buggers so that the ABC technicians will see I've absorbed what they taught me about not giving in to the temptation of the zoom. But the moment I'm in place the radio woman shrieks out to the Dole staff and makes to cover the shrimp with a sheet of paper. "It's okay," I say, gently. "I'm just seeing if this thing still works." I keep shooting for a good five seconds. Then I put the camera away.

Suddenly, a Dole lady is in my face, teeth gritted, breath blowing. *"We told you seven times not to film on the plane!"* she shouts. *"You don't know how serious this is!"* "But it was just shrimp—" I begin to say, before she cuts me off. *"We told you. . . ."* I want to protest that it's not my fault her guy is twenty points down in the polls and she's on the fast track to not being the next Dee Dee Myers. It's not worth the trouble. I return to *The New York Times*, where Dole's campaign manager, Scott Reed, is quoted as saying that some major event is about to transform public opinion. "We deserve a break and we're going to have one," he explained.

Asked to be more specific, he said, "Something. World affairs." It's hard to see how the shrimp fit into this scenario.

O C T O B E R   2 – 5

Morry Taylor says he's calling because he has a great deal for me. Some months ago he agreed to speak at a conference in Palm Springs for bigshot manufacturing executives, the heads of such illustrious companies as Caterpillar and John Deere. America's CEOs want to know what it was like to run for president, and Morry thinks that once he tells them they might decide to run, too. Now it seems that on the very day he is scheduled to speak he must undergo tests on his liver. The deal he is offering is that I go in his place and give his speech. What I really want to do, he explains, is to fly across the country and talk to a bunch of people I don't know and probably will never see again and who in any case are deeply disappointed that I am not Morry Taylor. I laugh into the phone.

But Morry can be persuasive when he wants to be. For instance, he is normally withering on the subject of journalism; asked to define "journalist" he will say, "People who can't add." Now he tells me that I'm different from other journalists because "unlike those other guys you're not inserting your private opinion. You just listen and tell people the truth." I nod to myself: How true. "Look," he says, "you can be me for a day. Then you can write about what it was like to be me." I agree to do it; twenty-four hours later I change my mind. When I call to tell him, however, I'm told that Morry has vanished into the bowels of the former Soviet empire. In spite of his bum liver he's squeezing in visits to the president of Ukraine, the president of Belarus, and the mayor of St. Petersburg to sell them tires.

On the plane to Palm Springs I review both the package provided by the conference planners and the first draft of Morry's political manifesto. "Successfully Managing the New Realities!" is what they're calling the conference. The kickoff speakers are former labor secretary Lynn Martin and Morry. The inside flap of the brochure bears a photo of Morry wearing his tight-lipped commander-in-chief grin plus a description of his talk. The paw marks of the Grizz are all over it:

Been There! Done That! Learned Something! Morry Taylor dared to do what no executive of an institute member company

250

has ever done before: become a candidate and campaign for President of the United States of America! Using his own money and his interpretation of the ideas, wants and wishes of a constituency he identified among his fellow citizens, Morry learned a lot about "politics in America." He will share these insights from the perspective "What most business executives don't know about politics can hurt us."

A few hours later I am standing in a ballroom in the dark beside a stage, waiting to be Morry. A host of well-known executives are introduced—to the same tune that accompanies Bob Hope's College Football All-American Team. One by one they parade through a multicolored spotlight while the audience claps. Over the titters of the crowd I can just make out the distant squawk of the parrots chained to posts in the hotel lobby. Then the man at the podium calls for silence. He tells the audience about Morry's campaign and delivers the sad news about Morry's liver. What is striking about the introduction is not its content but its solemnity: here is one place the Taylor campaign is no joke. The audience is filled with big shots from the Midwest, just as Morry promised. My job is not only to be Morry but to explain to them why they should want to be Morry, too. The only help I have from Morry is a four-page handwritten fax, decorated from top to bottom with Have a Nice Day smiley faces. Mostly illegible, it contains only two policy prescriptions, beneath the subhead "Two Things We Could Do to Help This Nation": (1) *Close the Law Schools for Ten Years.* (2) *Elect Just Women for Ten Years.*

I decide to tread gently with the businessmen and tell them first not about Morry's idea for replacing jail terms with public whippings but about Morry's plans for slashing government waste. "The Census Bureau," he says. "They count you every ten years. What do they do the other nine years?" The businessmen don't laugh. I am afraid to look any closer and see what species of bemusement has settled on their faces: in the Midwest jokes that might also be serious are thought queer.

Not for the first time it occurs to me how unlikely it was that Morry pole-vaulted himself out of this culture and into politics. He wasn't like Ross Perot, whose career had as much to do with manipulating government officials as with mixing it up with free-market types. Onstage with the other candidates in Iowa and New Hampshire Morry was a different species, as I am here. But unlike Morry I do not have rubber tires to fall back upon; I'm a talker, not a doer. And so I do what all talkers do in the Midwest when their jokes are hitting nothing but air. "But seriously . . . ," I say, and then for the next thirty minutes bore the hell out of everyone. As I speak some part of my brain drifts away to a prettier place, a happier time. This is the natural conclusion of politics; the follower seeks to meld himself into the leader. When he appears onstage or on television George Stephanopoulos *becomes* Bill Clinton.

I have become Morry Taylor.

OCTOBER 6

When the businessman beside me on the flight from Palm Springs to Hartford asks me what I do for a living I'm embarrassed to say that I'm a journalist. A day of being Morry Taylor has caused me to forget my place in the world. That is, until I pull down from the overhead rack and fiddle conspicuously with my Sony Digital Super SteadyShot Handycam DCR-VX1000 with its 3CCD Digital Zoom (20X!) festooned with various stickers that say ABC NEWS. He becomes interested; he asks me if I've ever met Ted Koppel. I haven't, but I hope to.

On the streets outside the debate hall in Hartford the Super SteadyShot wreaks havoc. Many hundreds of previously listless protesters leap into action at the sight of it. "Let's Have Some Action for ABC!" I shout, and the effect is distinctly more dramatic than if I'd said "Let's Have Some Action for *The New Republic*." They rise as one and proclaim their causes. One moment they are an undifferentiated jumble of people shivering in the cold; the next they are ardent supporters of Nader and Perot, pro-life and antivivisection, antideficit and pro-welfare.

Of course the SteadyShot is not permitted inside the Bushnell Theater. It is too powerful a weapon to be permitted close to the candidates. So after a brief altercation with a security guard, I retire to Spin Alley. Spin Alley is what the debate organizers have renamed the Hartford Civic Center, until a few journalists start pointing out that only a few years ago political hacks actually denied that they "spun" at all. The signs saying SPIN ALLEY are then ripped down—which, when you think about it, is itself a form of spin.

At any rate, the Super SteadyShot penetrates Spin Alley, emanating its extraordinary force field. When she enters the frame the comely Maureen Dowd of *The New York Times* dives behind her notepad, and who can blame her? Once you are in the camera's eye you no longer have control of your soul. Truly it is astonishing the way all of the important people cave to the camera. I point it at White House press director Mike McCurry, then at Pennsylvania governor Tom Ridge. They answer questions that they might ignore if it were just me and mine eye—How do you feel as you stand there spinning me? If you truly felt your candidate had lost would you say as much? They are not talking to me, of course, but to some notional audience, "the American people." And whatever they might be thinking they treat the camera with deference. In the same way that ordinary people feel obliged to smile when they have their picture taken, even when they are unhappy, important people feel pressured to answer sincerely even when they are insincere.

I miss the debate entirely; I am too busy taking pictures of people assessing the debate, which they do from the moment the debate starts. No matter. I am able to track its effect between the lines of Scott Reed's quotes. Tomorrow in *The New York Times* Reed will revise his mental picture of the campaign. "This is going to be a steady building process for the next 30 days," he will say. "There's not going to be an overnight shift." All of a sudden it's looking as if every little shrimp might matter.

OCTOBER 9

This evening I stumble into my Washington apartment and remember that Gore and Kemp are meant to be having a debate. I flip on the tube and there they are, about to start. Kemp masks his nervousness with locker-room jocularity; Gore looks as if he is incapable of any feeling whatsoever. After a few minutes they are doing the usual thing of using the questions to score points off each other when suddenly something extraordinary occurs. Jim Lehrer asks Kemp an interesting question:

> Mr. Kemp, some are saying these days that something's gone terribly wrong with the American soul, that we've become too mean, too selfish, too uncaring, and the spitting incident, how it was handled, the baseball players used as a recent example. What do you think about that?

It isn't the question or Kemp's answer that inspires hope to leap into my heart. It is Gore's rebuttal. In every other instance in every other debate the rebuttal is used to score points in whatever way possible. Gore for once declines to do this:

> I think, Mr. Lehrer [Gore says], that throughout much of his career Jack Kemp has been a powerful and needed voice against the kind of coarseness and incivility that you referred to in the question. I think it's an extremely valuable service to have a voice within the Republican Party who says, "We ought to be one nation. We ought to cross all the racial and ethnic and cultural barriers." I think that is a very important message to deliver. And we ought to speak out against these violations of civility when they do occur. You asked about the incident involving Roberto Alomar. I won't hesitate to tell you what I think. I think he should have been severely disciplined, suspended perhaps, immediately. I don't understand why that action was not taken. But the same could be said of so many incidents in all kinds of institutions in our society. But I compliment Mr. Kemp for the leadership he has shown in moving us away from that kind of attitude.

The politics of our time are so petty and rivalrous that you forget there is another way of disagreeing with people. It was the first time in months that I had heard anything like the voice of leadership from those who are meant to be leading.

TWENTY-ONE

Abroad and at Home

We don't need embassies all over the world. They were estab-
lished years ago before televisions, telephones, e-mail and faxes
existed. We're spending millions of dollars on pigs-in-a-blanket
happy hours overseas. Iran and Iraq serve as proof that we don't
need these operations. Watch CNN if you want to know what's
going on abroad, that's what the President does.

—MORRY TAYLOR,
"Kill All the Lawyers and Other Ways
to Fix Washington" (unpublished manuscript)

OCTOBER 17

The great connoisseur Bernard Berenson understood that the surest way
to attribute a painting was to study its seemingly insignificant details. The
Italian Renaissance painter was more likely to express his idiosyncrasies
when painting, say, the Virgin's toenails than when painting, say, the Virgin's smile. The equivalent of the Virgin's toenails here in San Diego are
the signs in the media center after the debate. They bob up and down
over the heads of the spin doctors like the flags over golf holes to call attention to the people beneath them. The spinners' names—Scott Reed,
Mike McCurry, Clinton economic adviser Laura Tyson—are printed on
them, and they would hardly be worth mentioning except that they be-
tray so clearly the different styles of the two campaigns.

After the Hartford debate the Dole spinners merely stood around,
hoping to be recognized by journalists, until panic set in. "They've got
signs; they've got signs," a Dole staffer hissed before running back into

the Dole offices to grab a few signs they could raise over the spinners' heads. Here at the second debate, the Dole campaign turned up with their own small square (blue) signs, near-perfect imitations of the Clinton campaign's (pink) Hartford signs. But as usual the Clinton campaign stays one step ahead: now they have dramatic prism-shaped signs, two feet long. It's as if the Clinton people knew that the Dole people were going to copy them and planned accordingly.

When the debate ends and the spinners appear in the media center, I am behind one of the Clinton signs holding the Sony Digital Super SteadyShot Handycam DCR-VX1000. Normally I would relax after the debate, but the Handycam's magical force field keeps me moving until the place has emptied. I follow it like a dowser with a divining rod and soon find myself staring up at a sign: DOLE PERSONNEL ONLY/NO MEDIA ALLOWED. Here is the private room where the Dole spinners watched the debate. The Handycam barely pauses before marching me inside. In the viewfinder, I see two dozen empty black swivel chairs all jammed together around the television. Otherwise the room looks as if a tropical storm has just passed through. The floor is littered with a disgusting mixture of papers and sandwich shards. The Handycam examines the refuse for the briefest moment before it lights on something truly interesting: a stack of leftover Xeroxes. Clearly they were passed around to the Dole spinners so they would know precisely what to say to reporters. The document consists of six bulleted points:

We won. Not even close. Dole was loose and Clinton uptight, smug, and bristling with contempt. Dole rocks Clinton on ethics, his Medicare tactics, trial lawyers, defense cuts, tax increases, and so many issues. Dole was in charge. Clinton in retreat.

This is a real race. A real race in California, and a real race nationwide. This was a brilliant performance by Dole, a passionate performance, a humorous performance. This is a new race.

And so on.

A few minutes later, thanks to the miracle of modern technology, I am back in Spin Alley during the debate, watching the Dole spinners in action. The first face in my viewfinder is George Shultz's. "I think Senator Dole was on a roll when he came here, and he's really rolling now," he says, his face pressed right up against the lens. "If you thought he had lost the debate," asks the Handycam, "would you be willing to say that?" "Sure, but I don't have to because he clearly ran away with it."

Shultz vanishes as suddenly as he appeared and is replaced by a man under a blue Dole sign that reads MICHAEL ANTONOVICH. "There's panic on the Clinton side!" this man jeers before insisting, like Shultz, that Dole ran away with the debate.

Soon I've seen enough to know that these people are sticking pretty closely to the memo in my hand. The Handycam and I are pulled toward a stack of papers. Faxes! To Haley Barbour! Actually, they are just Barbour's cover sheets. But alongside them in what looks suspiciously like Barbour's handwriting is a pad of scribbled notes. It turns out to be a running commentary on the debate—and a rough draft for the memo. "CNN—*USA TODAY*" is written across the top of the first page. "10/6: –21; 10/16: –9." Poll data. What's interesting about the writer's clear attempt to boost his own spirits is its implicit admission: eleven days ago no Republican ever admitted that Dole was down by twenty-one points. "Dole opens well," the author goes on to write. "Good humor, warm. Not a hard sell at all." Many times since January I have felt bad for Dole, who seems driven by some desire to prove he'll never be president. Now I almost feel bad for his campaign. Almost.

A thin blue curtain taped between silver poles separates the Dole people from the Clinton people. The Handycam tears the curtain from its supports and plunges into the inner sanctum of the leader of the Free World. But the room has already been cleaned. One campaign is being run by criminals who deep down want to be caught; the other by criminals who sincerely don't. The lone scrap of paper on the floor reads "'Worst economy in a century'—including Great Depression???" referring to one of the less plausible claims made by Dole during the debate. The Handycam nose-dives into the Clinton trash basket to see what else might have been left behind when suddenly a shrill reproach pulls it up short.

"Excuse me, what are you doing in here?"

"I was supposed to meet George here for drinks," I say. "He's long gone," she says, then waits quietly until I leave. I have found that whenever I am caught where I shouldn't be in the Clinton campaign I only need to say in a casual, familiar tone that I am looking for George Stephanopoulos and I am immediately released.

All around me in the empty media room are televisions replaying the debate. But there's no point watching other people's television shows when you can watch your own. I retire and review the rest of the Handy-

cam's tape. On it I am able to discern another major difference between
the two campaigns. Time and again the Clinton spinners create the illusion that their campaign has risen above the level of a crude sales pitch.
They actually praise Dole for his performance. They carry in their palms
tiny plastic tops, to show you that they know how silly and mendacious
spinning is. The effect of their irony is to undermine not only their own
spinning but the far more necessary spinning of the Dole campaign,
which is now entirely dependent on spin to persuade the world that its
guy won the debate.

The Clinton campaign is beginning to grapple with the voters' need
to feel that they are not being sold anything. Indeed, one of the odder aspects of our current politics is that even though campaigns are deploying
ever more sophisticated marketing techniques—many of them pilfered
from Madison Avenue—the customers want ever less to do with the
product.

OCTOBER 18

It's hard to say whether either candidate is running for president any
longer or just pretending to while actually focusing on congressional
races. After the debate Dole remains in California, of all places, and delivers what is billed by the Dole campaign as "a major policy address."
Major policy addresses occur at regular intervals to stir the reporters'
juices and make them feel like something important is happening, which
it isn't. Today Dole just wants to reiterate his commitment to keeping
Mexicans in Mexico. Like much of Dole's rapidly expanding agenda, his
outrage about illegal immigration is not truly his own. Like Pat Buchanan, Dole attempts to paint his opponent as the patron saint of illegal immigrants. The trouble is that, since pretty much everyone is against
illegal immigration, all that's left is the rhetorical contest. Buchanan can
win this because even if he has no novel policies to offer, he genuinely is
a lot angrier about the problem than just about anyone you know.

As Dole rails meekly in Riverside I head for Mexico. A young reporter
with the Associated Press named Dana Calvo has agreed to take me to
the place I've wanted to visit for months. In late March when the primaries came to California I followed Pat Buchanan to the fourteen-mile
fence that runs along the border between California and Mexico; "the
Buchanan fence," Buchanan calls it, though nowadays just about every-

one in elective office including Dole and Clinton has visited the same spot and claimed credit for the thing. Back in March, though, it was mainly Buchanan's issue. He stood beside the fence while hordes of television cameramen pushed and shoved to film him against the background of Mexico and the Mexicans whose legs dangled over the levee across the border. At the time I wondered what on earth these people thought the gringos were up to. Tonight I am going to find out.

On the way Dana gives me a bit of background, which is probably boring to anyone who knows anything about the subject but is interesting to me. I didn't know, for instance, that since January the Border Patrol has been nabbing illegals at a rate of fifty-five thousand a month. Nor did I know that the main consequence of beefing up the Border Patrol at Tijuana, and cramming lots of electronic surveillance into the landscape, is to shift the thrust of activity east, toward Arizona. There was a time not long ago when Mexicans would gather in big crowds at Tijuana and, in a strategy well known to anyone who has played kick-the-can, rush the border simultaneously. The few who got through justified the many who got caught. These days they employ the same tactic but fifty miles east.

At length we arrive on the levee facing the Buchanan fence. It is built on a pile of dust and loose rocks and overlooks on one side the Tijuana offices of the ruling political party and on the other a tan concrete gully maybe one hundred yards across. Dana points to the thin channel a few feet wide that bisects the gully and says, "That's where Mexico ends and the United States begins." Facing us from the other side of that gully are the headlights of the U.S. Border Patrol trucks.

But, late as it is, there remains a crowd that looks pretty much like the crowd that gazed across at Buchanan in broad daylight. Dozens of young Mexican men sit dangling their legs over the levee staring into the headlights and beyond them at the Buchanan fence. Before we have a chance to decide which way to turn we are met by three stragglers, one of whom is a small bearded man with a black duffel bag of the sort airlines are forever misplacing. What happens next must be taken with a grain of salt, since I am scribbling in the dark, not the man's exact words, but the man's words as Dana translates them.

The small bearded man explains he's making a dash for it tonight. He's come up from southern Mexico for just this purpose—he's thirty-two, has a wife and two children, and believes he can find a job picking crops in California. "I know it is hard work," he says. "But it pays well." In his bag he carries a blanket but no water and no money. He has been caught by the Border Patrol each of the last eight nights but reckons it is better to be caught here than to die in the desert to the east. "It is more efficient this way. They catch me and hold me for twenty minutes and then let me go." There was a time when he might have hired a guide to escort him, but since the beefing up of the Border Patrol the going rate for guides has more than doubled, from three hundred dollars to seven hundred dollars.

As we speak a thuggish young man in a sleeveless shirt sets rubber tires on fire and rolls them into the concrete gully. The idea is that the U.S. Border Patrol will become so consumed with fire extinguishing that the Mexicans will have time to dash across. If that doesn't work they will wait until dawn. "Dawn is the best time to cross," the bearded man explains. "The Border Patrol officers play Nintendo and Game Boy in their cars and by dawn they often have fallen asleep."

"But what about the fence?" I ask. "How do you get over it?" I recall the pride with which Buchanan leaned up against the cold metal and said, "This wasn't here the last time we were here. And if you give me a victory in California you'll see this fence all the way to Florida, where I want it."

"It is easily climbed," says the man, laughing loudly. *Easily climbed?* "It has toeholds even," says his friend, joining in the joke.

For some reason just then I think of the signs over the sinks in restaurant bathrooms across America: EMPLOYEES MUST WASH HANDS. Those signs exist obviously not for the benefit of the cook, whose decision to wash is not likely to be affected by the sign, but for the customers who, after reading it, are perhaps a bit more satisfied that the cook is clean. The fence is an extension into politics of the instinct to place signs that say EMPLOYEES MUST WASH HANDS over restaurant sinks. It exists not so much to prevent Mexicans from entering the United States as to placate those people who are especially disturbed by the idea of Mexicans entering the United States. Put up the sign in the restaurant bathroom and you don't have to subject the cook's hygiene to spot inspections. Give Buchanan and his followers the fence and you don't have to give them laws against hiring illegal immigrants. In such times as these much of the loudest political activity results in a similar symbolic response, from the abortion plank in the Republican platform to the banning of the Confederate flag. Appeasing the minority, and ensuring that even as it is losing out steadily to the majority it does not feel entirely ignored by the democracy, are important political activities.

The Mexican man about to make his dash across the border, I now notice, is wearing a Harley-Davidson sweatshirt that says MADE IN THE U.S.A. I ask him if he has seen politicians on the other side turn up with hordes of cameras to defend the border. He has. "They're just doing their jobs," he says, "making more and more laws." And it's true. Not three weeks ago Congress passed a bill adding five thousand men to the Border Patrol and approving the funds to add two more tiers to the Buchanan fence. Nevertheless, the man explains, the crossing will become much easier after the election. "November fifth is a very important night," he says. The night after the next president is chosen, the thinking here goes, the Border Patrol will dwindle and everyone will get across.

Another burning tire is rolled into the gully; Dana is getting a bit tense. Interviewing prospective illegal immigrants in the dead of night is as fraught as interviewing vice-presidential candidates. I have time for one more question, she says, before we should leave. "Do you know the man inside that car?" I ask, pointing to the nearest Border Patrol vehicle. The men shake their heads. "He's bald and he looks Puerto Rican," one says. "Do you even have a nickname for him?" I ask. "Motherfucker," he says.

On the way home Dana points out that the man with the black duffel bag could make good money running drugs, but he has chosen instead to risk his life looking for hard, honest work. Does anyone doubt that if Pat Buchanan were Mexican he'd be one of the first across the border? Does anyone doubt that to say this is a compliment?

OCTOBER 24

Last night my father took a poll in the locker room of the place where he plays tennis, and not one of the men there had any idea that either Bill Clinton or Bob Dole was coming to New Orleans today, which they are. Twelve days before the 1996 presidential election the two candidates can land in a medium-sized city without making a dent. The front page of the *Times-Picayune* reflects the general apathy. Beneath a huge story about who will be the next coach of the New Orleans Saints is a tiny map showing how traffic will be affected by the candidates. After a brief discussion of the various roads being closed to make way for Clinton's motorcade the story says, simply, "No roads will be closed for Dole."

When projected onto one's hometown, presidential politics shrinks, dramatically. One of the first people to arrive at the Dole rally on the banks of the Mississippi this afternoon is Jay Batt, who was in my class from nursery school until college. Jay is a colorful character of the sort that you are always hearing about in New Orleans. He stands maybe six foot three and weighs between 270 and 350, depending on when you catch up to him. The men's clothing store Jay runs downtown is not like normal clothing stores. It has a happy hour, for instance, when Jay wheels in a bar from a back room and turns on music. The one time in my life I was thrown in an American jail I was thrown in jail with Jay. While I used my first call from the dingy chamber filled with dangerous-looking men to contact loved ones, Jay used his to order a delivery pizza. He didn't mean to be funny, either; he was really hungry.

But even a character as robust as Jay is no match for the modern media. The powers that be at ABC have hired a camera crew to follow me around and film me while I film with the SteadyShot. People filming people filming people. Amused by the sight, Republicans with video cameras glom on: people filming people filming people filming people. People who ordinarily would be slightly timid in the SteadyShot's force field are completely spooked by the SteadyShot backed up by a team of hard-bitten pros wielding their Cyclopses. I also feel that my amateur's touch is being compromised.

At any rate, one of the first things the crew asks me as I head toward Jay is if I plan "to do a few MOSs" "What is an MOS?" I ask. "Man on the street," says the soundman. Since I know he'll eventually tell me what he actually thinks, I put the (two) cameras on Jay and ask him his political views. He becomes a different person than the man I know. He explains that he has been a Republican ever since he shook hands with Richard Nixon on Canal Street in the early 1970s. He has come to the Dole rally, he says, sounding exactly like every other man on the street, because it is very important to him that the right man become president. I never knew any of this. Indeed, I never thought it was possible for Jay to sound like every other man on the street being interviewed about politics. But he does.

Once I put the camera down, however, Jay comes clean. He explains that the only reason he turned up to the Dole rally was, "Kearney called and asked me to come and it's only four blocks from the office." Bill Kearney is another old classmate of ours. He runs the Dole campaign in Louisiana.

OCTOBER 25

In one final test of the discrepancy between politics as it is experienced in real life and politics as it is experienced through a TV camera (or screen), I take Jay and Bill—perhaps Dole's two most rabid supporters in New Orleans—to lunch at a restaurant called the Palace Cafe, owned and run by another former classmate named Ti Martin. Jay and Bill know that Ti is as adamantly Democratic as they are Republican. When Clinton came to town a few months back, he descended on the restaurant unannounced. "Men with large guns wanted to know how to get to the roof," Ti recalls. "The president's dietitian wanted only one person to cook for him and only one person to serve him. By the time I went outside, Canal Street was blocked off in both directions and red velvet ropes were holding back hundreds of onlookers. When the Secret Service wanted to see the reservation book, I explained that much of our lunch business was walk-in, so he passed. Later we noticed one of the names on the reservation book was Oswald."

In the same way that you don't realize how essentially wrong the newspaper is until you read a story on a subject with which you are intimately familiar, you don't know what is wrong in a political campaign until you see it come to your hometown. Even the two most ardent Dole supporters place politics so far down on the list of what they'd like to talk about that it becomes invisible. I could stand there until Election Day asking them questions designed to force them to lock horns and they won't do it. Ti wants Jay to keep coming to her restaurant; Jay wants Ti to keep buying clothes from his store downtown; and in any case they like each other too much to let politics come between them. Precisely because they have a shared history they have no interest in discussing who will be president. There are so many better things to talk about.

I think the main reason most political journalism seems so remote from life as we know it in America is that in life politics is far down on the list of concerns, whereas political journalism operates on the assumption that politics is the most important thing in the world. Ordinary people understand they are meant to exhibit a certain tedious seriousness when they talk to a journalist about presidential candidates, and so they do. I don't mean this as an insult. Apathy is a perfectly intelligent response to our current politics. And it is a sign of a stable society when who gets to be president makes no difference in your life. It is also a vindication of old-fashioned conservatism. The debate between conservatives and liberals boils down to which comes first, politics or culture. Conservatives argue that the culture drives our politics, that a politician can do only what the culture allows him to. Liberals argue that government policies shape the culture. Obviously each holds some claim on the truth. But in these uneventful times the conservatives are more right.

Before I leave Ti hands me a list of what Clinton ate the last time he came to the Palace Cafe:

Marinated crab claws
Crawfish gazpacho
Pan-seared yellowfin tuna with Creole tomato cream and Louisiana crawfish tails
Catfish pecan
Country apple pie with house-made cinnamon ice cream and caramel sauce
White chocolate bread pudding (a few bites)
House-made raspberry yogurt (a few bites)

This isn't an accurate reflection of his intake, she says, because the president kept reaching across the table and spearing food off the plates of people he barely knew. But even the official list of Clinton's consumption prompted a local columnist to write that "anybody who can eat like that and then address the legislature is an inspiration." Other than that, nobody much noticed that he'd been in town.

TWENTY-TWO

The Clinton Chronicles

*I am ridiculed all day long; everyone mocks me. Whenever I
speak out, I cry out proclaiming violence and destruction.*

—Jeremiah 20:7–8

OCTOBER 28

I had planned to spend the final week of the campaign in Little Rock and
Hot Springs looking into the many Clinton-related scandals and outrages
that, I assume, will define his inexorable second term. I had even gone
so far as to book the Governor's Suite at the Excelsior Hotel for the occasion. But then the letters started to arrive in response to my previous
attempt to dip my wick into these fires: pamphlets purporting to prove
that Clinton had Commerce Secretary Ron Brown killed; disquisitions
on Clinton's cocaine habit; further evidence that White House counsel
Vince Foster could not possibly have committed suicide. "Mike," wrote
one concerned reader in an attempt to discover where I stood on these
matters, generally, "do you believe or tend to believe that Lee Oswald
acted alone on Nov. 22, 1963 in murdering JFK? Are you comfortable
about accepting that both the Croatian airport mechanic's and air traffic
control officer's death shortly before the April crash [of Brown's plane]
were suicides?"

Then Murray started calling again.

My problems with Murray began a month or so ago when I decided
that there was no point in dwelling much on Clinton's official campaign,
as it consisted merely of Clinton's repeating himself ad nauseam for the
next couple of months over a sound track of $150 million in political

ads. I decided instead to explore various groups of people whose lives Clinton has shaped, starting with the long list of those who have written books and made movies to warn the world about Bill Clinton. No sitting president has been responsible for so many new careers in the arts.

I set out first to find Larry Nichols, the Little Rock narrator of *The Clinton Chronicles*, the famed samizdat video that has sold more than five hundred thousand copies, according to its producer, the aptly named Jeremiah Films. *The Clinton Chronicles* seeks to demonstrate that Clinton was (a) a heavy user of cocaine, (b) a philanderer far worse than we know, (c) the aider and abettor of an international drug ring, and (d) the mastermind of a criminal conspiracy responsible for the murder of many innocent people. Probably for good reasons in his mind, Larry Nichols (whose information about Clinton comes from his stint at the Arkansas Development Finance Authority) is not listed in the Little Rock phone book, so I left a message for the investigative journalist Murray Waas, asking him for Nichols's number. (I had heard through the grapevine that Waas has been down in Arkansas working for *The Nation* on some complicated story involving the Clinton conspiracists.) Waas called back and left a message for me saying he would love to help, but failed to leave the phone number.

A few hours later, thanks to the Arkansas journalist Gene Lyons, who now earns his living debunking Clinton conspiracy theories, I reached Nichols. "Murray Waas called me a little while ago," said the nasal voice familiar to me from the *Chronicles*. "He told me that you are writing a hatchet job on me for *The New Republic*." I was stunned. Not only was I not writing a hatchet job about Nichols, I was not even quite sure why I was calling him. Faced with the possibility that Waas was out to get me, there were two possible responses, I figured. I could respond as Hillary Clinton would and engage Murray on his terms, in which case I'd wind up pickled in my own paranoia. Or I could respond as Bill would and operate on the assumption that Murray was ultimately prepared to love me. I opted for the Hillary approach.

That's when things became complicated.

I called Waas, got his infernal machine, and left one of those threats intended to make him quake with fear for his life but which nine seconds after you hang up strike you as completely asinine. He called back immediately. "Did you do this to me?" I asked. "I find that an insulting question," he said. He's too amused to be outraged. The mere suggestion that I would *believe* Larry Nichols about anything is *comical.* Murray did *call* Nichols, he says, but he didn't talk to him about me.

Only then, feeling embarrassed for having been taken in by Nichols, did I switch to the Bill approach. I apologized to Murray, and we shared a short laugh about the nut cases down in Arkansas who dream up these stories about President Clinton. "I talk to a lot of crazies down there," he said. "And they have a lot of crazy, crazy stories."

The penny dropped only after I'd hung up: Waas called Nichols, which means he had his phone number. But if he had his phone number, and was sincere in his desire to help, why didn't he give it to me when he called the first time?

That's when things became *really* complicated.

Twenty-four hours later I worked up the nerve to call Nichols again. A long weekend had put the things Murray told him about me into perspective. He had a bad taste in his mouth about Washington journalists. He said that Murray kept calling him on the pretense of looking into the Helen Dickey story while in fact he was looking into him, Larry Nichols.

"Who's Helen Dickey?" I ask.

"Helen Dickey," says Nichols, "is the former Clinton nanny who made the call from Washington telling people that Vince Foster had killed himself." He paused in just the same way he does on *The Clinton Chronicles* video, before dropping the bomb.

"The problem was that she made the call fifteen minutes before the body was found."

Helen Dickey is well worth looking into, he said, but Murray was only *pretending* to look into her. Instead:

> Murray would say he was looking into the Helen Dickey affair, but then after a while he says, "By the way, Larry, you got ten million dollars for *The Clinton Chronicles,* right?" And I'd say, "What?" Then Murray'd talk some more about Helen Dickey, and after a bit he'd say, "By the way, how much money did you make off the tapes?" I said, "Murray, what are you talking about? I didn't make any money." Then he'd call again and say, "This Helen Dickey thing is looking really good. And here's a tip for you Larry: the Washington *Post* has been contracted to attack your credibility. So please will you call me as soon as the *Post* calls you?" And so I say, "Murray, the *Post* ain't never going to call me." Then Murray would go off and tell people in Little Rock something against me,

you know, try to Ping-Pong us, trying to put one person against the other. So finally I'd had enough. He calls one last time as I was about to get in the shower. I said, "Murray, I'm not going to *put up* with you fabricating one thing and then another." And I hang up. Then he calls back and says, "Larry, I'm going to do you a favor: This guy Lewis from *The New Republic* is going to call you. He's been assigned to write a hatchet job on you." Sure enough, three hours later you call.

"Wait," I said, my mind reeling again in the way it does when I try for the tenth time to follow the labyrinthine connections of *The Clinton Chronicles*. On the one hand, Nichols, who claims to be personally responsible for thirty-two *major* Clinton scandals, makes Deep Throat look like a piker. On the other hand at least a few of his allegations have proved to be way ahead of the curve and ended up eventually in the Washington *Post*. Increasingly, for instance, it appears that Paula Jones— the woman who claims Clinton exposed himself to her while he was governor—is telling the truth. And the gist of Nichols's complaints about Clinton's character sounds very much like everyone else's. "Michael, you can love Bill Clinton," he said, quite reasonably, "but you need to know that Bill Clinton doesn't tell the truth."

Before he hung up he was kind enough to give me the phone number for Gennifer Flowers.

In this loquacious, conspiracy-drenched environment it seemed only appropriate that I meet Murray Waas for coffee. In person he is very agreeable, and I ended up buying him dinner. We talked of this and that, scarcely mentioning Larry Nichols. But before I left him, Murray cautioned me about Little Rock, where I planned to go. "If Larry Nichols asks you to meet him at a truck stop at one in the morning . . ." he began.

Don't worry, I said, I was now savvy to the ways of Arkansas.

"It's just that they—the Clinton haters—are a little bit pissed off," he said, "and crazier than they usually are."

"You mean, because Clinton is about to win a second term?" I asked.

Murray didn't immediately respond but instead smiled, knowingly. Creepily.

"Is there some other reason they are especially pissed off and crazy?" I asked.

"I'm sorry," he said. "But I'm working on the story about it."

Who wasn't? As Clinton rolled toward a second term the Clinton scandal industry was booming. By the end of that day two new rumors about the Clintons were gathering steam. The on-line publication *Conspiracy Nation* reported that Hillary had hired people in the Pentagon to assassinate Dick Morris. And then a friend called to tell me that a friend told him that Clinton was sitting on his medical records to hide an old nose operation, which was necessary to repair the damage from his cocaine habit.

Which brings us up to date. Almost. I forgot to mention that I wrote an article about my first brush with the scandal industry. After it appeared Murray bombarded me with phone calls and messages, ranging from death threats to apologies for saying he planned to have me killed. Soon I took to letting other people answer my phone. But even that didn't do much good. "It's Mike Samuels for you," said my houseguest, as she handed me the receiver. It was Murray, of course, using one of his pseudonyms. "I can't believe all you said to me about Hillary Clinton," he said ominously. In the end I unplugged the phones. As I did, it crossed my mind that people who apologize for making death threats are possibly more dangerous than people who don't.

The signature qualities of both Clinton conspiracists and their chroniclers, I now know, are their determination and their abundant leisure time. They never give up. Murray has now taken to calling my employers to inform them he tape-recorded our phone conversations and plans to release the transcripts to the Washington *Post* and *The New York Times.* Apparently I said some pretty damning things about Hillary Clinton. I also fabricated his quotes, he says. One of Murray's last calls came to Sydney, a new intern in the magazine's office, who is polite and pleasant almost to a fault. Murray took Sydney's formality as a sign that Sydney was trying to keep him at arm's length. "You don't have to be so formal with me," Murray yelled on the phone. But Sydney is formal with everyone. (After he had addressed me as "sir" for the fourth time, I said, "Sydney, you're going to have to stop calling me that." "I'm afraid that is going to be difficult, sir.")

On balance, I have decided, it is better to let Clinton get away with everything than to become further involved in his conspiracies, and I wonder how many other journalists have arrived at the same conclusion, and whether a lot of scandals are going undetected because the emotional and psychological cost of getting to them is prohibitive. And so as the campaign heads into its final week, instead of going to Little Rock and finding the dirt that will end Clinton's career and start mine, I head out on the road to witness what the Clinton campaign is calling "a summing up of his argument for reelection."

When I arrive in St. Louis the Clinton campaign plane is waiting empty on a tarmac. Clinton is speaking downtown. The only other people on board are the four stewards, who are watching reruns of Barbra Streisand's tribute to the Clintons. I pass the time reading *Unlimited Access,* the book about the Clinton White House by a former FBI man named Gary Aldrich, who was moved to write, he says, to prevent a security disaster in the White House. One of the reasons it is sitting at the top of the best-seller lists is that it can be finished in two hours. Another is that it pushes the genre into new territory. According to Aldrich, the women in the Clinton White House are not really women and the men not really men:

> There was a uni-sex quality to the Clinton staff that set it far apart from the Bush administration. It was the shape of their bodies. In the Clinton administration, the broadshouldered, pants-wearing women and the pear-shaped, bowling pin men blurred distinctions between the sexes. I was used to athletic types, physically fit persons who took pride in body image and good health. Arnold Schwarzenegger called the Clinton friends "girlie men" during the campaign in 1992. I now knew what he was getting at.

The people who are consumed by their hatred of the Clintons—only some of whom believe that they sit at the center of many conspiracies—can be broken down into schools. There is the Bad Investment School, which consists of people who have lost a great deal of money on an investment sold to them by someone who reminds them of Clinton. There is the Sublimated Sexual Jealousy School, which comprises mainly men aged thirty to fifty-five who are vaguely aware that Clinton is getting women to vote for him and to sleep with him in the most unmanly ways, by feigning a kind of female sensibility—feeling their pain and all that—and thus transgressing the basic rules of the game. The hostility this breeds in some is akin to the hostility of the striking union member toward the scab.

Aldrich is a good example of a third school of Clinton haters: the Law & Order School. The Law & Order School is defined in part by its weird precision. Aldrich notes all sorts of seemingly irrelevant details—the exact time of day, the names of Vince Foster's children—which of course lends credence to his account. But at the same time he is counting carpet fibers he is repeating every wild rumor he has ever heard: that two male staffers were caught having sex by a White House security guard; that the president sneaks off to sexual trysts at the Marriott, hiding under a blanket in the backseat of a car; that the first lady has busted another lamp in the West Wing. Aldrich's main charge, which he makes repeatedly, is that the Clintons and their employees are counterculture types with counterculture morals, which is to say few morals at all. Once he lands onto this line of inquiry he can reveal all sorts of seemingly innocent behavior for what it is:

> It appears that Al and Tipper Gore decided to reward their "incredibly hardworking staff" after the inauguration by inviting them to a Grateful Dead concert. The Gores were described by a Gore spokesperson as dedicated "Deadheads." As an FBI agent, I knew the parking lots of Grateful Dead concerts were notorious open air drug markets.

Unlimited Access seems to be inspired by a very modern form of resentment, the kind of resentment that a man who has spent his life climbing the ranks of a large bureaucracy feels toward a man who leapfrogs up the career ladder through a special and obnoxious blend of deferments and degrees. Duty, loyalty, and discretion are the qualities most highly valued in Aldrich's world. Glibness, shrewdness, and nerve are the qualities required to jump from Hot Springs to Oxford, then back to the governor's office and on to the White House. The Law & Order mind-set is easy to make fun of, but you do so at your peril, as Clinton has learned the hard way, struggling to gain control of his salute, his security detail, and his generals. A status structure is a powerful thing. It can lead a man whose job is to protect the president to sound as if he'd rather kill him.

By the time I finish the Aldrich book, Clinton has given speeches in Chicago and Minneapolis. It is well past midnight. We're flying to Columbus, Ohio. A reporter in the seat in front of me is staring into his computer screen and the abyss of the 1996 campaign. Tomorrow's first sentence glows back: "In an abrupt departure from his remarks here four years ago, President . . ."

271

I wake up in Columbus, Ohio, after five fitful hours in a second-string Hyatt, and stumble onto the press bus heading for Ohio State University and another Clinton rally. Within moments the press filing center is hosting a press conference, and press secretary Mike McCurry is making press-conference noises. "By now you know fully well the president's positions on pardons . . . I have to check further . . . pure speculation . . . on prior occasions." He then introduces Bruce Reed, who explains how every third grader should be required to pass a reading test. Bruce Reed was in my class in college. It's good to see him doing so well. At length the reporters are briefed on how much more money the Clinton campaign has to spend in the final week in Ohio than the Dole campaign. This no doubt will lead to even more stories about how Dole can't win, making it even more likely that he won't.

Today's airplane reading is *The Seduction of Hillary Rodham*, David Brock's new book, which ostensibly is addressed to the sane reader. But the more hysterical the anti-Clinton propaganda becomes, the harder it is to pay attention to any of it, except as a joke. You can't say that Clinton had Vince Foster murdered and then expect people to feel the same outrage when you say that Bill Clinton took 4 million bucks from a shady Indonesian. Gresham's Law applies to political insults as well as it does to anything else: The bad drives out the good.

Brock, the past master of the genre, understands this; indeed in some ways *The Seduction of Hillary Rodham* was shaped by *Unlimited Access*. A few months ago Brock went so far as to disclose that Gary Aldrich had gotten his information about Clinton's visits to the Marriott from *him*, and that it was a fourth-hand rumor that should never have seen print. Now the man who brought us Troopergate and magazine covers depicting Hillary Clinton as a witch has written a *sympathetic* biography about the first lady. Hillary may be a Commie and a pinko, Brock says, but she is nevertheless principled. It is therefore an even greater shame that her career was derailed by Bill, who, we learn again, through repetition of the usual charges, is scum.

But in a gymnasium in Ohio, as Clinton winds up his speech, it's hard even to remember those charges. He's speaking off the top of his head and turning the world's most bitter hatreds into a very private matter:

I was in Detroit the other day and I was told that in Wayne County there are people from 141 different racial and ethnic groups . . . 141 in one county in America. There are only 192 different national groups represented at the Olympics. Amazing. But you look at the rest of the world. Pick up the paper on any day. And you read about the Middle East, or Bosnia, or Northern Ireland. Or Rwanda. Or Burundi. All over the world people literally torn apart by their differences. Why? Because there's something in human nature that makes people have to believe that they can only be important if they're looking down on someone else. Well, whatever is wrong with me, at least I'm not them. Now, we're trying to beat that rap. And that's why we cannot tolerate hatred or intolerance in this country.

After his speech Clinton reaches into the crowd with both hands. With just a few days left in his life as a campaigner he's no longer shaking hands so much as grabbing at people as if he were kneading dough. Working the rope line he stumbles on a Dole supporter, a former employee of the Coast Guard. After a few minutes of discussing his idea to use the Coast Guard to support the Immigration and Naturalization Service, the man is transformed. "I was a Dole supporter," he tells Clinton. "But I've changed my mind." The president turns to one of his aides and like an excited little boy says, "Did you hear that guy? He said, 'When I came here I was voting for Dole, but I changed my mind.' Did you hear him say that? Did you hear him?"

I accept a ride on *Air Force One* back to Washington, which is to say that I begged so hard they couldn't refuse. I'm not even forced to sit in the press section, which resembles ordinary first class, but am allowed into the forward section, which is more like a fancy living room. A white phone beside each chair is answered by an operator who places your calls, and you can order up just about any bad movie you want. Mike McCurry glides back and forth a couple of times, but I am so far from the man in the front of the plane I might as well be back in New Orleans. I pass the trip finishing *The Seduction of Hillary Rodham*. Think of it: the leader of the free world sits in his office playing hearts a mere few yards in front of me while a reporter sits reading a nasty book about his wife, the chief purpose of which is to strip him of whatever moral authority he retains. Such are the pleasures of life in a free society, where the losers become lobbyists rather than corpses.

OCTOBER 30

I am nearly seduced. But then suddenly I'm not. It's like this every time with Clinton. Just as I am being drawn to him my instincts of self-preservation take over and I pull back. It's not the character issue. Like Clinton I don't have much interest in facing the character issue head-on except to say that it is more complicated than its politics. On the one hand it appears the president routinely cheated on his wife; on the other he's still married to her and seems to have been a pretty good father to their daughter. On the one hand, he's adopted a set of socially conservative beliefs purely out of political expediency, to prevent Dole from having an issue on which to campaign. On the other hand, he's taken some big political risks in his career—such as his attempt to reform health care or secure gays in the military—and paid the price. The current fashion in politics is to brand any insider who tries and fails to advance a new agenda a fool. But it stands to reason that such failures require more courage than do successes.

No, the problem with embracing Clinton is that you know that you'll come to regret it. Maybe the weirdest aspect of his presidency is that his friends, and their ideas, have suffered while his enemies, and their ideas, have prospered. Not since Nixon composed his list of enemies has there been such a frightening and shadowy idea as Clinton's list of friends: Lani Guinier, Webster Hubbell, Vince Foster, Marian Wright Edelman, Susan McDougal, Mack McLarty, Hillary Clinton. Only a fool would take a bullet for our president. But maybe this is okay for now. The challenge for the sane person who wishes to keep politics in its proper place is to define some new space in which to live with our once and future president—somewhere between outrage and adoration. We can't beat him. We can't join him either. But we can use him—withholding our adulation while sending him off to do the dirty work of making the world a little bit better. So let's do it. It's the ultimate revenge on someone who is so adept at manipulating others.

OCTOBER 30 (VERY LATE)

My first *Nightline* segment aired immediately after *Monday Night Football*. Mercifully, no one I know watched it, so far as I can tell. The contrast between the power of the force field emanating from the SteadyShot and the pale vibes of the final product was astonishing. Jay Batt ended up on the cutting-room floor, together with Haley Barbour's faxes. Afterward, the *Nightline* producer calls and, as politely as possible, gives me to understand that my future in television may be limited.

It is nearly one-thirty in the morning and I'm alone in bed. There is no denying that I was excited by working alongside Ted Koppel, driven less by a Fallovian (as in James Fallows, editor of *U.S. News & World Report,* who believes that political journalists need to spend more time thinking of the public interest and less time thinking of their careers) desire to inform the public than a lust to become rich and famous. A winner. It is not to be.

The whole point of taking along the SteadyShot, I now remember, was not to become rich and famous but to insinuate myself into the world of the insiders. I also had some vague hope that the SteadyShot would give me a better chance of getting in to have a heart-to-heart with Ross Perot. There was no way Ross was going to give an interview to a print person, or so I was led to believe by the People. But television was another matter. With only $29 million to blow on infomercials Ross needed as much free TV as he could get. So I called and put in a request I thought he couldn't refuse: Would Ross give me a tour of his private art museum? One thing about rich people is that they like to show people what they own, I figured. But no.

And so here I lie, a *Nightline* washout watching Perot's infomercials, which turn out to be less info and more mercial than their predecessors four years ago. Perot has been reduced to replaying his greatest hits from 1992; he is a parody of himself, which is saying something. "Yes, folks," he says, in the most recent one I have seen, "we predicted it. There is a *giant sucking sound* coming out of Mexico. They're sucking your jobs down there. They're sucking our dollars down there. . . ." As I watch him rant on it occurs to me that four years from now all three of the finalists could very well be institutionalized. Perot will be in a mental asylum, Dole will be in an old folks' home, and Clinton will be in jail.

At least some of Perot's original appeal was the sense that the White House would be a sacrifice for him, a step down from his palace in Dallas. Now he seems to want to be president just as badly as the next guy who will never be president. With perhaps one exception.

TWENTY-THREE

The End

I have been around long enough to know it is going to be the candidate's fault. If I lose, the rest of them [the rented strangers] are going to be home free.

—BOB DOLE,
on CNN

NOVEMBER 1

The first day of Dole's final campaign swing is devoted to warmed-over endorsements from the former presidents who are traveling with Dole on *Citizen's Ship*. Gerald Ford had the window seat, George Bush the aisle. While Dole blared jokes over the microphone Bush picked up the latest campaign T-shirt and read it aloud, as a question: "Ninety-six hours to victory?" Ford responded, softly: "Once you get there, is there skiing?" This and many other damning anecdotes are told and retold by the journalists. The momentum of a losing campaign is as unstoppable as it is unfortunate.

Everyone has stopped looking for politics and started looking for disaster. A week or so ago *The New York Times* ran a story about all the important Republicans who had given up on Dole. The story quoted Florida party chair Tom Slade as saying that if Dole took the state "it will be nothing short of a political miracle." A couple of days later the *Times* printed a correction in which it quoted what Slade actually had said: "I am more optimistic than I have ever been that Dole will carry Florida. Because we were down substantially, if he does, it will be nothing short of a political miracle." And so when John Kasich wanders onto the parked press bus in Columbus, Ohio, he is actually walking into a trap.

276

He thinks he is there to make everyone feel a bit better about Dole and perhaps improve his own standing with the press. But the press is way beyond that—all anyone wants from Kasich now is more evidence that Dole is doomed.

Kasich stands boyishly in the aisle of the bus for a few happy minutes, answering very good questions about the budget and defending with great confidence everything Bob Dole stands for. Clearly he wants badly to be portrayed as a team player, the sort of guy who never, ever would flee a losing cause. But when pressed about the 15 percent tax cut Dole has promised every American, and Dole's inability to make it sound appealing, Kasich slips, albeit for the briefest moment. "They never sold it right," he says. "They've got to get into more fundamental cultural terms." He has dipped his toe in the whirlpool; before he knows it he's swimming for his life. Here is how the subsequent exchange is described in the pool report, written immediately after the encounter and passed out to a hundred journalists, many of whom use it in their stories today:

> Asked what he meant [Kasich] replied "if people have money in their pocket, they have more power over what happens to their family. . . ." Continuing in this supportive vein Mr. Kasich opined that—referencing Ohio—"If [Dole] wins, it will be a real upset. [But hey, I'm okay!]"

None of this is exactly inaccurate. But Kasich spent maybe ten minutes pretending that Dole was going to win Ohio and maybe ten seconds saying that Ohio was a long shot. About the last thing he wanted was to say anything that could be interpreted as fainthearted. But when you are surrounded by journalists badgering you about the sort of poll numbers Dole faces, eventually you say something that can be used against you. Thus, a mere few hours into Dole's ninety-six-hour journey, the press has the defector it's been looking for.

NOVEMBER 2

Dole's public appearances quickly become a blur of weird theme songs ("Play That Funky Music White Boy"), odd slogans suspended over the back of the stage behind Dole (HONEST ENERGY!), and strange rhetoric from the podium. (Dole in Indianapolis pointing to a race car: "That's what we're doing. Five hundred. Ninety-six hours. Nonstop. Nonstop. Nonstop. Nonstop.") Mainly what is noticeable to the naked eye is how much less pleasant the Dole campaign has become—which is saying something. The crowds flip the finger at the busloads of journalists and chant rude things at them as they enter each arena. The journalists slink meekly past them, but the television cameramen are having none of it. Television cameramen are a different breed, less like journalists than defensive tackles. They walk right up to protesters, thrust out their chins, and shout: *Fuck off, asshole!* They wear buttons that say YEAH, I'M THE MEDIA. SCREW YOU.

The artillery aimed at Clinton from the podium gets heavier by the hour. "I never saw an FBI file," former president Bush tells the crowd. "But then I never had a barroom bouncer right there to look them over for me." Five hours later Bush's barroom bouncer has become President Ford's bartender. A few hours after that Dole himself picks it up and describes Clinton's bartender looking through files: "He looks at a FBI file, then has a beer. Looks at another file. Has another beer."

On one of the shorter hops between cities, one of Dole's better-known strategists, Charlie Black, rides in the press plane. Black was the brains behind Phil Gramm's presidential bid, which by comparison made Morry Taylor's campaign seem a magnificent success. Now he takes his new place in one of the big seats up front and waits until there's about twenty minutes left before wandering back to do business. He sits immediately behind me so that if I swivel in my seat I can look over the fine bristles of his carefully groomed hair and the clean press of his madras shirt. Everything except the expression on Charlie Black's face says that he is on his way to a country club social. His expression tells you that, whatever he's about to do, he can hardly wait until it is over.

Joylessly Charlie announces that we are all deluded in thinking that Clinton is ahead in the polls; the true poll numbers show that Dole is gaining in popularity three percentage points a day and there is nothing Clinton can do about it. "They're in a desperate gambit to turn out their base because they see the election slipping away from them—and it is," he says, with total certainty.

This sort of behavior has become routine in the Dole campaign; indeed, from the beginning the Dole people have preferred to insult your intelligence than to craft more plausible lies. The disjuncture between the persona of the candidate (straight talker) and the behavior of his campaign (big liars) dates back to the very start of the primaries. Remember those phony polls, and the Dole campaign's explanation that Forbes and Buchanan were hiring pollsters to slander *themselves,* so that they could accuse the Dole campaign of dirty tactics. Dole's attitude seems to have been: Whatever these people I've hired do in my name is not my responsibility. He never seems to have realized there's a problem with selling honesty dishonestly. And so now Charlie Black has been sent back to tell the journalists not merely that the election is tightening but that Clinton is clearly doomed. "Do you think that Clinton has even a chance of winning?" I ask, in an attempt to enter into his mood. "Oh, he has a *chance,*" says Charlie, dubiously.

I am told by one of the Dole staffers that I'm no longer welcome on *Citizen's Ship* but must fly for the duration on the press plane. I am the only journalist in America excluded from the pool duty that enables you to get a bit closer to Dole than the cameras. "To be honest with you," says the staffer, signaling the likelihood she is lying, "some of the press got angry with you because of the camera." She is referring to the episode of the shrimp. The campaign managers have held a meeting to decide my fate, I'm told by a fellow journalist who overheard the meeting. "I'd like to push him out the back of the plane," said the Dole woman who had been in charge of yelling at me.

NOVEMBER 3

Since I stood in for him in Palm Springs the only news I've had from Morry Taylor came in the form of a press release. "Former GOP candidate Morry Taylor offers employees incentive to vote," it announced, then went on to explain that he was giving each of his 3,200 employees who voted one extra day of vacation. Morry figured that if city hall could let its employees off on Election Day to vote for Democrats, then he should be able to do more or less the same thing. His employees more or less agreed. "It hit with such a bang," Morry says when I call him, for old time's sake. The fantastic number of Titan employees in Des Moines who turned up to register to vote caused county officials to phone the company to ask what was going on. Soon enough the secretary of state in Illinois was calling Morry to say that his scheme sounded illegal. In turn Morry called somebody at the Federal Election Commission, who told him, again, that it *was* illegal. Imagine—the FEC has nothing to say when every one of the major candidates fiddles the spending rules dur-

Who says you have to be a Washington Politico to be President? Seems to me they're the guys who got us in the mess we're in. I'm not a professional politician and I'm not a lawyer. I'm a businessman. America needs a hard-nosed businessman to shake things up in Washington.

1 RETURN POWER TO THE STATES

For too many years the arrogant Washington insiders and bureaucrats have been taking more and more power away from the states. It's time to return power back to the local level so each state can decide how to use its own resources and how best to solve its problems. Instead of closing military bases we should mothball the Pentagon. We should move the Department of Agriculture out of Washington to where the agriculture is. There's no need for the federal government to be meddling with education — close the Department of Education.

2 CUT THE FEDERAL BUREAUCRACY AND BALANCE THE BUDGET

Washington is crawling with bureaucrats! They get 25% more money than workers in the private sector for the privilege of making your life miserable. I'd eliminate one third of federal management employees — starting at the top, but not anyone who is doing the work. I wouldn't lay off any mailmen, for example, but the mailman doesn't need eight layers of management to tell him how to deliver the mail. Cutting one third of management would save enough to balance the budget in eighteen months. President Clinton proved this can be done. He temporarily sent 800,000 nonessential employees home. Did you miss any of them?

3 THIS IS AMERICA — WE SPEAK ENGLISH HERE

Our ancestors came to America for freedom and opportunity. For most of them, learning English was a struggle. But they wanted to be Americans and they understood the American dream. Today, our government — by brushing aside English as our official language — is stealing the American dream and that's unfair and it's wrong. Elect me President and English will be our language.

4 FAIR TRADE, NOT FREE TRADE — LOOK OUT FOR AMERICANS FIRST

I'm the only guy running who's sat across from the Japanese and gotten my products into their markets. American trade policy is a disaster — we're too soft and we're getting shafted. It's time to get tough, **MORRY TAYLOR TOUGH**, and play hardball with the countries that want to sell their products to us but won't reciprocate. If they pull those stunts with me, they'll find themselves trying to clear customs through an abandoned military base in Sidney, Nebraska.

5 DON'T HIRE A POLITICIAN TO DO A BUSINESSMAN'S JOB

The federal government is the biggest business on earth, and the worst run. Why in heaven's name would we choose a Washington politician to run things? The only thing they're good at is spending other people's money and raising other people's taxes. They've stuck us with a five trillion dollar debt and they haven't balanced the budget in twenty-six years. I've never run for office before in my life. I consider that an asset, don't you?

6 END FOREIGN LOBBYISTS, CONGRESSIONAL JUNKETS, AND JUICY POLITICAL PENSIONS

This Republican Congress did something the Democrats wouldn't do in forty years - it reformed itself. As far as I'm concerned, that's just a start. As President, I'd get rid of foreign lobbyists, ban the junkets, and end juicy political pensions. Since her appointment, Energy Secretary O'Leary has spent more than $1.2 million on lavish trips around the world. It's time to end this madness. Our country's going to be a lot better off when the special favors and the special interests are long gone.

7 SET TERM LIMITS FOR POLITICIANS

I'm the only guy running with the guts to say we need a six- year term limit for Congressmen and Senators. Any longer and the "representative" forgets who he's representing; he starts thinking Washington has all of the answers and that throwing money at the problems gets them solved. As President, I'd lead by example and serve just a single four-year term.

8 WE DESERVE A FAIRER, FLATTER, SIMPLER TAX CODE

Who the heck designed the IRS Tax Code? Any of us could have done a much better job. On Day One, I'd scrap the IRS and replace it with a tax system that's fair, flat, simple, and written in plain English. There would be no loopholes, no deductions, no tax credits, no tax attorneys, and no free rides. Everyone will pay something because we're all Americans. Taxpayers would pay 2% on income under $20,000, then 10% on income between $20,000 and $35,000, and 17% on income over $35,000.

9 THAT'S IT FOR PAC'S

I'm using my own money to run this campaign. PAC money is dirty and there are strings attached. I don't want to have anything to do with it. I don't believe in federal matching funds either because that money should go to reduce the national debt. I'm willing to put my money where my mouth is--the Washington Boys are willing to put your money where their mouth is. That says a lot about the professional politicians. They're skilled in the art of taking care of themselves.

10 SMALLER GOVERNMENT LESS REGULATION

American businesses are suffocating under a blanket of idiotic rules. Every family in America pays $3,200 in taxes for federal bureaucrats. That's obscene! I'd mothball the EPA. I'd dismantle OSHA. I'd fire a million federal management bureaucrats, starting with the throne-sitters at the top. I'd end government funding for the NEA and PBS. Government has gotten too big, too bloated, too burdensome, and too bureaucratic. Washington's going to be a far simpler place when I get done with it.

MORRY TAYLOR ★ ★ ★

is is where I stand on the issues. Let me know where you stand. Return your completed
estionnaire and you'll be eligible for our prize drawing in February. Go to your neighborhood
ucus on February 12th and everybody wins!

DO YOU AGREE THAT POWER SHOULD BE BROUGHT BACK TO THE STATE AND LOCAL LEVEL?

☐ You're Right, Morry   ☐ You're Wrong, Morry

**DO YOU AGREE WITH MY PLAN TO CUT THE BUREAUCRACY BY ONE THIRD AND BALANCE THE
DGET?**

☐ You're Right, Morry   ☐ You're Wrong, Morry

DO YOU AGREE WITH ME THAT OUR NATIONAL LANGUAGE SHOULD BE ENGLISH?

☐ You're Right, Morry   ☐ You're Wrong, Morry

DO YOU AGREE WITH MY GET TOUGH TRADE POLICIES?

☐ You're Right, Morry   ☐ You're Wrong, Morry

**DO YOU AGREE THAT WE NEED AN OUTSIDER
CLEAN UP THE MESS IN WASHINGTON?**

You're Right, Morry ☐ You're Wrong, Morry

**DO YOU AGREE WITH MY PLAN TO TRULY
ORM GOVERNMENT?**

You're Right, Morry ☐ You're Wrong, Morry

**DO YOU AGREE WITH MY PLAN TO LIMIT
RMS?**

You're Right, Morry ☐ You're Wrong, Morry

**DO YOU AGREE WITH MY PLAN TO SCRAP
IRS?**

You're Right, Morry ☐ You're Wrong, Morry

**DO YOU AGREE NO PAC MONEY AND NO TAX
NEY FOR POLITICAL CAMPAIGNS ?**

You're Right, Morry ☐ You're Wrong, Morry

**DO YOU AGREE WITH ME THAT WE NEED
STOP THE REGULATORY MADNESS AND CUT
SIZE OF OUR GOVERNMENT ?**

You're Right, Morry ☐ You're Wrong, Morry

FOLD ON THIS LINE FIRST

NO POSTAGE
NECESSARY
IF MAILED
IN THE
UNITED STATES

BUSINESS REPLY MAIL
FIRST CLASS MAIL   PERMIT NO. 8745   DES MOINES, IOWA

POSTAGE WILL BE PAID BY ADDRESSEE

TAYLOR FOR PRESIDENT
2345 E MARKET ST
DES MOINES IA 50317-9940

FOLD ON THIS LINE SECOND

The Morry Poll: a distant memory of a better time.

281

ing the primaries. It has nothing to say when an Indonesian businessman channels millions of dollars to the Clinton campaign through a man who worked at the Department of Commerce. But when Morry Taylor tries to give his employees a day off, the bureaucrats leap into action.

It seems that word has spread among the Dole troops that I am to be held responsible for all of their unhappiness. Returning to the plane I find that I have been moved from an aisle to a middle seat, and that once-friendly staffers now are avoiding my lonesome gaze. Meanwhile the Dole lady who wants to push me out the back of the plane is unable to fill the seats on *Citizen's Ship*. It turns out that a lot of the journalists prefer the press plane, where the seats are bigger, the company is better, and the electrical outlets work. I seem to be the one journalist who is longing to ride on Dole's plane, and yet I can't get within a hundred yards of the thing. Clearly I have no choice but to strike out on my own. I can think of only one place worth going.

NOVEMBER 4

It's nearly two in the morning by the time I find wheels and drive out of the Kansas City airport, and well past four by the time I reach Abilene and spot the signs for the Eisenhower Presidential Library. At this hour on a lonely stretch of I-70 I can come up with any number of reasons to stop for the night, but the main one is a conversation I had several months ago with my one friend in the Dole campaign. This person accepted Dole's offer of work after the primaries, even though there were a lot of other ways he could have made a living. On his way to start the job he paid a visit to the library mainly because he thought it might give him some insight into his new boss; Eisenhower is Dole's favorite president. Though not by nature a sentimentalist, my friend in the Dole campaign had been left fairly well choked up by an exhibit at the museum.

After a few hours in a Best Western I find my way to the library, and a helpful curator. He shows me the old Eisenhower campaign posters (LET'S CLEAN HOUSE WITH IKE AND DICK!) and the letter imploring Eisenhower to run for president signed by nineteen Republicans, including Gerald Ford of Michigan. It nicely illustrates that the longing in our democracy for the Unpolitical Politician, the man who doesn't seek power but instead has power thrust upon him, has been around awhile: ". . . if our own country is torn asunder by corruption and greed, by disloyalties and opportunism, by the avarice of selfish men, by the lack of vision of pseudo-statesmen greedy to retain public office, all the good and constructive work you have done will be destroyed."

The curator explains that Eisenhower's presidency had triggered a boom in Abilene much like Dole's is meant to in Russell. By the end of the Second World War Abilene looked to be headed toward extinction. What saved it was first the Eisenhower Museum, created in 1946, and then the Eisenhower Library, which now draws about 125,000 visitors a year. Once tourists began to come, the town built further attractions to divert them: the Greyhound Hall of Fame, the Museum of Independent Telephony, and other places that no one in his right mind would build a vacation around but that perhaps lend dimension to a visit to Abilene. The people of Russell have Abilene as their model. One of the biggest Dole authorities in Russell even gave me a tour of the site for the presidential library. It would be shaped like a silo, he said, and built entirely of glass.

It only takes a few minutes to find the exhibit my friend in the Dole campaign had described. Before every major engagement of the war General Eisenhower penned what amounted to a press release in which he took full responsibility for failure. Every time but one he tore up his note and threw it away. But after D-Day an aide with a sense of history fished one of the notes from the trash can. "The thing of it is," my friend had explained, "is that it was all in the first person—I, I, I. Then he wrote another press release in the event of victory in which it is all we, we, we." To my friend this pattern said something not just about Eisenhower but about Dole. It represented an entire way of life that has fallen from fashion. The actual press release sits behind a pane of glass:

> Our landings in the Cherbourg and Le Havre area have failed to gain a satisfactory foothold and I have withdrawn the troops. My decision to attack at this time and place was based upon the best information available. The troops, the Air and the Navy did all that bravery and devotion to duty could do. If any blame or fault attaches to the attempt it is mine alone.

There is no second note announcing the success of the operation in the first-person plural, however. The curator tells me that Eisenhower never bothered to declare D-Day a success, which, when you think about it, makes his personal admission of failure even more striking. My friend in the Dole campaign embellished the story, no doubt unconsciously, so that I might feel what he wished me to feel. Such is the power of stoicism over stoics. Such is the current weakness of the creed that it must be compromised if it is to survive.

NOVEMBER 5

The mood on Election Day in Russell, Kansas, is much like the mood of the Dole campaign: on the surface, a great deal of hope and, just below it, a lot of anger. In nineteen speeches over two days Dole failed even to mention Russell or his upbringing. I first realized that Russell was being phased out of the Dole campaign, and out of Dole's life, when I asked Scott Reed how long Dole was planning to be there on Election Day. Reed made a sign with his hands of a plane touching down and taking off again, quickly. That the Dole campaign would not spend a night in town would come as news to the local motels, which the Dole campaign had reserved.

Still, I think people here really believe it when they say Dole is going to win. Bub Dawson, whose family drugstore employed Dole, talks about the "hoopla" that will overwhelm the town after the victory. But resentment is swelling in Russell—of Clinton, who only a few months ago was more laughed at here than hated, and of everything and everyone who is perceived to have helped him. After breakfast I am assaulted by a woman who accuses me of being a member of the liberal media. "He's a sleazy draft dodger!" she hollers, until finally I am forced to tell her that I didn't vote for Clinton. "You voted for Dole?" she says, incredulously. "Ralph Nader," I say. "Well, that's just stupid," she says, but the fury has gone out of her.

By 10:30 a.m. Main Street is lined on both sides with the town residents, who, curiously, seem to be either very young children or very old people. In Russell you always wonder where the parents have gone. At noon the Dole motorcade pulls up to the First Christian Church, and the Doles go inside to vote. One look at the reporters' drawn faces and I'm grateful for being non grata on the Dole plane, though of course in these situations you always wonder what might have been. Dole walks into the church, picks up his ballot from five elderly ladies, mentions that he is nervous because he's never voted for himself for president, and then vanishes behind a blue cloth curtain. There he stands at a metal shelf, steadying his ballot with a miniature limestone fence post that is, aside from Dole memorabilia, about the only souvenir you can buy in a Russell gift shop.

Until now in the campaign Dole usually has been surrounded by bigwigs. Everywhere he goes Dole is accompanied by governors and senators. But today, the final day of the campaign, the day Dole will discover that he never will be president, the governors and the senators seem to have vanished. At his side in the church there is no one but his wife and daughter. Even the rented strangers are thin on the ground. The paper today reports that Dole's former media adviser, Don Sipple, has suddenly realized that Dole shouldn't be running for president. "I don't think he would be a particularly good president," said Sipple. "There's the lack of communication skills, the indecisiveness, the obsession with self-reliance."

But just as it appears that Dole has been left by himself to carry the carpetbag of defeat I notice Senator John McCain, standing off to one side in aviator sunglasses and a baseball cap pulled down low over his brow. A few weeks ago in Phoenix I watched McCain rearrange his schedule over the protest of his staff so that he could be with Dole on Election Day. The staffers thought the senator should be back in Arizona celebrating probable victory with Republican freshman J. D. Hayworth. (Hayworth won by six hundred votes.) McCain thought he should be on the road coping with probable defeat with Dole. "I would think the time he might need a friend would be that night," he said back then. And so here he is, in Russell, Kansas, lecturing a reporter who would rather hear about the despair in the front of the plane than Bob Dole's place in American history. "I predict to you," I can hear him saying, "that Bob Dole's picture, win or lose, will one day hang in the lobby of the U.S. Senate."

I slip through the Russell police force to say hello. McCain tells me with real wonder in his voice that he's just heard that Lamar Alexander planned to be in Des Moines tomorrow to be followed by Steve Forbes on Thursday, laying the foundation for their presidential campaigns in 2000. Even before the campaign ends it is starting again, which of course means that it never ends. We talk about this and that until finally McCain says, by the by, almost apologetically, "I wouldn't be here if I thought he was going to win."

That evening the town of Russell gathers to watch the returns at the local offices of the Veterans of Foreign Wars. By the time I arrive Clinton has won Florida, and maybe four hundred mostly old people sit on orange vinyl chairs at long cafeteria tables hoping for more, different news. The walls are papered over with Dole-Kemp signs, and the people are all done up in patriotic reds and blues. A few wear Eisenhower pins beside their Dole pins. Beneath a banner for the Republican Party is a tote board to keep track of local voting. While the big-screen TV announces the national results, the tote board will tell everyone how Bob is doing in Russell County. No one so far as I can tell believes Dole is about to lose in either race. How can they, when no one knows anyone who didn't vote for him?

At some point in the first twenty minutes I mention something about the conspicuous absence of Democrats, and I am directed to the back of the hall. "The Democrats are back there," says an elderly woman. Sure enough, they are. A dozen or so of them sit together in a small private room. At their center sipping a scotch and soda is a man who introduces himself as Leroy Jaggers, a retired Russell school superintendent running on the Democratic ticket for the Kansas legislature. He and his fellow Democrats, it seems, have been shuffled off to this cold, forgotten place. "How many black votes you think you got, Leroy?" someone shouts. "Hey!" shouts Leroy. "I got a lot. 'Cause I went to the cemetery today. I know *all* the tricks." It's a running joke in Russell that the Democrat gets the black vote, because there isn't any black vote to speak of.

But there is a difference between Democrats in Russell, Kansas, and Democrats everywhere else: Democrats in Russell vote for Bob Dole. And they don't advertise their affiliation very loudly; the donkey on Leroy's campaign posters looks nothing like a donkey and a great deal like a giraffe. This raises a question, which I put to him: Why bother being a Democrat? "You know why I'm a Democrat?" asks Leroy, slurpily. "Out of respect for my father. My father was a very big Democrat." He doesn't think it hurts him much in Russell, "'cause here people take you for what you are. You vote for the person, not the party." At which point Leroy and everyone else in the room bombard me with explanations about the unimportance of political parties in Russell. And it is true that while outside Russell County Leroy seems to be getting shellacked by his Republican opponent, inside Russell he's doing fine. Leroy understood that there was no need to sell yourself in Russell, that people knew who he was. He may even be right. It may be safe to assume that people know who you are when you run for office in Russell, that you don't have to bother with telling them. But it is disastrous when you run for president.

In the giant hall the TV and the tote board are now moving in opposite directions: as Dole widens his lead over Clinton in Russell (451 to 72 at the moment) he falls further behind on the TV (204 to 35 electoral votes). What's odd is that, as the night proceeds, it brings with it only the most subtle signs of disappointment. No one weeps or howls in despair. No one talks about the unfolding election—or anything else, for that matter. By nine o'clock the few reporters who bothered to turn up have gone. The brief and glorious ability of Russell to project itself onto the world's television screens is rapidly dwindling to nothing; it is the last time that anyone in town will be asked for his opinion by Barbara Walters. Half an hour later—well before Dole concedes—his campaign posters are being stripped from the walls by the man who drove him seventy-five thousand miles during his first Senate race. By the time Dole arrives on the big screen, with John McCain standing directly behind him, to tell the world that tomorrow for the first time in his life he will have nothing to do, no one in Russell is around to watch. The hall is empty. I can't help but wonder if Dole didn't wait so late to spare the folks back home.

On the way out into the Kansas night I notice a display on the wall, a series of boards that bear the names of the life members of the VFW. There on the first board is the small black enamel rectangle bearing the name of Robert J. Dole. There is nothing to distinguish it from the other names; if you knew nothing of politics you'd think Robert J. Dole was just another citizen of Russell. Gold stars adorn several of the surrounding rectangles, and it quickly becomes clear that these denote the life members who have died. The passage of time is a sad thing. We can never return to the green garden of our youth. Fifty years from now all the names on the boards will be decorated with gold stars, and maybe one evening, maybe just like this one, two people will stumble upon them, and one of them will point to Dole's name and inquire, "Didn't he run for president?" "I don't know," the other will say. "I never heard of him."

Tonight in Russell, Kansas, World War II finally ended.

EPILOGUE

Postmortems

I've received a nice letter from Bob Dole. "Dear Michael," it begins. "Perhaps our paths will cross in the future, but in any event, please let me know if I can ever be of assistance—maybe get you tickets to a Brooklyn Dodgers game." But when I call his headquarters Dole remains as unavailable as ever for serious interviews. I am reduced to watching him flog Visa cards on my television set. The joke in the commercial is that Bob Dole returns to Russell, Kansas, to find that his check is no good—unless accompanied by a Visa check-cashing card. The commercial appears to be filmed in Russell, but it is not. It is filmed on a stage set in California that reproduces Russell's more charming locations. For much of his political career Dole has used Russell more or less as a stage set. Now the process is complete.

This morning Clinton delivers his Inaugural Address on the steps of the nation's Capitol, after which a choir belts out "The Battle Hymn of the Republic." Before it finishes the first stanza, however, the phone rings. It's Ralph Nader. I realize that I haven't heard a peep from him since the Green Party convention last August, but he quickly makes up for lost time. He's beyond outrage at the emptiness of Clinton's inaugural rhetoric. "He's planning to run in 2008, you know," he says. I think he must be joking, but no: word is circulating that Clinton intends to take two terms off and then return to the White House.

The Nader for President campaign didn't reach many Americans. Ralph didn't run any commercials, for instance, though he did travel to eighteen states. He claims he spent less than five thousand dollars doing this, however. His enemies say that he limited his expenditures to avoid having to disclose to the Federal Election Commission the millions he has stuffed away in secret bank accounts. Ralph says that he limited his expenditures because spending more money would have undermined the spirit of his campaign. "How many votes did I get?" he asks. "Five hundred and eighty thousand? Six hundred and seventy thousand? I don't know. But what would I have done with more money? I might have gotten four or five hundred thousand more votes, but I wanted people to see they did it for themselves."

Like many people who seriously want to change the world Ralph clearly has a different view of elections than either Clinton or Dole. Like most professional politicians Clinton and Dole view elections as contests to be won at all costs. They mean no harm by this. If they lose, they reason, they won't be able to do anything for anybody. Ralph views elections as public referenda on the direction the society is heading. In this respect, he says, the 1996 presidential campaign was the worst he has ever seen. "Content free," as he puts it, and then starts to list the issues that neither candidate addressed: energy policy, health insurance, mass transit, tax fairness, consumer fraud. "Look at where they campaigned," he continues. "They never campaigned with *people*. They never used their appearances to further a cause. They never campaigned in the lower-income areas. It was malls. It was suburbs. It was Hilton Hotels." I point out that Jack Kemp made one trip to Harlem. "Exactly," he says, "and he got so much attention because it was so exceptional."

And it's true. The campaign trail is not typical of America, mainly because the people on it are obsessed with seeming typical. In their efforts to blend in, the candidates avoided rich neighborhoods as assiduously as they did poor neighborhoods. The goal in both cases was to avoid being photographed against backdrops that might alienate the middle class. The reason for this, of course, is that the middle class is where the votes are. But in their efforts to seem in touch, the candidates greatly reduced the chances they would learn much from their travels. Once you've seen one typical middle-class setting you've seen them all, by definition.

"Whatever else you say about these two guys," Ralph says, "haven't they failed the excitement test?"

JANUARY 23

I eat lunch with John McCain just a few hours before he's meant to go meet in the Oval Office with President Clinton. McCain's campaign finance reform bill, which failed to pass the last Congress, is the flavor of the month, especially with a White House plagued with campaign finance scandals. Clinton wants to be seen to support reform; and perhaps he actually does support it. But he is a very new crusader against the need for big money in politics: He himself spent a record $175 million on his reelection campaign. And he has a new reason to posture in front of McCain. When South Dakota senator Larry Pressler lost his race for reelection McCain ascended to the chairmanship of the Senate Commerce Committee. Immediately he announced his intention to hold investigative hearings into the Commerce Department. Under Clinton, we now know, the Commerce Department has been used to raise money from various shady foreigners for the Democratic Party. The smartest thing Clinton could do at this point is to court McCain.

As McCain explains how his bill—even with Clinton's support—will probably be killed, I am reminded once more that he is unlike most people who do what he does for a living in his taste for a losing or unpopular cause. I understand that this benefits him at some level in that it distinguishes him from the great mass of politicians and leads many people to admire him. I understand that he cannot push his courage too far without ending his career. Nevertheless, there is something extraordinary about the way he seeks out trouble to avoid violating his sense of who he must be. And it never fails to allay somewhat my general misgivings about democracy as currently practiced.

I have an image of McCain fixed in my mind that I can't quite shake. He is standing alone in the dark on the wrong side of a chain-link fence outside the Democratic convention. Inside, CNN is waiting to interview him, only he doesn't have a pass to get to them. The guards drop their pose of callous indifference and begin to shift uneasily. Their admiration for the senator's war record (they all know about it) exceeds their interest in their immediate authority. If McCain made the slightest issue of being blocked from entering they'd let him by. But he doesn't. He just stands there waiting, for maybe twenty minutes, with his hands shoved deep in his pockets.

And then a young woman who works for him rushes up, carrying a cell phone. McCain takes a series of calls from Arizona reporters. The mayor of Tempe has just been exposed as a homosexual. The revelation, in Arizona, could kill a politician; indeed, it might tarnish a politician too closely associated with the victim. All of the reporters are calling to see what McCain thinks, and McCain doesn't hesitate to tell them. Standing in the dark beside the chain-link fence outside the United Center he takes the phone and says, over and over, "The mayor of Tempe is a friend of mine. He is a fine man. Who the hell cares if he is gay?"

JANUARY 28

Alan Keyes has gone back to his radio show. Bob Dornan, having lost his congressional seat, has formed an organization dedicated to impeaching Bill Clinton. For the past few months Pat Buchanan's people have put off my request to see him with the claim that Buchanan wasn't seeing anyone. He was holed up in his basement, they said, writing that book about the history of American trade policy. Until this afternoon, when I drive out to Buchanan's home in Virginia, I assumed that this was hyperbole. But the man who opens the door looks as if he has spent the past six months in his cellar. His hair juts out in odd ways and his shirttail extrudes from his wrinkled slacks. He wears white sneakers and matching tube socks. Buchanan apologizes for leaving me standing on the porch. He was downstairs in the basement, he says, working on his book.

After a tour of the cellar Buchanan leads me into his living room, where he begins to reminisce about his campaign. One of his most vivid memories, he says, is the evening of the New Hampshire primary. After it was clear he was going to win, he left his room at the Holiday Inn and set off for his victory rally. Surrounded by his entourage he took the elevator to the basement and headed out. But coming the other way was Bob Dole, surrounded by his entourage. The corridor wasn't more than a few feet wide. The two sides passed without saying a word to each other.

At that moment, Buchanan says, he thought he might win. Just as Dole now says that with a few more breaks he'd have beaten Clinton, Buchanan is now telling me that with a few more breaks he'd have beaten Dole. "If Keyes hadn't been in Iowa," he says, "we'd have won that thing. We'd have beaten Dole twice and that would have finished him." He even drew up a fall strategy, and as he describes it I feel I am hearing about one of those contingency plans drawn up by the U.S. Army during the Second World War in the event of a Japanese landing in California. "I'd have tried to put the Republican Party back together," he says. "You have to do what Goldwater did *not* do—turn a rebellion into a party. Go to all the statehouses. Go to all the Senate offices. Get as many of them to come with you as you can. Then you gotta talk Perot out of running. Then you go to Howie's convention (the Taxpayers Party fiasco). Then you choose a running mate." I don't ask him who that would be, on the assumption that he would never tell me. He tells me anyway: "J. C. Watts"(the black House member from Oklahoma). "Or maybe Rick Santorum" (the Pennsylvania senator).

Most of the commentary about the 1996 campaign now overlooks Buchanan; he's rarely mentioned as a force to reckon with in 2000. But he is. Maybe the most striking thing about his campaign is that it triumphed, however briefly, in prosperous times. Buchanan was selling anger when there wasn't a great deal to be angry about. You can imagine all sorts of events that could change that: a stock market collapse; a recession; a war in which Americans die wearing U.N. blue; a revolution in Mexico. A medium-sized economic downturn and the people at the Buchanan rallies will be not unemployed textile workers but lawyers and doctors. Anger would become respectable. And any man with the capacity to speak to it could go far.

"Do you think you could have beaten Clinton?" I ask him now.

Buchanan thinks about it a minute. "I'm a figure of some controversy," he says, "and that works against me. But I tell you one thing: you could have scalped tickets to those presidential debates."

Which brings us to his new book. The winner of the 1996 New Hampshire Republican primary has been investigating the history of American trade policy and American military interventions on foreign soil. He's proved to his satisfaction that Washington, Lincoln, and Jackson were proud protectionists. You might wonder why he bothers to prove this, unless you'd watched him campaign. His great gift is for deploying the past as a political weapon. In the truce of 1997 he's manufacturing his own ammo for the next war.

"The research could be useful four years from now," I say.

"That's right," he says. "I got these people calling and saying, 'Look, who cares what these people thought.' But they don't understand. If you can put Washington and Lincoln and Jackson in the tradition, you're halfway home with the American people. It puts me in a great tradition and puts my critics in the tradition of Wilson and FDR."

As he speaks I notice that the room is choked with history: portraits of Civil War generals, long rows of books invariably about the distant past. On the coffee table in front of me rest a portrait of Lenin and busts of Sir Thomas Moore and War Chief Joseph. Buchanan is indiscriminate in his taste for troublemakers.

I point to War Chief Joseph, the leader of the Nez Percé. Instantly Buchanan recites Chief Joseph's pithy surrender at the end of his dramatic last stand: "I will fight no more forever." Then he laughs, but it is not a happy laugh. It is the laugh of someone trying to disguise how moved he is by the failure of a man who was so obviously great-souled.

JANUARY 30

Morry Taylor was walking from a clubhouse to a first tee outside of Naples, Florida, when a man came up to him and introduced himself. It's now an everyday thing for Morry to run into people who admired his campaign from afar and were poised to vote for him. He never tires of the experience, however. And though he doesn't recall the name of the man who intercepted him on the way to the first tee, he remembers what he said. He says: "This guy says to me, 'The Dole campaign asked me to be you in preparing Dole for the debate.' " Morry could not quite believe that Dole went to the trouble of staging a trial run with all eight of his rivals. "So I say to him: 'What?' And he says, 'I was supposed to play you. But then I go to see you speak—out in Vegas. I listen to you and I says to myself: *"He's real!* I *like* this guy." So I call the Dole campaign and I say, "Regretfully, I like this guy and I'm gonna vote for him. So I can't be him in your practice debate. I'm not going to do it." I told the Dole campaign I'm voting for Morry Taylor.'

"Better for him," says Morry now, as he finishes this curious anecdote. "How could he play me? I just walk out there and let it fly. I don't know what I'm gonna say myself until I say it. I never prepare for anything. I couldn't even prepare to play myself."

It's not a bad definition of the genuine man, I think: one who couldn't even prepare to play himself.

Of course I make a final trip to see him. It wasn't easy. Since the election last November Morry has been nearly as elusive as Dole and Clinton. In the past few months he's been off to buy companies in China, Ukraine, Croatia, France, and Germany. Business has been so good that last month he was named Executive of the Year by *Rubber and Plastic News.* "Taylor Flops in Politics but Moves Titan Forward" read the headline announcing Morry's selection.

When I arrive in Detroit I find Morry brandishing the dust jacket he's designed for his political manifesto. On it a giant grizzly bear perches, obscuring the name of the author and the title. The only name you can read clearly is the ghostwriter's: "As Told to Barbara Feinman," it reads in giant letters.° Morry's wife, Michelle, gazes at it without interest. She has had enough of the Taylor for President campaign. "Everywhere we go," she says, wearily, "people come up to Morry. The only people who will tell Morry he was a fool to run are his friends. The strangers all want to tell him how great he is." "The biggest thing is," says Morry, interrupting, "they want to know whether you're gonna run in 2000. How the hell do I know what's going to happen in the year 2000? They say, 'The other guys, Forbsey and Lamar, they're already running.' And I say, They're already running because they don't know what else to do."

Getting back to business has not been easy for him; much as he has tried he has been unable to escape the politicians. Not long ago, for instance, he had a call from former Colorado governor Richard Lamm, who ran for the nomination of the Reform Party and ever since has been a useful critic of Ross Perot. "He wanted me to join him and Bill Bradley in some think tank," says Morry. "You know, the boys in Washington who never want to leave. They don't have a friggin' idea how to manage anything and they want to start this tank to manage government. " Morry declined Lamm's invitation. "If you said yes," he says, "they'd get you out there. You'd be sittin' around some table and one of them would say—'Well, I guess we need some money.' Shit. 'I got my money. Where's yours?'"

But just when I think Morry has been lost to politics forever he lets slip that he's been working privately on a new project, a plan to reform the way we elect our presidents. I'm not allowed to spill it all here. But the gist of it is to eliminate the advantage of money, office, and political parties, and turn the campaign into a free-for-all in which the most ferocious competitor wins. If Morry has his way the presidential primary will look a lot like the NCAA basketball championship. The problem with politics, he feels, is that it is not an honest competition. It is more like a

---

°This will shock Barbara, I think; in her dealings with Hillary Clinton she became used to receiving no credit at all for her work.

rigged fight. And this puts it at odds with American values. If politics were more like the NCAA, he feels, most everyone would take an interest in the outcomes. But Morry's taking no chances. "Here's the deal," he explains, "if you don't vote you pay either five hundred bucks or ten percent of the income declared on that year's tax return, whichever is greater. That way some Hollywood guy doesn't vote it might cost him a hundred grand." Here we arrive at the root of Morry's interest in politics: his belief that if everyone voted the results would take care of themselves. In Morry's imagination it is mainly Washington insiders who voted in 1996. The rest of the country must have stayed home. Otherwise he would have won.

As I sit puzzling over the structure of future presidential elections Morry vanishes into the past. His mind wanders back into the 1996 campaign. Only this time it's *his* campaign: two-hour debates without a moderator. *Mano a mano.* Single elimination. He sits in his Barcalounger thinking up winning sallies, and they come tumbling out of him without the slightest prompting from me:

"Senator Dole, why would you want to be president? You never managed anything!

"Okay, Steve, you wanna talk about entrepreneurs. What the hell have you ever done, Steve?

"Pat. You wanna preach family values. You're the last person. You don't got any kids. You could have adopted kids. You didn't."

On and on he goes, sharpening the zingers that will bring the professional politicians to their knees.

Morry's lopsided loss to the pros seems only to have reinforced his disdain for their business. He remains unwilling to concede that the fight he lost was fair; and in this he is once again sounding much like the voice of the People. Political professionals have a taste for laughing at failure (and the more they laugh at it the more they fear it). But these days it is not only the loser who is scorned: the winner is often reviled. It's no accident that the biggest political issue in the months following the election was the laws broken by the winners to raise the money required to get themselves elected. The winners—and their ideas—have been at least partly discredited by what they did to win.

We seem to have arrived at a point in our politics where the means (how politicians win elections) are so all-consuming that the ends (what politicians do once they win) become obscured. Consider U.S. trade policy, for instance (though you might just as well consider tax policy, homosexual rights, judicial reform, abortion rights, or any other controversial issue). When he was a senator, Bob Dole led the fight to pass the North American Free Trade Agreement (NAFTA). That is, he took a clear, principled stand that the United States is better off opening its markets to foreigners. But once he became a presidential candidate, Dole muddied this view beyond recognition, until even the attentive voter couldn't really say what Dole would do if elected. "I think we're going to have to take a look at that again," he'd say of NAFTA, typically, when confronted. It was as if he felt a professional obligation not to say what he believed.

Clearly this is a big problem. During the Republican primary, for instance, it was no longer a simple matter for a free trader to support Dole over Buchanan, the enemy of free trade. A vote for Bob Dole—or for Clinton, or for any big-time national politician—was a vote for professional dishonesty, for low tactics, and for the rented strangers who dreamed them up. In general, the moderate center of American politics discredited itself with its blind faith in the power of deception. In doing so it raised the stature of the extremes—which was why Buchanan and Forbes enjoyed such good runs. By contrast Buchanan's straightforward opposition to free trade was so refreshing that it was tempting to concede him the issue just to encourage his attitude to public life. Even the most ardent free trader was forced into a dialogue between his head and his heart. The head said Dole; the heart said Buchanan.

This disjuncture between means and ends is one big reason the moderate, centrist majority is alienated from politics. Like any problem it is worth trying to fix; like any problem it is easier to diagnose than to solve. The most popular solution at the moment is to reform campaign finance: most everyone agrees that private money exercises too much influence in public life, and prompts big-time politicians to behave badly. But even if you take the money out of politics you still have to confront the reason money is so important in the first place: the terror of honest political speech. If you are the presidential nominee of a major political party you don't need a lot of money to tell people what you and your opponent really think. You need money to buy ads to distort what you and your opponent really think.

The 1996 presidential campaign represented the apotheosis of the paid political ad. Probably there was a more credulous time when television ads were more effective. But there can never have been a time when the faith in the power of TV ads was so great relative to other forms of communication. All three major candidates avoided the press, or at any rate granted only as many interviews as were required to avoid the appearance of dodging the press. All three feared frank and open exchange with knowledgeable, critical people. Instead they spent hundreds of millions of dollars—nearly half of their campaign budgets and far more than ever before—on ads that were, to an extent, a substitute for authentic public exposure. "But they campaigned!" you protest; and it is true that Clinton, Dole, and Perot stood before hundreds of crowds and delivered hundreds of speeches. But these public events were so carefully staged—right down to Democratic henchmen plucking the lone Perot supporter out of a crowd of twenty-five thousand Clinton enthusiasts— as to be indistinguishable from paid advertisements. Everyone in the frame of the camera followed the script. Of course, there were a few exceptions, like the refreshing town-hall debate in San Diego, for instance. But as a rule the candidates kept their characters, and their views on controversial matters, to themselves.

This was not the fault of the journalists, who, within the rules of the game, did all they could to learn all they could (though journalists don't help matters by treating doublespeak as straight talk and straight talk as scandal). It was not even the fault of the politicians, who were just doing what was required to win, according to the same strange rules. Ultimately the culprit was the culture that wrote the rules: an electorate grown numb to cynical candidates and their rented strangers. The phenomenon is circular: the less sentient the electorate, the more easily it can be cynically manipulated; the more cynical the manipulations, the less sentient the electorate. There is no obvious end to it, short of some sort of crisis or external shock. The television ad no big-time presidential candidate is ever likely to run is the ad attacking the idea of television ads. The poll no big-time presidential candidate is ever likely to take is the poll that asks, How do you feel about a president who decides what he believes by taking polls?

I don't see how you solve this problem. Or, rather, the solution is not the sort of thing that can be imposed from above. It must arise from within. You can't legislate more critical citizens or greater expectations. All you can do is howl and hope others will join in. And then maybe some big-time politician will step forward and do things differently.

But ideas and attitudes are judged not solely on their merits; they are judged also on their provenance. The cowardice and stupidity of winners will always be whitewashed, simply because they have won. The courage and ingenuity of losers will always be forgotten, simply because they have lost. All we can hope is that they don't let us get to them.

ACKNOWLEDGMENTS

I seem destined to thank Marty Peretz at the end of every book I ever write. This time I am more grateful to him than usual. One of the joys of writing for *The New Republic*—which Marty owns—is being edited by people who are overqualified for the job; sadly, they are forever finding better things to do with their time. Andrew Sullivan first proposed that I travel into American politics and see what I might find. David Greenberg stepped in when Andrew stepped out. Margaret Talbot stepped in when David stepped out. Peter Beinart stepped in when Margaret stepped out. Margaret stepped in—again!—when Peter stepped out. Debra Durocher worked on this project from beginning to end and saved me from myself more times than I can count. Leon Wieseltier offered sage counsel, and put into my hands James T. Havel's delightful survey *U.S. Presidential Candidates and the Elections*. It served as a constant reminder that in a democracy you never can tell who the messenger will be.

Jennifer Bradley, Jonathan Chait, Michael Crowley, Stephen Glass, Catherine Elton, Sydney Freedberg, Romesh Ratnesar, Anya Richards, and Elissa Silverman checked my facts and helped me to make more sense. Jackie McCullough fought honorably against me as I strived to test the limits of a small magazine's expense account (racquetball shoes!). Betty Billups saved me from the airlines more than once.

Since I started writing books I have been luckier than most in my publishers. I would like to thank Sonny Mehta at Alfred A. Knopf for his leap of faith and Jon Segal for his help in turning a rough draft into a book. I have also been lucky in my friends. Nicholas Lemann, acting dean of the State Street school of writers, read and improved the manuscript without unnerving its author. Tabitha Sornberger read and improved the author without unnerving his manuscript. Some interviews never end.

A NOTE ABOUT THE AUTHOR

Michael Lewis pursued a career on Wall Street for several years until he left to write a book about it—*Liar's Poker.* He is also the author of *The Money Culture.* A regular columnist for *The New York Times Magazine,* he has been a senior editor at *The New Republic,* as well as the American editor of *The Spectator.* He grew up in New Orleans, and now lives in Cold Spring, New York.

A NOTE ON THE TYPE

This book was set in Caledonia, a face designed by W. A. Dwiggins (1880–1956). It belongs to the family of printing types called "modern face" by printers—a term used to mark the change in style of the type letters that occurred around 1800. Caledonia borders on the general design of Scotch Roman, but it is more freely drawn than that letter.

Composed by Merri Ann Morrell,
Chester, Connecticut
Printed and bound by R. R. Donnelley & Sons,
Harrisonburg, Virginia
Designed by Virginia Tan